North Meols and Southport

A History

by Peter Aughton

North Meols and Southport: A History
by Peter Aughton

First edition (case), 1988
Reprinted (flush), 1989, 1998

Published by Carnegie Publishing Ltd
Chatsworth Road, Lancaster LA1 4SL

Typeset by T. Snape & Co. and Perfect Print, Preston
Printed by Pindar Graphics, Walton Summit, Preston

Copyright © Peter Aughton, 1988

ISBN 0 948789 38 7

NOTE ON THE ILLUSTRATIONS

The illustrations marked 'E.W. Collection' are reproduced by kind permission of Eric Whiteley of Birkdale, whose help has been invaluable. Those marked 'Southport Library' and 'Botanic Gardens Museum' are reproduced by kind permission of the Metropolitan Borough of Sefton Libraries and Arts Services Department.

COVER ILLUSTRATIONS

Front: A section of Yates's *Map of Lancashire*, 1786, showing the area from North Meols in the north to Ainsdale in the south. At this date, Southport did not yet exist. The ancient settlement at Churchtown can be seen.
(*Lancashire Record Office, by courtesy of the County Archivist*)
Also, a photograph of Lord Street around the turn of the century, showing shoppers and promenaders strolling along outside the Wayfarers Arcade.
Back: A painting of William Sutton's 'South Port Hotel'. Sutton's first enterprise, a bathing house constructed without a building licence in 1792, stood alone among the sandhills near where a small stream (the 'Nile') flowed into the Irish Sea. This rickety wooden structure was the first building of Southport. This painting dates from around 1845 and shows a later building on the same site.
(*Botanic Gardens Museum, Southport*)

ABOUT THE AUTHOR

Peter Aughton was born in Southport in 1940 to a local family with a fairly respectable number of generations of settlement. He lived in the town until he was seventeen and became a lecturer at Bristol Polytechnic. He is a founder member of the Liverpool and District Family History Society and a member of the Southport Civic Society; now retired, he comes back to Southport as often as he can. He has also written the acclaimed *Liverpool: A People's History*, also by Carnegie Publishing.

To Dilys, Jackie and Julie

Contents

Many people have contributed to this history and, in particular, I would like to acknowledge the following:
Mrs Emily Aughton, who has sent me news cuttings for 20 years and Dilys, Jackie and Julie, who have suffered my obsession for what seems almost as long; Mr Joe Bagley of Southport for encouragement, professional help and many useful suggestions; the late Col Roger Hesketh for a copy of Farrar and for his work on the Hesketh pedigree; Eric Whiteley for very kindly lending us his astonishing postcard collection and for permission to reproduce many of them in this book; Cedric Greenwood, one of Southport's best ever journalists, for the use of several excellent photographs; Alan Rimmer of Churchtown for sending me Paul Lloyd's memoirs and Miss Zellie Sale of Canada for permission to publish extracts from them; Jennifer Sutton of Marshside for the use of Richard Sutton's research; many officers and members of the Southport and Formby branch of the Liverpool and District Family History Society - if I must single out any members in particular I would like to mention John Turner and Geoffrey Barnes; I also wish to thank the staff at the Atkinson Library, Lord Street, the Lancashire County Record Office at Preston, Liverpool City Library and the University of St Andrews Library; Anthony Wray, the curator of the Botanic Gardens Museum, deserves special thanks for his help with illustrations, along with his predecessors Messrs Forshaw, Burrows and Morrison; Jack Sankey and Laurie Hardman of Broadhursts, Southport, for their kind help in finding illustrations, as well as general encouragement and good advice. Family tree data is mostly from parish registers, census returns and family records. The following people in particular have been most helpful: the late Col Roger Hesketh; Miles Blundell of Congleton; Margaret Irvine of Manchester; Harry Linaker of Churchtown; the late Richard Sutton of Marshside; Alan Rimmer of Churchtown and David Pearson of Hillside; branches of the Aughtons have been supplied by Mary Aughton of Hitchin, Verna Aughton of Southport, Peter William Aughton of Coventry and David Aughton of Connecticut, USA.

Foreword

by Ronnie Fearn, M.P.

Southport has always been my home and I love it. But, then, I have never met any resident who hasn't fallen for it, hook, line and sinker. That is why I commend this excellent, bright and entertaining book, *North Meols and Southport* to you, for no one could fail to enjoy page after page of our history, told in a way which makes any novel fade into obscurity. Peter Aughton has found the knack of telling true stories about our ancestors and ourselves which add to the growing belief that Southport is, and always has been, the right place to live.

There is much in this book which I can relate to. As a child, I remember standing at the Churchtown smithy watching my grandfather, Hugh Hodge, shoeing horses and I listened intently to stories of his family, including those of the devastating lifeboat disaster when *Mexico* foundered off Southport shore. Some of his relatives lost their lives in the gallant lifeboat which went to the rescue. On the Fearn side, in High Park, the main issues were football and politics, with grandfather heavily involved in local affairs, as a Liberal agent and organising much of the footballing in the area - indeed, one of his sons went on to play professionally.

As a Sandgrounder, I therefore feel well qualified to introduce this book. Southport people have always had a very keen sense of history and tangible reminders of the past exist in every corner of the town. Of course, Churchtown is the jewel in the crown. This is the centre of the real North Meols. For centuries, Churchtown was the only settlement in the area - hence the title of Peter Aughton's book, *North Meols and Southport.* Like the author, I too was taken to St. Cuthbert's churchyard to view the ancestors but I always ended up in front of the grave with the skull and crossbones on it. I still like to believe I was connected to the old pirate fraternity, although that seems highly unlikely.

Recently, I had the pleasure of opening our mobile Tourism

Office constructed from one of the original Southport bathing cabins of the Victorian era and this set me off on a tour of our lovely Lord Street. As the author points out, we can only admire the way in which, over the years, so much of the past has been retained - our Victorian facades, our splendid old buildings and the elegant shopping street, a unique and charming mall which, some would argue, is unrivalled anywhere in the country.

As a resident, a councillor, county councillor and now Member of Parliament, I have had ample time to take stock of our well planned town, from Woodvale and Ainsdale to Churchtown and Crossens. Tourism continues to develop as the major industry of the town. Indeed, one authority has just ranked it as the second resort in Great Britain for the number of visitors. As you travel from one end to the other, you cannot help but fall for the place - for the beach and nature reserve (though not the bathing waters), the dunes, the excellent houses of character, the village life, the parks and flowers, the hotels, the pubs, the shops, the art, the entertainment and, most of all, the people who I still find to be the friendliest in the world.

During the time of the many campaigns I have taken part in, endeavouring to return the town to Liberalism, I have always done what I could to help promote Southport. The future seems bright. The unfortunate decline of Liverpool in recent years has benefited our town from a business point of view and shops and offices now find ideal premises and markets to work within. Southerners are beginning to find the town and, on a recent House of Commons Select Committee tour of Canada, I found that many Canadians were very eager to visit the town, further proof that the good name of Southport is known in every corner of the world.

I heartily commend Peter Aughton's book. It has been a long time since the last full length history of Southport and this one, so easy to read and full of so much genuine and human interest, looks set to satisfy that deficiency for some time to come.

Introduction

North Meols Ancestry

E found the gravestone without too much difficulty. It was near the west wall of the churchyard and close to the main entrance of the church. A flat reddish-coloured sandstone slab, full of moss and lichen and very badly worn by the passage of time. It was overlooked by the eighteenth-century clocktower and spire; tufts of grass had crept around the edge and the moss had made inroads into the ancient lettering. Because I had some idea of what to expect, I was able to make out the words 'John Aughton of Marshside' and eventually I made out a date of decease which appeared to be 1844.

As I fumbled for paper and pencil I saw my wife put up the collar of her coat and I felt the first cold spots of rain on my face. The north-westerly had increased in strength since our arrival and our infant daughter, the third member of our little party, was making onerous grumbling noises which gave me second thoughts about having brought her along. We had harboured visions of sunny pathways between the gravestones and a happy toddler cooing and pointing at the bright flowers left in remembrance, but the stark reality of that overcast spring day was a leaden sky and a chill wind straight from the Irish Sea.

'Jane, relict of the above,' I managed to decipher. I rested my piece of paper against the low pebble-built wall. It flapped in the wind as I tried to write on it and the rain, now building up to a persistent drizzle, created a random pattern of blotches on my record. My daughter's grumblings had turned into open defiance and lusty red-faced screaming. My wife took her small charge into the shelter of the church porch and was looking dolefully at me through the lashings of rain that lay between us. I looked up at the spire against the dark skies and it looked back impassively. The cold and the rain had penetrated my enthusiasm. I questioned the purpose of the whole expedition. I looked at the soggy scrap of paper which represented the total sum of my researches. I felt a trickle of rain finding its way down my back. As I looked one more time at the worn and illegible lettering on the sandstone, I made up my mind to abandon the whole project. 'If this is what tracing your ancestors is all about', I thought, 'then it's not for me'.

That night sleep evaded me for a long time and as I tossed fitfully between consciousness and unconsciousness I was haunted by memories from my past. Three childhood scenes came back to me and, although the details might be out of focus, they were all real events.

The first was in one of the long peaceful summers of the late forties. I was pedalling hard on my new bicycle to catch up with my father who waited at the crest of a small humpbacked bridge which spanned the Leeds and Liverpool canal near Halsall. We stopped to admire the view and he pointed out the squat tower of Ormskirk Church on the skyline and told me to look for the little spire. To the right was another church standing prominently on the brow of a hill.

'That's Aughton Church', he said. (It was in fact Christ Church Aughton, the parish church was not visible from where we were.) I already knew that there was a place of that name out beyond the horizon somewhere and I had often wondered about the seeming co-incidence.

'Did our family come from there'?

'I suppose they might have done'.

'But how long ago'?

'A long time ago', he shook his head, 'Long, long ago. We'll never know the answer to that question'.

The second memory which returned to me as I lay there sleepless was an indoor scene in the winter months when I was about seven. Perhaps it was Christmas, for I was sitting around a bright coal fire with the family. The children listened fascinated as father and grandfather conversed with each other in the dialect; the conversation went something like the following.

'Didta know Pluggin Tum's feyther's gone deeod'?

'Does t'mean Owd William's Bob, 'im as lived on t'broo '?

'Aye, 'im as wed Owd Stem's youngest'.

'That's reet, 'e wus a proper Sond-grounder'.

'What's a Sondgrounder'?, I piped up.

My father only used the dialect in conversation with his father. He changed to ordinary speech when he wanted to address anybody else.

'To be a Sandgrounder', he said, 'you've got to be born on the sand land around these parts. And your father and mother must be born on the sand land too'.

Mother was born in Cheshire. Grandad had married a Cheshire lass too. Father explained that this meant he and his children were disqualified from using the title. Only grandad with his red face, white whiskers and old-fashioned speech was a true Sandgrounder. Grandad sensed the slight disappointment in his grandson.

'Duant thee worry lad', he said kindly, 'Tha' canst call thisel a Sond-grounder if tha' wants ter'.

The third scene was in Churchtown, when my age had still not reached double figures. My father took me through the lychgate and into the grounds of St. Cuthbert's churchyard. This, he explained, was where my ancestors were buried. He pointed out a well preserved stone of blue slate which lay near to the main pathway.

'Your great-grandparents', he said.

It was a legible stone with deep clear lettering. I noticed the names Edward and Mary; both were familiar to me for one was my brother's middle name and the other my sister's middle name.

On observing that he had kindled a spark of interest, my father walked nearer the church and away from the path, scanning the ground as he walked. Soon he found the object of his search and he beckoned me to come over.

'He's one of your ancestors too'. He pointed to an ancient slab of red sandstone, covered with moss and lichen.

At first I thought the writing on the slab was illegible but, by finding the right viewpoint and by searching for patterns of grooves in the sandstone, I discovered that the family name was indeed carved upon it. This time, the forename was that of my father himself.

'John Aughton of Marshside', I read with difficulty, 'who was *he?*'

It took my father a few moments to answer this question and when the answer came the reason for his delay became apparent - he had to work out a precise form of words for his offspring to understand.

'He', pointing to the old grave before us, 'was *his'*, pointing to the more recent grave, 'grandfather'.

Great grandfather's grandfather! I counted the generations on my fingers but when I tried to put the names to the generations I found a name was missing. I have a feeling that my father supplied me with the missing name and thus completed a genealogy which reached back to the eighteenth century, but there the memory of my earliest researches into the family history ends. I have no recollection of what my next question was.

The night after my much later visit to the churchyard the memory of my childhood visit haunted me and I didn't finally get to sleep until the birds were heralding the dawn. We were staying at my mother's house and I eventually made a very late appearance at the breakfast table.

I was greeted with a bout of spoon banging from my infant daughter, a happy smiling child in complete contrast to the red-faced screamer of the day before. I heard somebody enter through the front door of the house. There followed a second bout of spoon banging as my wife Dilys entered carrying two hardbacked notebooks and some pencils.

'I couldn't sleep with you tossing and turning all night', she said. 'So I got up early and I've been out to the shops. I've decided that you're completely disorganised with your bits of paper. We're going to put everything in the notebooks from now on'.

My mouth was full of breakfast cereal. Before I could tell her that I had decided to abandon our family history project she spoke again.

'I thought we could go to the library today and see if we can find any local histories. Then perhaps I could do some shopping in Lord Street. We can leave Jackie with her Granny. We need to be on our own if we're going to make any progress'.

Overspending the family budget on Lord Street was a well known occupational hazard for visitors to Southport, but her other suggestion seemed a reasonable thing to do. We had previously agreed that the local histories might contain some things of interest, and I would therefore lose face if I didn't agree to the suggestion. We left our firstborn with her doting granny and, whilst these alternate generations made ridiculous cooing and chortling noises at each other, we headed for the hallowed hall of the Atkinson Reference Library. There I was presented with a copy of Bailey's 'History of Southport' and I was interested to find several references to the family name in the index. Browsing through the book I was surprised at how well written it was. I spent most of the time browsing through the early chapters and I found I was haunted again by thoughts of my ancestors.

After an hour or so in the library we decided to have a drink of coffee in the gardens outside the town hall; the weather had picked up remarkably since the previous day and it was pleasant and relaxed under the trees. We exchanged findings. I was wondering if I should have one more try before giving up my search as I now had no doubt

This buttress is thought to be the only remaining part of the original medieval church of St Cuthbert, North Meols. So much has been rebuilt over the years that we now know little about the original fabric of the building.

A plaque in St Cuthbert's listing all the rectors since 1178.

that we were an old North Meols family. As for my wife, who suffered from large overdoses of feminine intuition, she had completely wasted her time on a reference to a family called 'Aghton' a name from the middle ages which happened to be a similar spelling to ours!

Across the road and through the trees I could see the facades of the Lord Street shops with their ornate ironwork canopies flanking the entrance to the Wayfarer's Arcade. All this, I thought, was part of the old parish of North Meols. My ancestors must have known this place when it was no more than a bathing village. But what was here before the bathing village? A few scattered fishermen's cottages, I supposed. And before that? I had little doubt that two hundred years ago the very spot where we sat was covered by the sea at high tide. Just how far back did I have to stretch my imagination? Was there any information at all which survived to show what it was like?

I found myself staring into the upper branches of the sycamore trees. John, John, Edward, somebody, John. What was the name of Edward's father? Perhaps there was another grave or a written record somewhere.

'Dilys', I said, 'That grave. I think John was my great great great grandfather'.

She had been searching for something in her handbag and she now produced a cutting from a glossy women's magazine and studied it very intently. She held her index finger on the cutting as she spoke.

'It says here that the Victoria County Histories are the place to look. I wonder if they will have them in the library'.

'I think we ought to go back to Churchtown tomorrow'.

'Our name is a Lancashire place name. It says in here that Lancashire is one of the counties which has been fully researched and published'.

'We've got to go back again. We might be able to see the parish registers'.

'You're not taking the slightest notice of what I'm saying', she complained. 'You never know what we might find. We could have a coat of arms. Or anything!'

We didn't manage to get to Churchtown the next day, but a little later in the same year we did find ourselves back again in much milder weather. This time we were free of the cares of parenthood and free to explore church and churchyard at our leisure.

'I suppose we should write to the rector if we want to study the parish records', I said. 'We can't very well expect to turn up out of the blue and to see them without an appointment'.

'No, but there's still plenty we can do. We've only looked at one corner of the graveyard so far; there's bound to be inscriptions inside the church - all churches are full of them'.

The parish church of North Meols has suffered more than most from the population explosion of the nineteenth century. It underwent a major rebuilding programme in mid-Victorian times and again in the early twentieth century. Apart from a single medieval buttress, the oldest part of the church is the fabric which survives from an earlier rebuilding which took place between·1730 and 1739. A plain and unpretentious structure was created at that time which was well suited to the needs of a small agricultural community and, for those who wish to find it, the cosy and intimate eighteenth-century atmosphere still remains at the west end of the church, around the spire and in the vestry.

We lifted the heavy latch and stepped into the cool interior. Dilys was right about the inscriptions. On the wall nearby was a list of rectors

St Cuthberts, North Meols, 1859. A well-known picture of Churchtown and one of the earliest photographs. Bland tells us that the wooden pump at Churchtown was replaced by an iron one in 1858. Beattie painted a picture from exactly the same angle which he claimed was a few years earlier and which shows the wooden pump.

beginning with the name of Adam the Clerk in 1178 and continuing almost unbroken down to the present time, a reminder that the church fabric was a misleading guide to the antiquity of the place. We were standing in a parish church which was as old as any in England. Another, less obvious list was that of the churchwardens, names of local men who had served in this office from the early eighteenth century up to the present time and it looked very worthy of study. We also spotted a table with leaflets on it, including a booklet giving a short history of the church. I took one of the booklets and put some coins in the box provided. Things seemed to be going as well as could be expected.

We heard the sound of a latch. The door opened and a man entered. He was in his sixties, with thinning hair, of medium build and with a kindly, bespectacled face. He greeted us.

'Can I help you? You look as though you are searching for something'. How right he was! I prepared my words carefully.

'My grandfather was buried here', I explained, 'and I thought we might find some references to the family name'.

'Ah yes. We often get visitors for that reason. What is the name?'

I told him. I sensed that he did not wish to disappoint me.

'Yes', he said slowly. 'There are a few here but not very many'. This reply, though I did not appreciate it at the time, is the best that the family historian can hope to get, far better than a cheerful reassurance that there are plenty of them around!

The font at St Cuthberts, with wooden cover and the names of local families visible in the wooden panels behind. Infants continue to be added to the long list of names in the North Meols baptismal register.

As we conversed, we progressed through the church and he pointed out items of interest. He took us down the nave where we were shown one of the pews. This particular pew was boxed around and was larger and grander than all the others. It was something which used to be quite common in the nineteenth century but which has now become extremely rare. It was, he explained, for Roger Hesketh and his family. Here, in North Meols, the people still proudly retained a resident lord of the manor.

We arrived at a point near the north-west corner of the nave where I spotted a board high on the wall with some lettering on it. The board was partly hidden by shadow but with difficulty, it could still be read. I could see something about a school, but what intrigued me was that I thought I could see my surname on it. The board gave a list of benefactors to the North Meols Grammar School; about ten people were listed, including several members of the Hesketh family. The latest benefaction was given in 1800 and the earliest, by James Starkie, the rector, in 1684. But the one which interested me most was a benefaction of £10 by John Aughton in 1719! An amazing find. I couldn't really take in the consequences: could the family really have been in North Meols for so long?

I busied myself with copying out the whole of the inscription. When I had finished I was a long way behind my companions. I badly wanted to tell my wife about this exciting new find, but she was deep in conversation with our new acquaintance. As I approached, it was with the smug feeling of having made an excellent discovery whilst she had been wasting away the time with idle gossip. But I did not manage to get the first word.

'Peter!' she said. 'Mr. Roberts is the parish clerk. He says we can look at the parish registers!'

Thus began our quest. We came to know the parish clerk quite well during the following summer. On the first of our appointments we arrived at the pre-arranged time, armed self-consciously with hardbacked notebooks and pencils. We were shown into a little room under the spire, a sort of ante-room to the vestry. Mr. Roberts produced a pair of steps on which he stood to unlock a cupboard high up in one corner of the room.

'Whereabouts would you like to start'?

'We thought we would start with the baptisms in 1870 and work backwards from there'. We had discussed this problem at some length. I knew exactly when my grandfather was born and this seemed the logical point at which to begin our search.

He handed down a number of heavy volumes and we placed them carefully on a table beneath a little window. Having passed down about five volumes, which looked to be more than adequate for the day's work, the parish clerk stepped down and found us a chair and a stool. On the table before us were records kept by his predecessors more than a hundred years ago. What would they reveal? What secrets were hidden in these volumes?

I shall never forget the thrill of our first discovery. In the baptismal register, recorded on January 15th 1871, was entered the name of John, the son of Edward and Mary Aughton.

It was grandad! Yes, it was grandad's baptism! But it was not the grandad I had known in the sixth and seventh ages of man; he was a babe 'mewling and puking in his nurse's arms'! Dilys, too, was quite moved by this, our very first discovery, and we sat stupidly entranced and savouring the moment for several minutes. The entry told me little that I did not already know, but it left me with a newfound respect for the traditions of the Church and the way in which the events of life and death were considered important enough to be celebrated and recorded. I felt something take seed inside me. It was the urge to know more. I had tasted the fruit from the tree of knowledge. There was to be no more turning back.

We decided that I should continue to search through the baptisms; Dilys would search the burial register. For some reason we were unable to find the marriage register for the Victorian period. Other findings followed quickly at first. My grandfather's brothers and sisters appeared one by one. Richard, George, Lilly, Ellen, Alice - slightly familiar names of people whom I remember him talking about. A whole Victorian family gradually came to light.

A wooden board in the church displays the benefactors to the North Meols Grammar School, beginning with James Starkie in 1684 and ending with Sarah Hesketh in 1800.

I worked backwards through the nineteenth century. There was a long gap where I found nothing of interest for several years. The gap stretched out to a decade. I was in the 1860s and then in the 1850s. We sat and searched in the stillness of the vestry, where it was so quiet that we could hear our own breathing and every small scratch of our pencils. Still nothing. I started on an older volume which took me back to before the reign of Victoria. Still nothing. But Dilys would occasionally whisper a find in the burial register of people whom we were as yet unable to identify. We recorded these finds for future reference.

Hours later, I was suffering badly from eyestrain and just beginning to lose heart when I quite suddenly found the object of my quest. Written unmistakeably in the register was the baptism of Edward, the son of Richard and Alice Aughton. The date was April 13th, 1834.

Richard! That was the missing name! Of course it was Richard! Hadn't my father told me all those years ago? I became aware that, although I had forgotten the name, my subconscious mind had remembered it. Here was some of the proof I needed. With this discovery I was surely within sight of the eighteenth century! My eyestrain had miraculously disappeared, I studied the page and the neatly penned handwriting. There was something very moving about it. I found that my fists were tightly clenched and that my stomach was knotted. My Adam's apple lodged in my throat. I felt the connection between this moment in time and the moment over a hundred and thirty years ago when the record was written in this very book and perhaps at this very spot.

'Are you feeling all right? You look as pale as a sheet'.

'Look'. I pointed at the baptisimal register.

'Richard', she said. 'Yes. I think I have found his burial. It was in 1879. He was eighty.'

I looked at what she had written in her notebook, then we carefully turned the pages of the burial register to check it out. She was right, it all seemed to fit together. By degrees I realised that if there was a Richard baptised in about 1799 and if his parents were called John and Jane then that would verify that the gravestone really was what my father claimed it to be.

'Don't get too carried away', said Dilys. 'There's still a lot more to be done. I think its about time to give ourselves a break. Let's put the registers away and take a walk around the church for some fresh air. I'm getting absolutely boss-eyed with all this searching'.

The stocks outside the chuchyard wall at St Cuthbert's. Made by John Linaker in 1741, they were last used in 1862 when a man was given six hours for drunkenness.

In Churchtown there was all the atmosphere of the English village. The lychgate led from the church to a small green with a cluster of horse chestnut and sweet chestnut trees giving shade to a stone obelisk. Standing in a recess of the church wall were the village stocks with the name of John Linaker and the date 1741 carved upon them, illegible except to those who knew exactly where to look. Across the lane next to the church was an old long low building with stone tablets set into the walls, announcing that it once housed the village school. Carefully preserved cottages with thatched roofs and gardens full of flowers stood next to the school building. The green was also flanked by Churchtown's two pubs, the Hesketh and the Bold, named after the two manorial families. Their walls were whitewashed and their cornerstones and windowframes were picked out in black; both pubs had yards and stables which had been converted long ago into car parks. We made use of both the Hesketh and the Bold when in Churchtown, and sometimes fell into conversation with local people. It was here that my wife, a Lincolnshire lass whom I met at a London party in the swinging sixties, made herself completely at home and displayed an amazing talent for extracting dubious anecdotes of local history from the other patrons.

The parish clerk lived in a house opposite the church, near the entrance gates to Meols Hall. He made us very welcome and we were given coffee and biscuits in the mornings, cups of tea in the afternoon. He helped us to find the right registers, and occasionally helped us to read some of the handwriting which varied a great deal in quality. On one occasion he noticed that we were slightly cramped for workspace and he struggled across the village green with a small table from his house. He was not a young man and it would have been a simple matter for two people to carry the table, but such was his nature that he wanted to give us a pleasant surprise and he did not wish to interrupt our researches.

These were welcome diversions from the strain of searching the parish registers. When we had worked back to the eighteenth century, Mr. Roberts explained that the registers had all been published up to the year 1812 and could be consulted in the central library on Lord Street. I was pleased to discover this, for I was apprehensive about handling the older documents and I felt that we had already taken up a lot of his time.

'The Blundells managed to get back to the seventeenth century', said Mr. Roberts on one of our later visits to Churchtown. 'It's very unusual to get back so far'.

'That's really quite something', I replied. 'I would love to find that we had been in the parish as long as that'.

'Let me show you something', he announced, and he disappeared into the adjoining room. He returned a few minutes later and proudly placed an astonishing object on the table.

Dilys and I were novices. We had come to accept the finely bound Victorian volumes with the copperplate handwriting which we had been studying, but we had never before seen an Elizabethan parish register in all its glory! Before us was an incredibly musty volume of wrinkled, yellowed and uneven parchments. It was grotesquely warped, battered by the centuries. It grinned horribly at us from between its ancient calfskin bindings. Dilys clutched her notebook to her bosom; white knuckles showed over the edges.

The parish clerk took no notice whatever of our dilemma.

'Of course you won't be needing this, but I thought you might enjoy seeing it'. He opened it at the first page. By some miracle the register did not fall apart. He was right, of course, it was impossible to think of ancestors who had been alive in Elizabethan times. I looked with curiosity at this, the oldest of the North Meols parish registers. The pages were crammed with spidery writing, there were scratches and blobs made by a sharpened quill plucked from a long forgotten goose. Here was a corner torn off a page, and here was something scrawled in the margin. Events of life and death from the age of Shakespeare filled the yellowed parchments. Was it possible that I could have an ancestor hiding somewhere in this ancient volume?

'You'll never manage to read *that!*' Dilys had recovered some of her composure. I had to confess that she was right − hard as I tried I could not read a single word of it. (I was to meet the register again, but not for over a decade, and on our second meeting it greeted me as an old friend. Greatly to my surprise, I discovered that in the years between it had somehow become quite legible!)

At the end of the week Dilys presented Mr. Roberts with a small token of our gratitude and I gave him a donation towards the church funds. He was torn between loyalties, for he did not want us to feel indebted to him in any way, but he knew that he could not refuse a gift and that it was his duty to accept the donation. The fact was that there was no way in which we could ever repay the riches which he helped us to find at St Cuthbert's.

Those summer days in Churchtown remain a golden memory. They left inside me a deep sense of satisfaction and belonging which many people can never know. North Meols had cast a spell on me, as strange and compelling as the song which drew Odysseus to the sirens. When North Meols called upon me, and as it revealed its secrets one by one, I could not resist that call. What had started off as a weekend recreation became an obsession. The more I managed to learn the more I became fascinated by life in North Meols. Not only did I meet my ancestors, but I came to know all the other people of the parish as well. I knew the past was full of poverty, hunger and hardship, but these combined to give life a sharper sense of reality, a real meaning to life, and a strong dependence on the local community. I met fishermen, shoemakers, blacksmiths, village craftsmen, schoolmasters, everybody from the farm labourers and yeomen to the rector and the village squire. Generation after generation, century after century, the great pageant of English history rolled back and a truth stranger than any fiction began to appear.

I came to know the other families of the parish. The Sumners, Gregsons, Peets and Rigbys who were well established families before Southport was born. I met the Bradshaws, Wignalls, Linakers and Hulmes all of whom remembered the time when Cromwell's ironsides ruled the length and breadth of England. The Suttons, Watkinsons, Brookfields and Blundells were old enough to remember when the beacons burned on the hilltops to warn of the approach of the Spanish Armada. The Wrights, Rimmers and Abrams were so ancient that they were scratching a living from the North Meols soil when the old world struggle for the crown was still being fought between the houses of Lancaster and York. The families of Bond, Ball, Jump, Haworth and Hodgson were even older, so old that their names originated in North Meols at some time deep in the Middle Ages when fathers first began to take a family name to pass on to their sons.

And what of my own family quest? It is sufficient to say that my interests expanded to include these other families, and they continued to expand until I found that what I was really studying was no longer a family history but the history of North Meols itself, and of the town to which it gave birth. It is that history which fills the following pages.

Chapter One

The Settlement in the Meols

O N the northern horizon lay the purple mountains of the Lake District. Across the sea to the south west could be seen the snowcapped peaks of Snowdonia, and by a trick of refraction the summit of Snaefell on the Isle of Man could be seen near the sunset, low in the western sky.

The whole of the coastal plane was dotted with shallow meres which were destined to acquire names like Gattern Mere, Barton Mere, White Otter and Black Otter Pool, but the greatest of these was Martin Mere. It measured over four miles from east to west and three miles from north to south, and at one point it came within a mile of the sea. In its time Martin Mere was numbered amongst the greatest meres in England. Great flocks of wild geese flew over its waters. Pike, perch and bream swam beneath the surface and the osprey nested in the rushes of its hinterland. The waters would rise and fall with the seasons and after heavy rains the acres of bog and marshland were reclaimed by the waters, dried up creeks filled with water and became part of the mere until the next dry spell. After particularly heavy rains Martin Mere would sometimes manage to find an outlet to the coast and spill over into the great salt waters of the sea.

North of the mere was a river estuary, another habitat of geese and wild fowl, a land of mudflats, salt marshes and sea-washed turf — but to the south the coastal regions were of an entirely different nature. Here blown sand accumulated into a wide band of desolate sandhills with ever changing contours sculpted by the wind. Here the land was in perpetual conflict with the sea. On the slopes of the sandhills sparse clumps of marram grass struggled for a hold on the sandy inclines but in the valleys between the dunes the sand in some places gave way to carpets of local vegetation where, at the lowest points, lay dark shallow pools of water. Here grew the marsh marigold, reedmace, burr reed, water mint and bog bean. Millions of years of evolution had produced the sand lizard which scurried through the coarse grass, and in the spring could be heard the croaking, unlovely mating call of the natterjack toad.

Between the sand dunes, the mud flats, and the mere, nature had created a stretch of fertile soil with woodlands for fuel, pasture for animals, and fresh water only a few feet below the ground. It was a suitable spot for human habitation, but the earliest settlers ignored the Meols. They had no need to colonise such a desolate and isolated region in a country which had an abundance of fine, fertile and virgin territory to choose from.

The forces of nature alone shaped this coastal region. Man made little impression on it and it was known only to isolated hunters and wandering nomads until the long, high-prowed vessels of the Vikings rounded the treacherous iron-bound coast of Scotland and created a base on the Isle of Man from where they could command the whole of the Irish Sea. The Vikings attempted to settle in Ireland but were driven out by the Celtic Irish, so they turned to the north-west coast of England where, in the ninth century, they were able to establish themselves into small communities without any apparant strife or bloodshed. From what little evidence we have, it seems that they came not as plunderers, raiders or rapists, but as peaceful settlers prepared to drain the land and to plough the soil, often soil which was inferior to that which was already under the ploughs of the Anglo-Saxon settlements further inland.

The Vikings, a hardy sea-going race, preferred the coastal regions to the inland valleys. They knew how to farm the harvest which the sea had to offer and they knew where to dig for shellfish on the sandy shore. They found natural banks and hollows and constructed turf dwellings roofed over with brushwood and foliage. They dug wells to the water table. They cut timber and brushwood. They dried turf and peat to heat their primitive homes in the winter months. They brought the virgin land under cultivation. They herded sheep and they tended cattle. Sometimes they built a turf wall around a small enclosure where they kept pigs and hens. They fished the great mere and they snared the wild fowl to add variety to their rude tables.

The written records of the Viking settlements are few, but they left a permanent legacy in the names of the places which they settled. Although these placenames have sometimes changed over the centuries, their Scandinavian origins are beyond dispute. Thus Meols itself was a Norse word for sandhills. Birkdale, Ainsdale, Formby, Altcar, Crosby, Litherland, and Kirkdale are all Norse in origin and show the wide extent of the coastal settlements.[1] Inland were Scandinavian names like Scarisbrick, Tarlscough, Ormskirk and Lathom, Kellamerg, Hesketh and many more. The Viking *Landamabok* mentions Crossens as 'Kross-Ness', a clear indication that a cross was erected there, probably for the guidance of travellers along the coast. Also in the *Landamabok* is mentioned an ancestor of Mark de Meols called Odda, the son of Grim, possibly the first Norse settler in the Meols - this tiny scrap of genealogy represents all that is known of the names of the settlers for several centuries.

When these first settlements were made the region between the Mersey and the Ribble was border country and belonged to the Kingdom of Northumbria. This was to change after a great battle was fought at an unidentified site called Brunanburgh in the year 937. The outcome of the battle was that the Mercians defeated the Northumbrians and their victorious King, Athelstan, was able to push the frontiers of Mercia northwards to the Ribble. We learn very little about the Meols settlement until many years later than Athelstan's reign, after the coming of the Normans and when sufficient generations had passed for much of the Viking blood of the early settlers to become mixed with that of the neighbouring Angles, Saxons, Picts and Scots.

In 1086 William the Conqueror sent out his scribes to collect information for his ambitious and invaluable survey which became known as the Domesday Survey. The Ribble was still recognised as a boundary, for the returns south of the Ribble were included with Cheshire and those to the north appear with the returns for Yorkshire. 'So narrowly did he cause the survey to be made', records the *Anglo-*

This boulder was excavated from a depth of 17ft when the new pumping station was built at Crossens. It is thought to have been carried from Dumfriesshire by glacial action. The Snoterstone, which marked the boundary of West Derby Hundred was a boulder very similar to this one.

Saxon Chronicle, 'that there was not one single hide nor rood of land nor − it is shameful to tell but he thought it no shame to do − was there an ox, cow, or swine that was not set down in the writ'. But the Meols lay far beyond the valleys of the South and the Midlands and, as the Norman commissioners worked further northwards collecting their data, the hamlets became more scattered, the population became thinner, the miles became longer, and it is shameful to tell that the details they returned became less and less. But what they *did* return was of very great interest, and far better than nothing at all.

'In Otringemele and Hershala and Hireton there were three hides quit of the geld of the ploughlands and of the forfeitures of bloodshed and rape, but they rendered all other customs' − thus reads a translation of the Domesday Book. The Otringemele of the survey can be identified as North Meols and was held by five Saxon thanes whose names were not recorded. It was free from the Danegeld − tax paid to the Danes as immunity against bloodshed and rape − because the land was badly drained and of no great value; the prefix 'otringe' is a Norse sounding name, not dissimilar to Odda, the son of Grim, and possibly a descendant. The regions called Hershala and Hireton are not so easy to identify but, nearby, the survey mentions two other places called Meols, both of which include Scandinavian names in their spellings − they are called Erengermeles and Argarmeles. In the same area was Einulvesdael, 'Einulve's Dale', which is just recognisable as the earliest mention of Ainsdale. It is known from later documents that Argarmeols was an area on the seaward side of Birkdale which was later inundated by the sea. In William the Conqueror's time it was valued, like Ainsdale, at two carucates of land.

The land was measured in practical units of how much could be ploughed by a team of eight oxen in a year − this crude measure was called a bovate or an oxgang. Eight bovates made one carucate, and there were six carucates to one hide. The latter figure causes some confusion because it varied between different parts of the country, and

The indefatigable cleric, amateur medic and antiquarian William T. Bulpit, returns from one of his expeditions in 1899 with a dugout canoe which once sailed the waters of Martin Mere. The canoe, probably the single most important archaeological discovery from the region, can still be seen at the Botanic Gardens Museum.
(Photo, Botanic Gardens Museum.)

in this part of the Domesday Survey the units are not always consistent. A hundred and fifty years after Brunanburgh the Northumbrian influence was still very evident for, although some figures are Mercian measures, others appear to be Northumbrian.

There was a point on the coast where the mud from the Ribble met the sand from the Mersey. It lay at the northern limit of the sandhills and was therefore the first point, travelling northwards along the coast, at which access to the interior was not hindered by mountains of blown sand. It was here that Kirktown or Churchtown was established as the main centre of population in the Meols.

The name implies the early existence of a kirk which may well have been of pre-Norman origin. Further evidence on this point is lacking but 'the chapel of moeles with all its appurtenances is' referenced in the records of the distant Abbey of Evesham as early as 1113, and soon after this date 'three brethren and a chaplain' were supposed to man the chapel.[2] It is possibly true that the original chapel, whenever it was founded, occupied the same site as the later buildings — but the coastline has changed so much over the centuries that if this supposition is true then the first chapel must have stood hard by the shore, perhaps on a little hillock lapped by the sea at high tide, or even on a small island. The earliest references imply that no more than a chapel existed, but this chapel was later elevated to the full status of a parish church.

From our knowledge of Norman England and from records which survive from subsequent centuries we can deduce a little about the people who lived and worked the land under Norman rule. The first of the cruck-built cottages which became a common form of construction in timber growing areas throughout the middle ages, were built at this time. The Meols had no local stone, the cottages had poor foundations and the fabric of the wall seldom lasted for more than one generation, but the method of construction survived for centuries and can be reconstructed from later knowledge of building techniques.

The crucks were made from a pair of large curved timbers, usually of oak or some other hardwood. They were supported at the base and joined at their upper ends to form a frame suitable for one end of the cottage. Pairs of crucks were placed at intervals, forming bays, and joined by a ridgepole which was fixed with wooden pins, the whole being supported by a timber framework. The cottage was built in a number of bays and the framework was developed to look like the frame of an upturned boat; the rectangular and triangular panels were then filled in with wattle and daub. In local terminology this became known as clamstaff and daub - the clamstaff was woven brushwood and the daub was a local concoction of sea slutch and mud mixed with straw or rye grass from the sandhills and trodden by foot. Mud was generally used because no clay was available locally.

The distance of between fifteen and twenty feet between the crucks varied little throughout the country. It was a suitable dimension for timber construction and a convenient size for human living space. Extra bays could easily be added, increasing the length and area available for human and animal accommodation; such a bay could provide standing room for a team of four oxen. In the early middle ages the living space was often shared with the farm animals. The thrifty occupants would never dream of wasting valuable body heat by building a partition between human and animal quarters.

Roofs were thatched with rushes from the mere. In later times the rushes were replaced with rye straw, but rushes were still used to thatch the barns and outbuildings. The medieval cottage had no ceiling and no such luxury as a chimney; smoke from the open fire was left to

One of the several thatched cottages which still survive in Churchtown today, providing a tangible link with the past of North Meols.

find its own way to the outside through the thatch and the roof timbers became blackened with a thick deposit of soot. Windows, originally 'wind holes', were small and unglazed — so that the cottages were dark inside and the pall of the smoke always hung around. In winter evenings the only light was from the yellow flickering of the fire. Chickens roosted on the blackened rafters and their droppings fell onto the rushes which lined the earthen floor. Rodents and other vermin lived in the thatch. Bedding consisted merely of straw, and the only furniture was a crude table with perhaps a form to sit on — a wooden chest was a great luxury. The serfs and villeins who dwelt in these cottages lived a brief, hard-working, extremely basic existence. They lived, laboured and died knowing nothing of life but to be tied to the land. Their life expectancy was just sufficient to survive and to give rise to another generation.

For over a century after the Norman Conquest the isolation of the Meols was only rarely disturbed by the occasional traveller with news from the outside world. Towards the end of the twelfth century we at last get a smattering of written records which give us a glimmer of what life was like. In 1178 we discover the name of the first known incumbent whose name, appropriately enough, was Adam the Clerk of Meols. Adam was not the most perfect of his calling and we only know of him because he fell foul of the forestry laws, a common enough offence in his time, and was fined the sum of half a mark. His offence was probably a case of poaching, or illegal cutting of timber to eke out his slender living, or perhaps to help out one of his flock.

The church thus provided the first nucleus of social life in Churchtown, but another less venerable but still ancient institution which is almost as old claims a mention. In a charter dated prior to 1186 there is a mention of 'the maintenance of a hospice for those who shall have need thereof'. The hospice was an inn to accommodate the thin trickle of travellers passing through the parish. It also provided a place at which to drink and gossip, and where local people and the wayfarers could exchange news with each other.

In 1194 the Baron of Penwortham granted North Meols to Richard, the son of Huctred, in a charter which between the more formal wording gives a tantalising, brief description of part of the parish:

> . . . all Normeles with its appurtenances for his homage and service, freely, quietly, wholly and honourably, in wood, ways, paths, mills, churches,

fisheries, viveries, marshes, pools and meres . . . by rendering yearly one mark of silver for all service to me belonging, save forinsec service: and for this grant the said Richard has given me five marks of silver, and one hunting boot . . .[3]

Perhaps the mention of a mill in this passage does not provide proof that such existed, but it makes it very probable that a primitive mill did indeed grind the corn at this time. In 1903 an archaeological find was made at Churchtown near the gates of Meols Hall. Excavations revealed part of a timber construction at a depth of twelve feet, corresponding roughly to ground level in the early middle ages, which appeared to be the remains of part of a water mill. Further investigation uncovered a structure of wooden planks mounted on piles driven into the ground, which appeared to be a wharf or a bridge. A wickerwork frame, thought to be an eel trap, was also excavated — giving more evidence that the stream had flowed past this point at some time in the past. It was no mean feat of medieval engineering to drive a mill wheel from the sluggish waters of the stream known as the Otter Pool (later known as the Old Pool) which flowed through Churchtown in the Middle Ages.

The first freeholder to be resident in the Meols was probably, as is indicated by his name, Alan de Meols, an ancestor of the Meols family. Only one generation later, a second family, the Coudrays, became owners of three quarters of the manor but the Meols family hung on to their surviving quarter for five generations until the two families were united by marriage in the fourteenth century. The original Meols family were not forgotten and their arms, consisting of 'Argent, three torteaux in fesse within a bordure gules', were borne and quartered by the later Lords of the Manor.*

The Coudray family probably came to North Meols direct from Normandy, for Robert de Coudray appears in the civic post of *praepositus* at Domfont, Normandy, in the year 1180,[4] and a man of the same name became Lord of the Manor of North Meols early in the thirteenth century. He was at one time in the service of King John

---

*There is some inconsistency about the Meols arms, which are known only from the quarterings of their descendants. In some cases no bordure is quoted and in other cases 'in fesse' is replaced by 'in chief'.

The brick-built mill situated in Mill Lane, Churchtown. By the sixteenth century, wind power had replaced water power in North Meols. This was the traditional site of the windmill; the water mill which it replaced was situated nearby, off Moss Lane.
(Photo, Botanic Gardens Museum)

Coudray of Meols
Sable, ten billets 4, 3, 2 and 1 argent
The Coudrays probably originated from Domfront in Normandy where a Robert de Coudray appears in 1180. Their male line came to a tragic end in 1350 when the Black Death reached northern England.

but he supported the barons against the king at the time of Magna Carta, for in 1217 (when Henry III was king) he was given 'sieson of his land as he had before he withdrew from the service of the king's father'.[5] Robert de Coudray did much for North Meols. Not only did he actually live in the parish, he probably built the first manor house, and he successfully obtained the right to hold a weekly market and an annual fair on his manor.

The right to hold a weekly market was granted only on the condition that it did not draw trade from other established markets at that time, and it seems that this proved to be the case for the market only lasted a few years. This meant that the annual fair, held on the eve and the day of St. Cuthbert, became quite an event in Churchtown and although we have no early accounts of the fair, it appears to have survived the centuries and was still being celebrated boisterously by local residents during the nineteenth century.

It is obviously dangerous to extrapolate from the nineteenth century to the thirteenth. But the custom of giving the arvel bread, a funeral loaf, and the beverage called the braggart drink, both appear to be very ancient survivals. The drunken orgy which accompanied the election of a local mayor at the annual fair could also, just possibly, be a medieval survival. The traditional rushbearing ceremony, known to have been practised in Birkdale, and which involved replacing the rushes lining the floor of the church, must have very ancient origins. The rushes were cut from the smaller meres like the White Otter Mere in Ainsdale and the rushbearers walked to the parish church along the old Kirkgate which, at that time, skirted the shoreline for part of its length.

Francis Bailey makes some interesting and perceptive comments on the fair. His remark about country people ignoring the calendar reform applies only to the dates of the fair and should not be taken too literally; there was no way in which country people could remain out of step with the rest of the world for very long:

> The Churchtown fair, on the Sunday succeeding August 16th, and the Birkdale rushbearing, a fortnight later, were presumably a survival of the ancient 'wakes' or festival in honour of the patron saint of the parish, one of whose feast days was September 4th. Churchtown and Birkdale were, of course, in the same parish, and it is curious that the fair and the rushbearing, which were both in practice much the same thing and probably once held on the same date, should have become duplicated in this way; the dates may have been affected by the calendar reform of 1752, which many country people ignored.[6]

The laws of primogeniture required that estates descended wholly to the firstborn son but, if no son existed, then the estate was divided equally between the daughters. Successful families were therefore those who were able to increase their estates by marriage to eligible heiresses with no brothers. The first generations of the Coudray family were moderately successful at the medieval marriage game — they acquired land nearby at Barton-juxta-Halsall through marriage to Amabel Blundell, and they added Thistleton on the Fylde to their estates through marriage to Anota de Whittingham.

Thus it was that early in the thirteenth century North Meols emerges as a very typical English community, complete with church and priest, manor house and lord of the manor, mill, ale-house, and an annual fair. The only thing missing was the manorial court, and throughout the Middle Ages all pleadings and court cases were heard at the baronial court in Penwortham — a precedent which continued until the sixteenth century.

Chapter Two

Church and Manor

VERY year when the winter had passed, a train of oxcarts led by men in rough-spun woollen habits, and with the crowns of their heads characteristically shaven, ground its way into the Meols along the muddy tracks from the north. The Cistercian monks from the Abbey of Sawley in the valley of the Ribble had been granted an acre of land to make a salt pit, and pasture for four oxen, six cows and two horses, required for the collecting and carriage of sand. For one period of a fortnight every year they had pasture rights for twenty oxen on the common land. The monks also obtained the right to cut turf and to boil seawater in lead pans to extract the salt from the brine, a valued commodity for those whose status put them above the salt cellar on the Abbot's table.[1]

The Cistercians, an old established order in the valleys of Lancashire and Yorkshire, were a practical and popular order and they were not above doing manual work with their own hands; indeed, it was obligatory for all members of the order to do some manual task every day. In North Meols the Abbey of Sawley had a right to 'all that the monks have gained from the sea or may gain hereafter' – showing that by about 1250 the monks had already built the first of several turf embankments which were constructed as defences against the sea and to claim land for agriculture. Land reclamation and drainage were typical of the projects with which the Cistercians became involved. Another of their interests, also of practical benefit to country communities, was the woollen industry, so that their presence in North Meols was a great asset to the populace. Evidence of their influence and popularity appears in 1250 when William de Coudray expressed his desire to be buried in the grounds of their abbey at Sawley.

The field name 'Salt Pit' was established at this time in Crossens, and the lane from Churchtown to Crossens became known as 'Bankfield Lane', showing both the line of the embankment and also the position of the coastline at that time. In the same vicinity was a field called 'Friars Nook', showing that friars as well as monks visited the area. It is possible that they were visitors from the Greyfriars Abbey near Preston.[2]

In terms of area, North Meols was a large manor, measuring seven miles in length and three to four miles in width, and the parish, which included Birkdale and Argarmeols, was longer than the manor by about four miles – but in terms of cultivated land and population the parish was small and in the times of the Coudrays it contained, at a very rough estimate, only 30 to 40 families tending their land in the infields and outfields. Apart from the lords of the manor, no family names survive from the thirteenth century and, even if they did, then the names were seldom passed down from father to son. Early in the next century, however, the court rolls for the County of Lancaster mention a number of offenders from North Meols who have managed to get their names recorded.[3] Most of them are known simply by a forename and a place of residence, but the exceptions give the families of Bond and Ball a claim to be the oldest families still extant in North Meols parish.

The extracts from the Lancaster court rolls in the reign of Edward II are very brief and most of the offences are of a common nature. William de Crossens and Thomas Baron are accused of fighting and found guilty of breach of the peace. Alan de Coudray was fined 3d for stealing brushwood. Adam Balle and William de Meols were fined 6d for trespassing, William de Meols was fined 5d for unjustly witholding a debt, and John, the son of John of Banks, was fined 3d for contempt of court.

Behind these charges are more interesting stories if only more details were available to embellish the bare facts. John Bonde of Bonke (Banks), for example, was fined 3d for default of service — this could be a simple case of a service not performed, or it could equally be the more serious offence of a bonded labourer trying to obtain his freedom. The name of the individual is close enough to the origin of surnames for us to assume that John Bonde really was bonded to his master; and we may even be witnessing a case of a surname being designated to a man.

The most common court cases, however, concern the important matter of the quality of the North Meols ale, and here it is a painful duty to report that in the reign of Edward II it did not pass the scrutiny of the official ale-tasters. William de Meols, no doubt the same man who was fined for trespass and for witholding his debts, must be held largely responsible for this deficiency. His daughter Margot was fined 3d in March 1324 for serving bad ale. In November of the same year we find William de Meols mentioned again, this time in connection with ale-wife Emma le Marescal — they were fined 6d for brewing and selling contrary to the assize (a statute dating from 1266 to control the price and quality of bread and ale). Dobyn Emmok and the wife of Walter de Meols were fined 6d for the same offence, and in 1325 Walter de Meols' wife again brewed contrary to the assize. It would appear that not only was there a lot of illegal brewing of ale taking place at this time but, if we are to judge by the 1324 entry, even the legal brew was not up to the required standard.

No contemporary account of the medieval ale-house survives, but if we are prepared to accept the description given by John Skelton, who was born towards the end of the Middle Ages, then we can add more detail to a scene which must have changed very little from the time of Emma le Marescal and Dobyn Emmok to the time of the infamous Elynour Rummynge.

Ms. Rummynge was not noted for high standards of hygiene, even allowing for the more primitive times. Skelton was doubtless guilty of some exaggeration, but the details he gives leave us with an uncomfortable impression that his account contains some seeds of truth:

> For as ill a patch as that
> The hennes run in the mash vat;
> For they go to roust
> Streight over the ale-joust,
> And dung, when it commes,

In the ale tunnes.
Then Elynour taketh
The mash bolle, and shaketh
The hennes' dung awaye,
And skommeth it into a tray
Wheras the yeest is,
With her maungy fistis:
And sometimes she blennes
The dung of her hennes
And the ale togider,
And sayth, 'Gossip, come hider,
This ale shall be thicker,
And flour the more quicker;
For I may tell you
I lerned it of a Jewe
When I began to brewe,
And I have found it trewe . . .

JOHN SKELTON

To the names of the alewives and other lawbenders we can add nine landowners who contributed to a lay subsidy in 1332. A total of exactly one pound was collected from North Meols. In one case a genealogy of three generations is given, but it seems that in the north of England it was the exception rather than the rule to have a surname in the 1330s. One exception is the earliest mention of a Hesketh living in the parish, an isolated case for it was still many years before the Heskeths came to Meols Hall:

LAY SUBSIDY NORTH MEOLS, 1332[4]

William de Coudray	6s 8d
William son of William	2s 0d
Richard de Swartbrek	2s 0d
Roger son of Thomas	16d
Robert de Heskeythe	14d
Adam son of William de Meols	3s 0d
William, son of William, son of Walter	18d
Adam son of Robert	12d
William son of Hugh	16d

William de Coudray, whose name appears first in this list, was the largest landowner and lord of the manor; he was married to Joan de Meols. It was a marriage which united the parts of the manor into one whole, and it was successful in as much as the couple produced no fewer than six sons. Of these, only four grew to manhood but, even so, the future of the Coudray family seemed very secure when Robert de Coudray inherited his estates in the year 1340 — but Robert did not live to enjoy his inheritance for very long. Two years later, Stephen de Claverley was appointed parson. He too was not destined to hold his post for long and his successor, William Abel, was appointed some time before 1352. The episcopal registers do not say exactly when William Abel was appointed and they do not record the reason for the vacancy, but students of the fourteenth century will not need to look far to find the most likely cause of the death of both Robert de Coudray and Stephen de Claverley.

North Meols, situated on the west coast and fanned by a clean sea breeze, was a much healthier place to live than the overcrowded and rat-infested alleyways of the medieval cities of Europe, and its isolation usually provided some insurance against pestilence and disease. But North Meols did not escape the Black Death.

It was in the summer of 1348 that a scurry of black rats ran ashore from the hold of a vessel which had crossed to Dorset from the continent. A few days later deaths occurred from a disease which produced hard dry swellings in the neck and the groin. The worst fears of the people were realised. It was the first outbreak in England of a plague which had caused havoc on the continent of Europe. Other outbreaks followed quickly. In an age which knew little of medicine and nothing of hygiene, the plague struck suddenly, drastically and fatally. Within a few months it had reached Bristol and the West, and by November it had gained a hold on London where the death toll climbed inexorably to twenty thousand. London's toll was light compared to Norwich where one of the most populous cities in England lost three quarters of its population.

In Scotland and the North they hoped the plague would die out before it reached them. They hoped in vain, for it moved relentlessly northwards in the summer of 1349. Estimates that half the population died seem to be no exaggeration. In the Yorkshire Abbey of Meaux only ten of fifty monks survived and in northern Lancashire records remain to show that there was a death toll totalling 13,000 covering ten country parishes.

Plague and pestilence were never far from the door in the Middle Ages, but the great plague of the fourteenth century was remembered as worse than anything in recorded history. All over the country bells tolled solemnly, humble carts carried the bodies of the dead to communal burial pits. The harvest lay rotting in the fields. Farm animals died. Cows lay bleating in agony as nobody came to relieve them of their milk. Swine ran wild through the crops. When man failed to feed them cats and dogs took to the wild to fend for themselves. In the worst places whole villages were wiped out, the number of living became too few to bury the dead, some fled from their stricken villages and carried the plague with them, the sick and infirm stayed behind to die - many who survived the pestilence faced a lingering death from starvation. Thriving little communities were changed within a few months to deserted ghost villages.

This was the England in which Kathryn de Coudray, a young woman of childbearing years, found herself a widow. Her husband, father, brother, sister and child were all dead. She found that she was the rightful owner of the manor of North Meols but it was by no means an enviable position to be in because the whole administrative structure of the country, the trade and the economy, had been brought to a virtual halt by the Black Death. The best course open to Kathryn was to remarry, to try and find a man who would stand by her and help with the many problems involved in getting the manor back on its feet again. Apart from one elderly uncle, Kathryn was the last of her dynasty. She found her man, but whether their marriage was one of choice or of necessity it is not possible to say. In due course she bore him a son and the blood of the Coudrays still flowed in North Meols.

The new lord of the manor was Richard, the second son of Walter, Lord of the Manor of Aughton, situated just a few miles inland from North Meols. Aughton (meaning 'oak town'), was a pre-conquest settlement and was English in the true sense of the word, being an 'Angle-ish' place name. The family of Aughton had been established in Lancashire for about four generations. Their male line came from Rhuddlan in North Wales where they were driven out by the Welsh risings in the thirteenth century and as compensation were given land at Aughton. They adopted the place name for their family name but clung to their Welsh ancestry for several generations using forenames such as Madoc, Bleddyn and Llewelyn. 'The lords of high Snowdon in great days of yore, were wont to make battle on Mona's fair shore', and in 1282 Wido (alias Guy) de Aughton renounced England for Wales and fought for Llewelyn ap Griffiths in Snowdonia against Edward I. His act of Welsh patriotism cost him his life and he fell in battle.[5]

Richard de Aughton was probably over thirty in the plague year, for in 1339 his name appears in connection with the death of Dionysia, the wife of William Bimmestone, for which he held a royal pardon. No details of Dionysia Bimmestone's death are recorded, but the pardon was granted 'in consideration of his having gone overseas in the king's service'. Thus Richard was a soldier of fortune, as were many of the younger sons of the minor gentry. His elder brother Thomas inherited the family estates at Aughton but Richard fared just as well as his brother. When he married Kathryn de Coudray he was able to give up his military career for the safer prospects of a family and lands of his own.

His marriage did not change the rebellious character of Richard de Aughton and in later life he appears in the law courts accused of breaking into a house in the neighbouring manor of Scarisbrick accompanied by John le Gardener, Roger the son of Robert Bonde, and William the son of Roger de Holmes. They carried off timber valued at ten pounds. The house was the property of the Abbey of Dieulacres in Staffordshire, and the abbot promptly sued him.

Soon after their marriage, Richard and Kathryn were involved in a sequence of law suits concerning their rights to North Meols and the boundary of their manor. The first action was brought against them by Thomas de Coudray, Kathryn's elderly uncle, who claimed to be the rightful heir of the quarter of the manor which had belonged to the Meols family. His claim was probably just, and seems to have been settled out of court with the agreement that the property reverted to Kathryn on his death. Another dispute concerned the northern boundary of the manor which was also the boundary between the hundreds of West Derby and Leyland. In 1354 Richard and Kathryn obtained a verdict which confirmed their right to the whole of North Meols and established where the northern boundary lay. The deed of settlement defines the boundary as running from 'Snoter-pool unto Snoterstone and so in a direct line to the midstream of the Ribble'. The 'Snoterpool' was a natural stream and the 'Snoterstone' a large limestone boulder deposited on the Ribble estuary by glacial action during the ice age. It was typical of a boundary stone, keeping its lonely vigil on the mudflats for centuries, and sometimes serving as a landmark for travellers along the coast.[6]*

Richard and Kathryn de Aughton had at least two children; their son and heir, William, became a soldier of fortune like his father. Perhaps, since William became a soldier, there had once been an older brother, but there is no record to show that this was the case. One day William arrived at Meols Hall accompanied by a young lady from a high-ranking Warwickshire family. Her name was Millicent Comyn. Exactly how William came to meet her is a matter of speculation and it is quite possible that their relationship was the rare event of a love match between two young people. This was unusual in an age when the local gentry went to great lengths to get their sons betrothed to daughters of the neighbouring gentry at the earliest possible convenience. But William's parents could hardly have disapproved of the match. Millicent had no brothers and this meant that she was the joint heiress of her father's estates at Newbold Comyn in Warwickshire and at Hall Moreton in Worcestershire. It was true that she had three sisters and she was therefore entitled to only a quarter of her father's estates, but this still made her a very marriagable young lady.*

*One of the last people to see the Snoterstone was the Rev. William Bulpit, who rediscovered it after a systematic search soon after 1900.

*Millicent Comyn's dower lands in Warwickshire and Worcestershire remained with the Aughtons of North Meols until the sixteenth century. Newbold Comyn is now a suburb of Leamington Spa. Holly Walk, which was the road to Newbold Comyn, was used by Charles

John Comyn, Millicent's father, also held land at Kinsale in Ireland, but a study of the Comyn family in Warwickshire shows them to be a branch of a very old and powerful Scottish family — that of the House of Badenoch.[7] To this family belonged John Comyn the Red, who early in the fourteenth century was Robert Bruce's main rival to the Scottish throne. The story of John Comyn's death must have been told and discussed heatedly at the fireside in Meols Hall, for it was an event which was still within living memory of the elders of Millicent's kin.

On the tenth of February 1306 Robert Bruce and John Comyn the Red met at the Franciscan Church of Greyfriars in Dumfries. Their meeting was prearranged and they were at variance over Scottish policy with the English. Hard words were exchanged which developed into a violent quarrel inside the church. Nobody witnessed exactly what happened, but Bruce came out of the building carrying a bloodstained dagger and his words were 'I doubt I ha' slain the Red Comyn!' Bruce's followers, who seem to have anticipated the event, shouted 'We'll make sickle [sure]', and they ran into the church drawing their swords. Robert Comyn, uncle of the Red Comyn, went to his nephew's assistance but both the Comyns were killed. Their blood was said to have run down the steps of the altar at Dumfries.

This bloody episode in Scottish history relates indirectly to the history of North Meols, for the three wheatsheaves of the Comyns were adopted by the Aughtons of North Meols in their own coat of arms (Sable, three garbs or). Perhaps when Millicent Comyn related her version of the murder of her kinsman at Dumfries her father in law told the story of the great Scottish raid which took place in 1322 when he was still a child at Aughton.

The County of Lancashire had been created with palatine rights in order to give the leading families the power to act quickly in the case of invasion from the north, but in the days after the Scottish victory at Bannockburn, when the threat of invasion was at its greatest, the county was pitifully organised and the Banastre family chose this worst possible moment to create a feud with the powerful Holland family — the result of which was a local civil war! The Scots under Robert Bruce and the Earl of Moray joined forces near the Solway and plundered southwards through the fells of the Lake District and into Lancashire. The country north of Preston was devastated and the Scots gained control of Preston itself. They crossed the Ribble and threw the rest of the county into panic. But the canny leader of the Scots knew exactly how far he could go before the English could organise their defences and he retreated back over the border before he could be brought to battle. This was the only time that the Scots penetrated so far to the south, yet the manor house at Aughton possessed a fortified pele tower like the houses of the border counties. It was in the pele tower that the family, the neighbours and the cattle gathered to take refuge when there was the threat of a raid. We cannot tell whether the pele was built in anticipation of raiders, or after the event as an insurance against a repeat performance.[8]

After the death of Richard de Aughton, it was the women who were left to run the manor whilst the son William followed in his father's footsteps as a soldier. It was in the early 1380s when the news arrived at Meols Hall that William had been declared an outlaw — this meant that all his estates were forfeited to the crown and he was doomed to live the rest of his life in exile. We have no idea what crime against

Dickens as the scene of the meeting between Mrs. Grainger and Carker in his novel 'Dombey and Son'. Hall Moreton, near the unspoilt village of Inkberrow, is still only ten miles from Evesham where the Abbey appointed the Rectors of North Meols still before the Reformation.

the state he was thought to be guilty of, but it is not difficult to imagine the dismay of his mother Kathryn and his wife Millicent with her small dependent children when they first heard the news. Perhaps the Comyns still had some influence with the crown, and it may be thanks to his wife that William de Aughton eventually did return to North Meols. What transpired was that in 1382 William was granted a royal pardon for his unknown offence; and the wording of the pardon is of particular interest, for it was granted 'at the special request of Anne, Queen of England, Our Consort'.[9]

It does appear, therefore, that the Queen intervened personally in the case of William de Aughton. This was a surprising move, especially as she was a mere slip of a girl at only fifteen years of age. She was the daughter of Emperor Charles IV of Bohemia, and she was not at first popular in court circles because many complained that the Emperor of Bohemia was unable to offer a large enough dowry. But Anne quickly increased her popularity, she stood by the King in the most difficult times and Richard II came to rely heavily on her. Anne of Bohemia is credited with much of the ladies' fashion of the times, including the quaint custom of wearing long toes which eventually became so long that they had to be tied to the wearers knees, and she also introduced a fashion for ladies to ride side-saddle through London. She granted many pardons after the Peasants' Revolt of 1381 and became known as 'Good Queen Anne'. One thing is certain — that however the Queen's popularity waxed and waned in court circles, there was one corner of the kingdom in which she would always be a very popular lady.

It may be significant that it was one of William de Aughton's near neighbours, Sir Ralph Standish, who struck the blow which killed Wat Tyler at the meeting between the rebel leader and King Richard II at Mile End.[10] This fact, together with the intervention of the queen and the coincidence of the date, seems to imply that William de Aughton's royal pardon was somehow connected with the Peasants' Revolt of 1381.

His narrow escape from exile made little difference to William de Aughton's way of life. In 1386 we find him still roving the country and serving Richard II during the king's campaigns in Ireland. The main burden of running the manor thus fell again on the shoulders of his mother Kathryn and his wife Millicent.

William died in 1388 leaving four children of whom the eldest was fourteen; both his wife and mother survived him by over twenty years and the latter (Kathryn de Coudray) was still alive in 1410 aged over eighty, an astonishing age for the times.

One of the main catalysts of the Peasant's Revolt was the poll tax of three groats (one shilling) per head levied by the Northampton Parliament in 1381. A married couple was obliged to pay two shillings. This was the heaviest and most unpopular tax ever levied and everybody over the age of fifteen, except the destitute and beggars, was expected to contribute. A bone of contention was that the rich paid no more than the poor, and in the home counties it was this very tax which lead to the Peasants Revolt. When the returns were counted the population of every county appeared to have fallen by half; there had been tax evasion on an hitherto unprecedented scale.

The returns for North Meols actually survive in the Public Record Office, and as a record of the families living on the manor at that time it is fascinating and invaluable. The returns cannot be taken as complete. Both the lord of the manor and the parson seem to have avoided paying the tax but we are still left with the names of some who lived in North Meols during the age of Chaucer.

THE TOWN OF NORTHMELES (1381)[11]

Robert Brekeale and his wife	ijs	
Adam Walle		xijd
Adam del Wodland and his wife	ijs	
Adam Jump and his wife	ijs	
John Bernard and his wife	ijs	
Symond Tybott and his wife	ijs	
William de Pilkynton and his wife	ijs	
Adam Robynson		xijd
Roger Gilyott		xijd
Robert le Haywart		xijd
Adam le Walys		xijd
Adam de Manne		xijd
William le Foler		xijd
William Hoggeson and his wife	ijs	
John Giliott and his wife	ijs	
John Diconson		xijd
Amott Smalcharr		xijd
Sum	xxvs	

Of these families contributing to the poll tax, the Breakills survived until the eighteenth century; their land near Martin Mere at Crossens became known as Brekill's Land and was farmed by them for many generations. The Jump family was never very numerous and they were reduced to virtually a single family for centuries, but amazingly they survived in North Meols until the twentieth century. The Hoggeson (Hodgeson) family became the Hodges, and they can make a similar claim — as can the Haywarts if we make the reasonable assumption that they became the Haywards and then the Howards. Robert le Haywart was in all probability the hayward of North Meols. His extensive and responsible manorial duties are defined by Walter of Henly:

> The hayward ought to be an active and sharp man, for he must, early and late, look after and go round and keep the woods, corn, and meadows and other things belonging to his office, and he ought to make attachments and improvements faithfully, and to take delivery by pledge before the reeve, and to deliver them to the bailiff to be heard. And he ought to sow the lands, and be over the ploughers and harrowers at the time of the sowing. And he ought to make all [those] who are accustomed to come, do so, to do the work they ought to do. And in hay time he ought to be over the mowers, the making and the carrying [of the hay], and in August assemble the reapers and the boon tenants and the labourers, and see that the corn be properly and cleanly gathered; and early and late watch so that nothing be stolen or eaten by beasts, or spoilt. And he ought to tally with the reeve all the seed, and boon-work, and customs, and labour which ought to be done on the manor throughout the year.

WALTER OF HENLEY

Other manorial officials were the lord's steward, the bailiff, the beadle and the reeve — sometimes one individual covered more than one of these tasks. Chaucer's thin-legged shaven reeve is an excellent example:

> Wel coude he keep a gerner and a binne;
> There was noon auditour coude on him winne,
> Wel wiste he, by the droghte, and by the reyne,
> The yelding of his seed, and of his greyn.

The textbook description of the medieval village surrounded by the communal fields, each divided into their strips, did not strictly apply to the North of England. There is evidence that part of the agricultural land in North Meols was indeed divided into strips, but an equally popular system was for the peasant to work from an 'infield' and an 'outfield', the former around his dwelling and the latter further away. He had the advantage over his southern counterpart in that he had less distance to travel for the working of his land, but this advantage was offset by the fact that the population became more scattered and villages like Churchtown would have been larger centres of population under the strip farming system. In many respects, however, the manor of North Meols was a very typical English community. It had its manorial customs, officers, boon work, the lord's mill, and all the 'appurtenances of the manor'. The church officials, too, were typical examples of their kind, and Chaucer's parson with his wide parish and houses far asunder could very easily have been the parson of Meols.

The parson's lot was often little better than that of his flock but many of the clergy came from wealthy families and had their own private means. When John de Lyverpull, who hailed from a fishing village at the mouth of the Mersey, was parson, word must have got around the countryside that he was a wealthy man with money and valuables hidden in the parsonage house at Crossens. One January night, when John de Lyverpull had gone to bed, a gang of men led by Roger de Blyth broke into the house and held the parson down in his bed. They proceeded to pour water into his mouth by means of a pipe, and they 'caused him so much torment that he should tell them where his treasure stood'. Whether the poor spluttering parson managed to tell them or not, they found what they wanted — about twenty pounds in money, some jewels and other valuables including a pyx containing communion bread. To the parson's dismay, they broke open the pyx 'and the body of Christ, being in the said pyx, took and threw away'.[12]

John de Lyverpull took his assailants to court and the case reached the Lancaster sessions in 1400. We do not know Roger Blyth's side of the story, but he either had friends in high places or he had a brilliant defence — he was found to be innocent!

Chapter Three

The High Middle Ages

I N 1377 William de Aughton and his neighbouring landowners drew up an agreement for joint grazing rights in 'Northmeles, Aynaltesdale, Byrkedale and Argarmeols'. Three of these four placenames are easily recognised, but the fourth is something of a mystery and difficult to identify. From the wording it appears that Argarmeols was considered to be a township in its own right and not a part of any of the other three. In the reign of Henry IV it is mentioned as a manor, and was granted by Robert Parre to Gilbert Halsall for life, 'with remainder to his sons and heirs male'. From the Domesday Survey we find that Argarmeols was valued at a quarter of a knight's fee, but evidence shows that by before 1500 it had completely disappeared and the nearest place name to survive is Birkdale.

It was in 1503 that the Duchy of Lancaster made enquiries of Sir Henry Halsall asking why he had not paid his dues on Argarmeols. Sir Henry replied indignantly that no such place had ever existed within living memory. He claimed that the land in question was 'within the hegh see and drowned and anichilate with the sayd see, and out of the lawgh water marke, and also out of bodye of the sayde countye'. He was called upon to find witnesses to support his claim, and he managed to bring forward some of the oldest men in the area. John Sherlock, claiming to be eighty, and Hugh Tuckwold, aged 77, deposed that they had heard of 'great lands within four miles of Halsall worn into the sea'. William Harryson gave evidence saying that he had 'heard say that such londes there were drowned in the sea, but wher ner in what parte he never heard tell'.[1]

The evidence thus shows that by the sixteenth century the loss of Argarmeols was very complete. It appeared to be situated on the seaward side of Birkdale, yet it did not consist merely of sand and scrubland; Argarmeols was not only worthwhile grazing land but it also had full manorial status. It was certainly considered of some value at the time of the Norman Conquest. Over the hundred years of the fifteenth century there may have been a gradual erosion of the coast, but the wording of the witnesses implies otherwise. Their evidence points to a sudden and violent inundation when the whole area was flooded and could not be reclaimed — a rare but not a unique event on this stretch of coastline.

The case of Argarmeols shows that throughout the Middle Ages land

Halsall of Halsall

*Argent, three serpents' heads raised azure langued gules
In Elizabethan times the Halsalls held much of Birkdale and Ainsdale. They have produced many interesting characters including the infamous spendthrift Sir Cuthbert Halsall. Many branches of the family still survive.*

was sometimes lost by inundation from the sea, but over the centuries of settlement these losses were more than compensated by the land which was drained and gained by man for agriculture. The first turf embankments, which began with the labours of the monks of Sawley, were strengthened and lengthened and eventually a new embankment was built further seaward to reclaim more agricultural land. Inland, too, more and more drainage channels were cut and crops were grown on land which had previously been little more than a watery fen.

The water table was known locally as the 'ream' and there is a tenable theory that the men who dug the ditches and built the dykes were known as reamers. If this is true, then it offers a possible explanation of the origin of the name 'Rimmer' (Rymer, Rimer) which became so prolific in the coastal parishes of South Lancashire. There are claims that the Rimmers have a much older, Norse origin from the name 'Grim' or 'Grimr',[2] but the earliest mention of the name comes from a different part of the county altogether and the name may not in fact have originated in the coastal parishes. So much conflicting evidence exists that it is impossible to give a certain answer to this question.

On the inland side of the parish was an arm or bay of Martin Mere which the local people called 'Black Wyke'. This name was eventually corrupted to the form 'Blowyke'. 'Wyke' in this sense refers to marshy land which was too wet and boggy to cultivate.[3] In 1354 Richard de Aughton charged two men from Rufford with taking fish from 'the Wyke in the Meols' — he evidently regarded this part of the mere as his property. The defendants claimed that the fishing rights were common to all the manors which bordered on the mere and that no part of it belonged with any manor. The court accepted this explanation and the Rufford men were acquitted.

In the following century the name 'Wyke' appears again, but this time it is no longer a stretch of water but 'a certain parcel of land' measuring about sixty acres — it was evidently drained in about the year 1400. Deeds from this time refer to a long moss ditch which was

A lovely photograph which was used as a postcard at the beginning of this century and which contains the handwritten note: 'This is a photo of some Marshside fishermen. It is awfull poor times amongst them…', a reference to the then rapid decline in the industry.
(E.W. Collection)

Vagaries of the Sea

he sea has always been of crucial importance to this stretch of coastline. Like many other coastal parishes North Meols has frequently felt the power and destructive force of the waves. High tides, floods and inundations have taken their toll of the land – one township, Argarmeols, was submerged and lost for ever, and storms have taken their toll of seafarers and lifeboatmen. But there is a positive side to the relationship between North Meols and the sea. As the sketch map overleaf shows, there has been a marked, if gradual, retreat of the sea over the centuries; this has released much valuable land for reclamation and development as part of the ever-growing Southport. More recently still, the discontinuance of dredging of the Ribble estuary following the closure of Preston dock may result in a further shifting of the balance between land and sea in the Southport area. In any case, the sea's vagaries are still being felt today, just as in centuries long gone.

Below - A sketch map of the Inundation of 1720. This was the worst inundation of the Lancashire coast in recorded history. North Meols was the worst affected part, with 5,000 acres of land flooded but Pilling, Cockerham, Formby and nearly every other coastal parish also suffered severe losses.

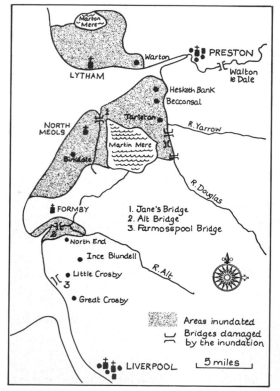

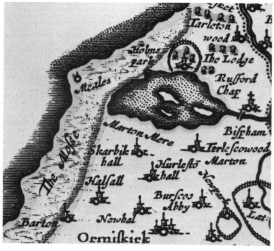

Above - A section of a 17th-century map of Lancashire, drawn by Johan Bleau in 1648. This shows the extent of Martin Mere at that time. Three islands are shown and the natural drainage into the River Douglas near Rufford can be seen.

Below - Children have always displayed an infinite capacity to enjoy the sea and sand. The generation shown here is no exception.
(E. W. Collection)

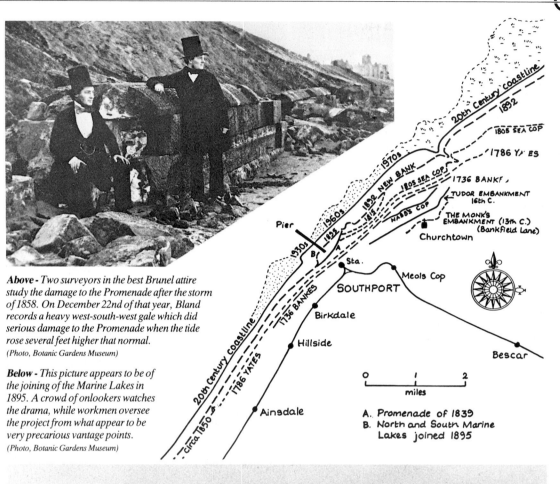

Above - Two surveyors in the best Brunel attire study the damage to the Promenade after the storm of 1858. On December 22nd of that year, Bland records a heavy west-south-west gale which did serious damage to the Promenade when the tide rose several feet higher that normal.
(Photo, Botanic Gardens Museum)

Below - This picture appears to be of the joining of the Marine Lakes in 1895. A crowd of onlookers watches the drama, while workmen oversee the project from what appear to be very precarious vantage points.
(Photo, Botanic Gardens Museum)

20th Century coastline

1892

1805 SEA COP

1786 YATES

1736 BANKF␣

TUDOR EMBANKMENT 16th C.

THE MONK'S EMBANKMENT (13th C.)
(Bankfield Lane)

1970s

1960s

1858 NEW BANK

1805 SEA COP

NABBS COP

Churchtown

Pier

1930s

B

Sta.

Meols Cop

SOUTHPORT

Birkdale

Hillside

Bescar

20th Century coastline

1736 BANKES

1786 YATES

circa 1850

Ainsdale

0   1   2
miles

A. Promenade of 1839
B. North and South Marine
   Lakes joined 1895

constructed to drain the water into the Otter Pool and subsequently through Churchtown.* More agricultural land was created and at the same time the miller gained a little more water with which to grind the corn. The Wyke, which had previously been of little value, now became a bone of contention. Which manor did it belong to? When it was part of the mere it belonged to nobody, but after it had been drained where did the new boundary between North Meols and Scarisbrick lie?

In 1410 we find mention of a dispute between Hugh de Aughton of North Meols and Henry de Scarisbrick regarding the ownership of the Wyke. At first the dispute seemed amicable enough and in 1410 it was agreed to draw up a legal document defining the boundaries, and in drawing up the boundaries both parties agreed to accept the decision of Henry the parson of Halsall and Nicholas Blundell of Crosby.*

In 1417, however, Hugh de Aughton died and this created another problem. The untimely death of the lord of the manor left three young children all under the age of ten. Their nearest relative was Millicent Mascy (nee Comyn). She was their grandmother, aged about seventy, who had remarried and was living at Nantwich in Cheshire. History was repeating itself for Millicent. She had faced a similar situation thirty years earlier when her husband died, but she was now too old to look after the children herself; she therefore chose to remain in Cheshire and to sell the wardship of the children jointly to Robert Halsall and Nicholas Blundell, an action which she lived to regret.

In the following year she complained bitterly that Nicholas Blundell had borrowed certain charters from her on the pretext of looking over them and examining them, and with a promise that she should have them back in good time. According to Millicent, as soon as Robert Halsall and Nicholas Blundell had purchased the wardship they 'tortuously ousted her out of her dower, and of the lands and tenements, not suffering her to take any money of the rent of the same for her maintenance'.[4] Millicent successfully obtained a grant from the Chancery Proceedings that writs be issued against the two offenders, summoning them to appear in court or pay a heavy fine of one hundred pounds.

In these times it was possible to purchase not only the wardship of an heir who was under age, but also the right to choose a marriage partner — and this is precisely what the guardians did in the case of the minor Hugh de Aughton. They arranged what on the face of things appeared to be an eminently sensible marriage between young Hugh and Joan, the daughter of Henry Scarisbrick. They were thus able to unite the neighbouring families and at the same time to settle the problem of the disputed boundary by including the Wyke as part of Joan Scarisbrick's dowry.

Nobody can be blamed for the fact that the arranged marriage proved to be childless. After the death of both partners the dispute over the Wyke flared up again and yet again with monotonous regularity, and ended with the affair of Balmondyhokes (1554) which almost became a battle between the manors of North Meols and Scarisbrick.

Amongst the gentry the normal custom was to arrange the marriage

Scarisbrick of Scarisbrick
Gules, three mullets in bend between two bendets engrailed argent
Scarisbrick bordered on North Meols and the Scarisbricks married into the North Meols families from the thirteenth century. In the nineteenth century Charles Scarisbrick became a major landowner in Southport after Sir Peter Hesketh Fleetwood was forced to sell his Meols estates.

---

*The ditch now forms part of the boundary between Lancashire and Merseyside.

*The deed was an indenture of covenant, cut into two portions with a serrated edge, as was the custom at that time. The part of the indentures which were handed over to Henry de Scarisbrick has an interesting octagonal seal, and bears a wheatsheaf on a helmet with a mantlet. On each side are the initials H.A., and below the helmet a heart pierced with an arrow. The wheatsheaf was part of the Aughton arms, and the seal was that used by Hugh de Aughton is sealing the part of the indentures given to the Scarisbricks.

of their sons and daughters conveniently between themselves at the earliest possible opportunity. It was obligatory for the children to be able to speak their marriage vows before witnesses, and this meant that some betrothals were delayed two or three years to give the intended time to acquire the rudiments of speech. A well known story is that of young John Rigmarden who, at the age of three, was carried in the arms of a clergyman and coaxed to repeat the words of matrimony to a bride of five years. Before the end of the ceremony young John struggled to escape saying he would learn no more that day, but the dutiful parson said 'You must speak a little more and then go play you'. The ceremony was completed.

The Lancashire families were no exception to the phenomenon of child marriages and in the fifteenth century there were at least three such unions in three generations of the Aughtons of North Meols. The first, between Hugh de Aughton and Joan de Scarisbrick, has already been mentioned. In 1469 Nicholas de Aughton (Hugh's brother) arranged the marriage of his son and heir Hugh to Matilda (alias Maud) Hesketh, the daughter of Robert Hesketh of Rufford. In this marriage Hugh took his marriage vows when he was about four and Matilda was a year older. When his turn came, Hugh arranged for his son Richard to repeat his marriage vows with Isabel, the daughter of James Boteler of Warrington; the groom was five and the bride was about the same age. In a thinly populated county, the choice of marriage partners amongst the gentry was always very limited but it must be said that many of these child marriages did turn out to be successful. Children grew up seeing their spouse only occasionally until they came of age and in the happier matches they saw their better half as a rather special cousin with whom they would one day share their lives.

The arranged marriage between Hugh de Aughton and Joan Scarisbrick produced no issue and when Hugh died in 1464 it was his sister Elizabeth who was found to be his heir. This seems to have been an error for, in a deed dated 1460, Hugh clearly named his brother Nicholas as the person to succeed him. Later in the decade we find that Nicholas did indeed become lord of the manor, but the fact that he was overlooked in favour of his sister has given rise to speculation that he was illegitimate[5]. The available evidence is not sufficient to prove his legitimacy but it does make a birth out of wedlock unlikely. Nicholas was mentioned without qualification as heir to Hugh, and seems to have been accepted as legitimate by neighbouring families like the Heskeths of Rufford.

Hesketh of Rufford
Hesketh of Meols
Argent, on a bend sable three garbs or, a chief azure, thereon an eagle with two heads displayed proper, all within a bordure arminois
The Heskeths inherited Meols Hall in 1603 after the death of Barnaby Kitchen. Their Meols estates were sequestered after the Civil War, but were reclaimed after the restoration. For many years they used the coat of arms of the Rufford Heskeths from whom they were descended. The Heskeths contributed much towards the development of Southport.

There is a more probable explanation for the finding of Elizabeth as heir. Nicholas was a younger son. He followed the family tradition, became a soldier of fortune, and wandered off to see the world, quite possibly crossing over to the continent. Communications were so bad in those times that messages took months to deliver and nobody in North Meols knew whether or not Nicholas was still alive when his brother died, still less how to contact him. Thus, when Nicholas finally sauntered home again to find his sister was installed at Meols Hall, it must have caused great surprise and embarrassment to all concerned.

Judging from a court case brought against him in 1465, Nicholas was a volatile character. In this year he gathered around him a band of armed men, farmers and farm labourers who forded the Ribble into the Fylde. There they were joined by other men as they made their way to the village of Thistleton. An irate widow called Margaret Bayne told the court what happened next:

. . . with force and arms they took and carried away goods and chattels which belonged to (the said) Richard Bayne to the value of twenty marks found at Thistleton, against the King's peace, etc., on March 25 of the fifth year of the now King [Edward IV] to wit, with swords, bows and arrows, viz., one quarter of wheat, two quarters of barley, three quarters of malt, half a quarter of sigali, one quarter of oatmeal, and four sacks, whereof they have done damage to the value of £20.[6]

We have here only one side of this story, and it certainly does not bring much credit to the lord of the manor. It is not difficult to deduce the other side of the story. Part of the manor of Thistleton had been the property of the owners of North Meols for some two hundred years before this incident in fact, since the time of the Coudrays. It is likely that because of his untimely death Richard Bayne's rent was in arrears. The custom of the manor would normally allow the widow a reasonable length of time in which to pay the arrears, though how long this time would be in the case of Margaret Bayne it is not possible to say. Thus Nicholas de Aughton had decided to take the law into his own hands to extract his rent, and he was possibly within his rights. This theory is supported by the evidence that a number of Thistleton men appear amongst his accomplices:

NORTH MEOLS MEN (1465)[7]

Richard, son of Thomas	Abram	labourer
Nicholas	Aghton	gentleman
James	Ball	labourer
Roger	Ball	labourer
Richard, son of William	Ball	labourer
Thomas	Hobbe	yeoman
William	Mathewe	labourer
Thomas	Wawen	yeoman

THISTLETON MEN (1465)

Roger	Herryson	webster
Robert	Kirkeham	yeoman
(late of Thistleton)		
Robert	Kirkeham	husbandman
John, son of Robert	Kirkeham	labourer
Thomas son of Robert	Kirkeham	labourer

From these names we discover that the families of Mathew and Abram were established by 1465. We also discover that Thomas Wawen and Thomas Hobbe were yeomen and therefore held their land freehold. In this same decade there appear the names of eleven men who held tenements 'at will' in the township of North Meols, meaning at the will of the lord of the manor. This was a small but very significant difference from the terms under which their ancestors held the land in the previous century. Their tenure was still subject to their lord's will but they paid rent as free men; they were not the serfs and villeins created by the Norman rule. They were well advanced along the tortuous road to the winning of their freedom, and some of their children would live to see the end of this, the last of the long centuries of the Middle Ages.

TENANTS AT WILL (1460)[8]

Henry Ball
Richard Ball
Thomas Ball
William Ball
John Blevyn
Thomas Coppock
Robert Haywarde
William Haywarde
Richard Henreson
Michael of Mann
Robert Matthew

It is significant that no Rimmer appears in any of the above lists of names. Had the Rimmers been as numerous as they became a few generations later then it would have been highly improbable that eighteen names from North Meols would not include at least one of them. The implication is that in the fifteenth century they were outnumbered by Balls and other families, although they were probably well established by that time.

The farming methods and the general standard of living had changed very little over the generations. Richard Ball and his ten colleagues shared a great medieval field called Meddehay which contained one messuage for each of the eleven, with 73 acres of agricultural land, 29 acres of meadow, and three acres of turbary. The name of another great field was the Townfield, and the Wyke was also a very large field of at least sixty acres, so that there could have been a three field system with all three of these fields used in rotation, or perhaps a two field system with land divided between the three. In other parts of the manor other similar field systems might have existed since we can deduce from data in the next century that the manor contained a total population of about three hundred at this time, and a very high proportion of these lived off the land.

The mainstay of the manorial economy was the farming and the fishing but the woollen industry was also of continued importance. A deed dated January 1488/9 makes mention of 'A close called Londheye in Northmelys which Hugh Aghton Squyer let to Hugh Schaue of Scaresbrek . . . for the [annual] rent of iiii s [payable] at the festys of the Anunciateon of our Lady Vygin and Saynt Michaell ye Archangell . . .'[9]

It is a reasonable assumption that 'Londheye' was the place where the London wool merchants, or their representatives, came to collect the raw wool to be fulled, dressed and woven into garments before finding its way to the European market at Flanders. Londheye is an isolated mention, but a part of North Meols become known for some reason as Little London and contained one of the parish's tithebarns. For part of the year the tithebarn could have been used to store the fleeces sheared from the flanks of the sheep which grazed on the common land of the parish, and on the coastal marshes to the north of Churchtown.

One detail of the Thistleton incident reminds us that the peasant farmers were armed with lethal weapons such as the longbow and sword - they were part of the bold peasantry of an England which counted Agincourt and Crecy amongst its greatest military victories. The longbow was not a mere ornament standing by the fireside, but was used for hunting and, if necessary, to defend home and property. Archery practice every Sunday was a statutory requirement and youngsters were shown by their fathers how to draw the longbow with the full strength of their bodies. The archery practice was a social event, a time of drinking, jousting, sport and courtship, and a welcome break from the dull routine of tending the fields and the cattle. It was a time when the parish came together for companionship, when the youngsters tried to outshoot their fathers and the lord of the manor. Archery was a statute of the realm for a very good reason: it ensured that every parish could provide a quota of men to fight for the country, and in times of war and rebellion there was an obligation to provide this quota.

In the second half of the fifteenth century the English had at last ended the Hundred Years War with the French, but the military men found plenty of employment in the long and often pointless struggle for the crown between the houses of Lancaster and York. Men from North Meols were sometimes mustered for service under the Stanleys of Lathom, and when Thomas Stanley arrived at Bosworth on that fateful morning in 1485 he must have had a handful of Meols men amongst his five thousand troops. They knew that a great battle was about to be fought which would decide the destiny of England, but as conflicting rumours reached them from all quarters they had no idea which side they were going to fight on.

Bosworth was an old world battle; an amateur historian from Stratford upon Avon described well enough the tactics of the Yorkist King Richard III:

> King Richard: Come, bustle, bustle; caparison my horse;
> Call up Lord Stanley, bid him bring his power.
> I will lead forth my soldiers to the plane,
> And thus my battle shall be ordered:
> My forward shall be drawn out all in length,
> Consisting equally of horse and foot
> Our archers shall be placed in the midst:
> John, Duke of Norfolk, Thomas Earl of Surrey,
> Shall have the leading of this foot and horse.
> They thus directed we ourself will follow
> In the main battle; whose puissance either side
> Shall be well winged with our chiefest horse.
> This and Saint George to boot!
>
> WILLIAM SHAKESPEARE

In the event, Lord Stanley did bring his power, but not on the side of Richard of York! After walking a hair raising political tightrope, he threw in his forces with the Earl of Richmond at the eleventh hour. That August morning the future of England hung in the balance for a few hours at Bosworth Field. Thomas, thankfully for the house of Stanley, managed to support the winning side.

Some of Stanley's young soldiers were able to return home soon after the battle. They esconced themselves in their favourite alehouses and told swaggering and exaggerated stories about their deeds at Bosworth. Lord Stanley, he that lives in Lathom House yonder, had plucked the Crown of England from a thorn bush and placed it on the head of Henry Tudor. To prove it, the Stanleys were rewarded with an earldom.

The Wars of the Roses were over. It was neither the Red Rose of Lancaster nor the White Rose of York which came to represent the English crown, but the Tudor Rose of the Earl of Richmond. A gradual realisation came over the people that at long last the country was at peace. The fifteenth century marked a turning point when the slowly evolving way of life known throughout the middle ages was on the threshold of change. At Rufford the Heskeths had already built a fine new manor house; at Lathom Thomas Stanley built a new chapel with some of the proceeds from Bosworth; in London the first of the Tudors was on the throne; and in Italy the Rennaisance had begun to flower. Europe was on the verge of a new age.

But when the initial excitement died away some began to wonder what all the fuss was about. The Wars of the Roses might be associated with Lancashire and Yorkshire, but it hardly mattered in the North whether Richard or Henry was King. The constant threat of invasion by the Scots was a far more imminent issue. It was another generation before victory at Flodden dispelled that fear, and for England north of the Trent the outcome at Flodden was considered more important than that at Bosworth.

The strips in the fields still had to be worked. The swine still had to be fed and the cows had to be milked. The weather and the state of the harvest were matters of life and death. In the silent winter nights, when fuel and food stocks ran low, the wolves still came down from their lairs in the hills to steal the sheep and to howl their eerie cry over the plains of the North. Was a new dynasty really going to make any difference to the centuries-old way of life in the countryside?

Chapter Four

Church versus Manor

HE news that Anne Boleyn had become queen was not exactly welcome to some of the king's Lancashire subjects. There was a stormy meeting at Croston, attended by many local clegy, where Richard Clerk, the vicar of Leigh, read out a proclamation which said that King Henry had divorced Catherine of Aragon and that she was now to be known by the title of Princess Dowager.

'Queen Catherine was queen!' shouted a priest by the name of James Harrison. 'Nan Boleyn shall be no queen, nor the king no king but in his bearing'.

The parish priests were not always the meek men we take them for, and as the meeting became more heated James Harrison's language became stronger. 'Who the devil made Nan Boleyn, that whore, queen?', he exploded. 'For I will never take her for queen!'[1]

Opinion on the matter was strongly divided, and in July 1533, at the coronation of the new queen, Henry the Eighth conferred a number of new knighthoods, and some of those to be so honoured had travelled all the way from the County Palatine of Lancaster. It is likely, but not proved, that one of those to be knighted was Richard Aughton of North Meols. In the 1530s he is referred to with the title of *Sir* Richard Aughton, and the most probable time and place for him to have been given this new title was with some of his fellow squires at the Coronation of Ann Boleyn.

This was the first occasion on which North Meols was able to boast a knight of the shire, although it is possible that Richard's father and others of his predecessors had declined the honour because of the military obligations which the knighthood carried with it. King Henry did not create the honours too lightly; knights were required to raise men in times of war and rebellion, and some of the more radical policies of our Soveriegn Lord and Greatly to be Dreaded Defender of the Faith proved, as we have seen, to be controversial and very effective at raising rebellion.

Thus, in 1536, we find that Sir Richard Aughton was called upon to raise 36 men from his estates in Meols to join a contingent of eight thousand troops who were given instructions to assemble near Clitheroe under the command of the Earl of Derby.[2] The assembly point was the Abbey of Sawley, where there lived the successors of the Cistercian monks who had once been a familiar sight earning their salt in the early history of North Meols. Lord Derby's troops were raised for the purpose of putting down the rising known as the Pilgrimage of Grace, which originated in Lincolnshire, spread northwards into Yorkshire and threatened to spread across the Pennines and gain a hold on Lancashire. In the northern and western counties there remained a great deal of sympathy and support for the monks and the rising was a direct consequence of Henry's decision to dissolve the monasteries.

The Pilgrimage of Grace was known to the King and his ministers by the less romantic name of the 'Northern Rebellion'. It gained ground very quickly and at one time it looked as though a full scale civil war could break out. It was feared that the 8,000 men under the Earl of Derby would not be sufficient to put down the rebels, whose numbers were rumoured to have reached nearly 20,000. Henry considered travelling north himself to direct the operations but his ministers advised against the idea.

The monks themselves played a large part in stirring up the rebellion. It is not difficult to imagine their feelings when they knew that their cloistered way of life was to disappear and they were to be thrown out to make their own way in the world. The Cistercians were better equipped than most to face the outside world, but they were strong supporters of the rebellion and the following ballad is thought to have been written by the Monks of Sawley. It was copied and circulated as a ballad sheet during the rising to try and muster support; it has sixteen verses in all but only six have been selected. These words, which describe the grievances of the rebels and of the monks when their monasteries were destroyed, are worthy of close study:

THE PILGRIMS' BALLAD 1536[3]

I   Crist crucified!
For they woundes wide
Us commens guyde!
Which pilgrames be,
Thrughe godes grace,
For to purchache
Olde welth and peax
Of the spiritualtie.

II   Gret godes fame
Doith Church proclame
Now to be lame
And fast in boundes
Robbyd, spoled and shorne
From catell and corne
And clene furth borne
Of housez and landes

X   Alacke! Alacke!
For the church sake
Pore comons wake,
And no marvell!
For cler it is
The decay of this
How the pore shall mys
No tong can tell.

XI   For ther they hadde
Boith ale and breyde
At tyme of nede,
And succor grete
In alle distresse
And hevyness
And wel intrete

XII   In troubil and care,
Where that we were
In maner all bere
Of our substance,
We found good bate
At churche men gate,
Without checkmate
Or varyaunce

XVI   Crim, crame, and riche
With thre ell and the liche
As sum men teache
God theym amend!
And that Aske may,
Without delay,
Here make a stay
And well to end.

The rebels assembled on Clitheroe Moor and Lòrd Derby moved forward to meet them, but Robert Aske of Norfolk negotiated a temporary truce before the parties got any nearer. The result was that no pitched battle took place, support for the rebels gradually faded away and Lord Derby's troops were found to be more than adequate to control the situation. Needless to say, the King was ruthless in his treatment of those who had risen against him. Rebels were hanged by the roadside and in the market places for all to see. Some of Sir Richard's 36 men who returned safely to their families must have had a lot of sympathy with the rebels, yet they must have been relieved on this occasion to find themselves on the side of the Crown.

The Aughtons of North Meols had strong connections with other Lancashire families. Richard Aughton's mother was Maud Hesketh, the daughter of Robert Hesketh of Rufford — as a child she had seen the building of the great hall at her family home in Rufford. From the age of five Richard had been married to Isobel Boteler, daughter of a prominent Warrington family so called because they had originally been butlers to the Earls of Chester.

Richard and Isobel's eldest son was John. He married Ellen Radcliffe, the daughter of William Radcliffe of Ordsall. Their second son Thomas married Alice Heaton from Heaton Mersey, and their daughter Elizabeth married William Heaton from the same family. Elizabeth was widowed whilst still a young woman and subsequently married John Bold, the son of Sir Richard Bold from another prominent Lancashire family. Ann, the youngest of Richard and Isobel's children, married Barnaby Kitchen from Pilling near Garstang, a man who was destined to be squire of North Meols for more than half a century.

Butler of Warrington
Azure, a bend between six covered cups or
In 1498 Hugh Aughton married his son and heir Richard to Isabel, daughter of James Butler of Warrington. The groom was about 8 years old and the bride was a few years younger. The Butlers were an old and prominent Lancashire family, so called because they had originally been butlers to the Earls of Chester.

John Aughton succeeded his father in 1543. He was lord of the manor for only seven years, but he was instrumental in what was an important development for the administration of the law in the manor. In 1549 a bill of complaint was brought against him by Sir Henry Farrington of Penwortham:[4]

> . . . notwithstanding that the plaintiff has kept the leet there [at Penwortham] according to ancient custom, to which leet John Awghton dwelling in Northmylez and all others dwelling there have time out of mind used to come and sue at the said leet at Penworthen, and although plaintiff has often warned the said John Awghton to show at the said leet, yet he has absented himself and has caused the constables of Northmylez at his court baron held at Northmylez to present all such wrongs, bloodsheds and other misdemeanors, which ought to have been presented at the King's said court, at his own court [in North Meols] . . .

This is a significant development. Sir Henry Farrington was right about the ancient custom of complaints from North Meols being brought to the court at Penwortham. The custom went back to the time before the twelfth century when the Baron of Penwortham gave the land to the first freeholder in North Meols. But it appears that John Aughton was not satisfied with the justice dealt out at Penwortham and he had decided to take matters into his own hands. A few brief details of the court proceedings are given, indicating the belligerent nature of some of the locals:

> . . . James Mathewe at the leet last was amerced 3s 4d for assaulting Thomas Balle, and the said Thomas Balle was amerced 3s 4d for the like cause, and Thomas Balle of Kyrktown [a different Thomas?] 3s 4d for assaulting Harry Haryson, and Thomas Coplond 3s 4d for assaulting Lawrence Ball . . .[5]

Sir Henry Farrington sent Robert Somener, his bailiff, to North Meols with instructions to bring the dissenters to court, but John Aughton made sure that they were well hidden so that the bailiff returned to Penwortham empty handed. A similar incident occurred some years later when Robert Sutton and Henry Bradshawe were the parish constables; they were both fined 3s 4d because they refused to assist the bailiff from Penwortham in the execution of his duties. Again, the constables were acting under the instructions of the lord of the manor. John Aughton won his point, the North Meols Court Leet and Court Baron became firmly established and continued to administer the law in the manor on a regular basis right up to the first decades of the twentieth century.

The Aughtons had been lords of the manor for six generations spanning two hundred years. They helped to bring North Meols out of the Middle Ages and into Tudor times. They had achieved their first knighthood and had successfully established a court baron. But, when John Aughton died in 1550, he left no issue, and the next few decades proved to be some of the most turbulent in the history of the parish.

John's brother was dead. This meant that his sisters, Elizabeth Bold and Ann Kitchen, became the joint owners of the manor. It was therefore necessary to divide the manor into two halves or, to use the correct legal term, two moieties. The division of the land proved to be a very complex affair and fields were allocated not by the simple expedient of drawing a boundary line, but more in the manner of a chessboard pattern, with Kitchen and Bold fields alternating side by side. One wonders, in the light of subsequent events, if it was John Bold who insisted on these complicated arrangements on the grounds that it was the only fair way to make the division.

The Kitchens took up residence in Meols Hall and the Bolds built a new house in Churchtown standing on Manor Place. John Bold took up residence, began to wield a new broom to sweep clean and proceeded to upset his neighbours, all the tenants, his sister-in-law, two rectors, about half the manor of Scarisbrick, and even his easy going fellow squire and brother-in-law Barnaby Kitchen.

First it seems that, after the death of John Aughton, his widow Ellen was left with nothing. She sued John Bold and successfully recovered her dower rights. The dower assignment contains much interesting detail and will be referred to later. Soon afterwards Ellen married Edward Standish, whereupon she wisely left North Meols to live on his estates at Standish.

In 1551 the rector, Lawrence Waterward, brought a court action against John Bold whom he described as of 'covetous and gredie mynde'. The rector held certain land known as the Parson's Meadow which . . .

> . . . he and his predecessors have always enjoyed without interruption from anybody, and which he has enjoyed as parson for 21 years last, and to which he and all his predecessors have always had free passage and carriage, as well with carts and wains, as horses and other carriages to pass to and from the same and to carry the hay on the same without disturbance.[6]

John Bold not only prevented the parson from gaining access to the meadow, but had 'taken from him all the hay growing on the said meadows, carried it with him to his own mansion and converted it to his own use'. In addition to the hay from Parson's Meadow, John Bold had somehow managed to commandeer all the tithe hay from other parts of the parish, which was due to the plaintiff in his capacity as rector.

Lawrence Waterward, the injured party, deserves a special mention in the history of North Meols. Not only was he the first parson to be appointed after the Reformation, but he was also the first married priest which the parish had ever known. Mrs Waterward must have been one of the earliest parson's wives in the whole of England, for it was not until the reign of Edward VI that members of the clergy were allowed to marry. In due course his marriage presented poor Lawrence Waterward with another problem, because when the Catholic Mary came to the throne the Church of Rome became once more the official religion, and married clergy could obviously no longer be tolerated. Clergymen were given a clear choice to make, between their living and their wife! Lawrence Waterward chose to remain with his wife. In fact, it was still many years before the idea of the parson's wife became

Bold of Bold
Argent, a griffin segreant sable, beaked and legged or
The Bolds held one moiety of the manor from 1550 and they built Bold House in Churchtown at about that time. After 1600 they were non-resident landlords, but they retained an interest in North Meols until the nineteenth century.

An early woodcut of a minister in his pulpit.

The Orthodox true Minister.

accepted. Good Queen Bess might have been greatly loved by her people, but she was not always the most tactful of souls. She took leave of the bishop's wife at Lambeth with the words *'Madam* I may call you, and *Mistress* I am ashamed to call you, so I know not *what* to call you'!

In 1554 a new, celibate and Catholic priest in the person of Peter Prescot was appointed to replace the married Lawrence Waterward. The first thing we discover about the new rector is that he took John Bold to court for an incident almost identical to the one involving his predecessor. This time we find that John Bold, perhaps working cleverly on the mind of the displaced rector, had somehow managed to get Lawrence Waterward on his side together with John Fleetwood of Bretherton. The latter had a vested interest in the affair for the Fleetwood family had bought the right to appoint the rector after the dissolution of the Abbey of Evesham under Henry the Eighth.

From the new pleadings we obtain the interesting information that the parson, in addition to the rectory, was entitled to glebe land measuring a hundred acres and containing six messuages. Peter Prescot alleged that . . .

> John Fletewood, John Bolde, gentleman, William Haywarde, husbandman, and the said Lawrence Waterward, of their covetous and extorte power, with force and arms not only entered the mansion house of the said parsonage and into all the glebe lands and tenements thereof for their own use, but have also gathered and taken all the tithes of all manner of corn and hay and other things tithable arising within the said parish since the deprivation of the said Lawrence . . .

John Bold replied to these accusations by claiming that he was not guilty of any riot or trespass. His defence was that Lawrence Waterward leased the land to John Fleetwood at a rental of £7 6s 8d per annum, the lease to be renewed at three year intervals over a term of 21 years.

> Therefore [argued John Bold] although plaintiff is parson there, yet the demise made to John Fleetwood concerning the tithes belonging to the parsonage is good and available in the law for six years next after the deprivation of the said Lawrence Waterward without that the defendant in riotous manner entered the said mansion house . . .

The implication here is that Lawrence Waterward won his case three

The ivy-covered walls of Meols Hall before the single-storey wing was added by Roger Hesketh in 1938.

(E.W. Collection)

years earlier.

Peter Prescot argued that 'the said Lawrence having been married before making the said lease, and then being deprived because of the marriage, the said lease or any other act by him done is of no avail'. The new incumbent was the legal rector and seems to have been within his rights, but the law had been harsh on Lawrence Waterward when his only sin was that he had chosen quite legally to take himself a wife. Peter Prescot remained as rector for another twelve years.

In the same year as the problem over the glebe land and the tithes, another more serious affair blew up over a meadow called Baldemeryhokes which lay near the edges of Martin Mere and between the boundary of North Meols and Scarisbrick. Referred to as 'alias

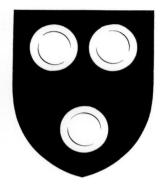

Standish of Standish

Sable, 3 torteaux argent

Edward Standish of Standish became a landowner in North Meols after his marriage to Ellen Aughton in the 1550s. The family included Sir Ralph Standish, who killed Wat Tyler during the Peasants' Revolt of 1382, and Captain Myles Standish of Ormskirk who sailed on the Mayflower with the Pilgrim Fathers.

Witnesses at Baldemeryhokes (1554)

Name		Age	Residence	Landlord
Adam Abraham			North Meols	
Edmund Abraham				
Will. Adamson		68	Huddlestone	Ric. Huddlestone Esq.
Nicholas Aughton		60	North Meols	Edmd. Standisshe Esq.
Edmund Ball		60	North Meols	Sir Thomas Hesketh
John Ball	about	106	Meols	Sir Thomas Hesketh
Lawrence Ball			North Meols	
Thos. Ball		60	North Meols	
Ric Ball		80	North Meols	John Bold
Robt. Ball		80	Hesketh	Hen. Banester Esq
Jas Balgshagh		38	Scarisbrick	
Hen. Blevyn		60		
Andrew Blundell		60	Scarisbrick	Thos. Barton Esq
Christ Blundell		60	North Meols	
Eglemowre Blundell		58	Scarisbrick	Will Spensar
Ric Blundell		47	Burscough	Thos Hallwurthe
Jas. Bonde				
Adam Breakyll		74	Scarisbrick	
[Grandson of Robt. Breakyll of North Meols]				
Percival Brekyll		60	Meols	
Ric. Brekyll		66	North Meols	
Will. Brekyll		60	North Meols	John Bold
Richard Byrch		89	Halsall	Hen. Halsall Esq
Richard Gilibrand, gent		36	Lathom	
Will Golburn		76	Scarisbrick	Jas. Skarsebreke Esq
Thos. Gorsuch, gent		41	Ormskirk	
Will Heyward		54	North Meols	
Rich. Henryson			North Meols	
Adam Hunter		66	Scarisbrick	Mr. Scarsebreke
Christ. Jamison		82	North Meols	Sir Thomas Hesketh
Thos. Jumpe		50	Birkdale	
James Kyd		60	Scarisbrick	Jas.Skarsebreke Esq
John Mathew		54	North Meols	
Will. Mawdisley		40	Burscough	Jas. Scarsebreke
Jno. Richardson		60	North Meols	Edwd. Standisse Esq
Nicholas Rimor			Birkdale	
Peter Rimer			Birkdale	
Ric. Rimor			Birkdale	
Thos. Rumur, the elder		56	North Meols	
Thos. Rumer, the younger		50	North Meols	
Jas. Rymor		60	Birkdale	Hen. Halsall Esq.
Hen. Skalsebreek, gent		30	Ormskirk	
Jas. Stopforth		24	Scarisbrick	
Jas. Such		60	Burscough	Mr. Scarsebreke
Peter Such		56	Scarisbrick	Mr. Scarsebreke
Roger Such		40	Burscough	Peter Rigbie
Peter Waryng		30	Scarisbrick	
Hen. Whitestones, gent		60	Burscough	'their Majesties'
Peter Wynstanl [Winstanley]				
John Wright				
Renald Wright		60	Meols	Peter Prescott, Priest
Robt. Wright		63	North Meols	
Robt. Wright			Blowicke	

the Wykes', this was the land which had been in dispute as long ago as 1410, and when the entitlement to the land came to be examined it proved to go right back to the quarter of the manor held by the Meols family who had married into the Scarisbricks in about 1340.[7]

William Stopforth from Marton in Burscough complained that certain charters had lately come into the hands of John Bold. After he had read them, John Bold, predictably enough, decided that the peaceful meadow of Baldemeryhokes in Scarisbrick was his property.

> . . .by colour whereof Robert Wright, servant to the said John and Elizabeth, Percival Brekyll, Thomas Ball, Edmund Mathue, and Edmond Ball, together with divers other riotous persons [unknown to the plaintiff], on or about the 16th day of June last, assembled at the said close of Baldemeryhokes and with stronge hand and multytude of men did mow and cut down the grass and hay growing there . . .

It was alleged that about fifty men arrayed with swords, bucklers and daggers came in a warlike manner, some being 'layed and placed in busshements' (in ambush). They carried off a hundred loads of hay valued at fifty pounds and took it to Bold House, the residence of John Bold.

In answer to these charges of illegal and warlike mowing of the meadow, John Bold marshalled his defences. He claimed a right to the land by virtue of his wife's inheritance from John Aughton and claimed that it was part of the moiety. He claimed that the labourers carried only scythes to mow the grass and that the hay was in any case in danger of being flooded and destroyed by the mere. There were seven or eight carts, with two men to each cart, and the reason given for the large number of mowers was that they 'com all upon one dai for because to have it mowen and ledde home whyle the wethere was fayre'. Or, as we might have put it in a later century, 'to make hay while the sun shines', an old saying which must have its origins in incidents like Baldemeryhokes.

North Meols at this time had two resident squires and the second squire, Barnaby Kitchen, was a complete contrast to his brother-in-law. Squire Kitchen was a considerate and model Tudor squire. In his will he left half a year's wages to every one of his house servants, he left twenty shillings and a heffer to Elizabeth Bullock, he left forty shillings and a cow to William Bullock, he gave £3 6s 8d to Thomas Snape and the same amount to William Watson. Thomas Brekill and John Rogerson were each given a jerkin. Jenett Blundell was given a coat. Lawrence Jump was also given a coat and John Kitchen of Forton was given a young bay mare with her colt, as well as a suit of clothing.[8] But John Bold was too abrasive for Barnaby Kitchen and in 1560 Barnaby sued him for trespassing on a meadow called the 'Shylds' and on a fishery called 'Water Dyche'. A few years later John Bold retaliated and accused Squire Kitchen of trespassing on his land called the 'Wykes', which was probably not Bold land at all but a part of Scarisbrick township.

Some of the differences between squire and rector were undoubtedly personality clashes, but part of the reason for the differences between Manor and Church was because of the fact that the gentry in the coastal parts of Lancashire did not readily embrace the new Protestant religion - they preferred to retain their old faith. In 1542 Sir Richard Aughton seems to have been concerned with the task of implementing the new religion when he appointed two stipendiary priests, Edmund Hodson and James Hodgkinson, to assist Lawrence Waterward with his duties. After the dissolution of the monasteries there existed many unemployed clergy in England and sometimes their learning could be put to good use by running a village school for the children of the parish. North Meols hardly needed the luxury of three priests to cater for the needs

Kitchen of Pilling and Meols
Argent, on a chevron quarterly gules and sable between three bustard gules, beaked and legged or, three bezants
Barnaby Kitchen of Pilling became lord of the manor soon after his marriage to Anne Aughton and remained so for over fifty years, including the whole of the reign of Elizabeth I. He became a Justice of the Peace and his daughter married Hugh Hesketh of Rufford. He seems to have been a very considerate squire and in his will he left half a year's wages to every one of his servants.

Early mapmakers and their craft

aps, plans and charts provide one of the most valuable sources for the local historian. From the 16th century onwards, the number and quality of maps increases until, by the end of the 18th century, mapmakers like Yates were producing the first truly reliable representations of this area. Before then, most maps were either lacking in detail, questionable in accuracy or selective in content. Many were produced for a particular purpose: estate maps, like that of Bankes, often showed only one man's holdings; Burghley's map of Lancashire showed only the seats of Roman Catholic gentlemen; Fearon and Eyes chart showed only those features which concerned the mariner, and so on. Nevertheless, we are greatly indebted to the early cartographers for much valuable information which would otherwise probably not exist in another form.

Left - *The map upon which this sketch is based is by George Lily and is one of the earliest we have of Lancashire dating from 1545. One prominent feature is a deep concave bay between the Ribble and the Mersey. The surveyor had probably seen Martin Mere from the high ground around Parbold and mistaken it for an inlet of the sea.*

Above right - *A small section of John Speed's map of 1610, showing Martin Mere and the sandy coastline around North Meols.*

Below - *Fearon and Eyes Chart of 1738. This chart was produced for navigation and gives some idea of what was visible to ships at sea. Note that Packington Bank was dry at high tide water at neap tides. The position of Fairclough's Lake, used by smugglers in the 17th and 18th centuries, is clearly seen, as is the position of the 'Sugar Houses', where slaving vessels unloaded their cargoes of sugar from the West Indies.*

(Reproduced by kind permission of Liverpool City Libraries)

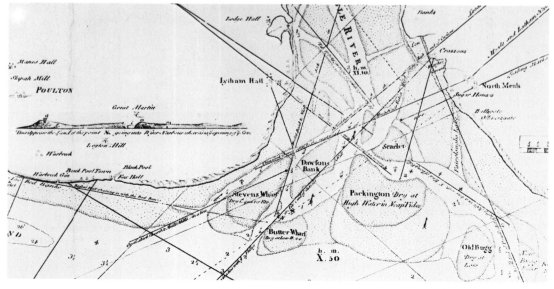

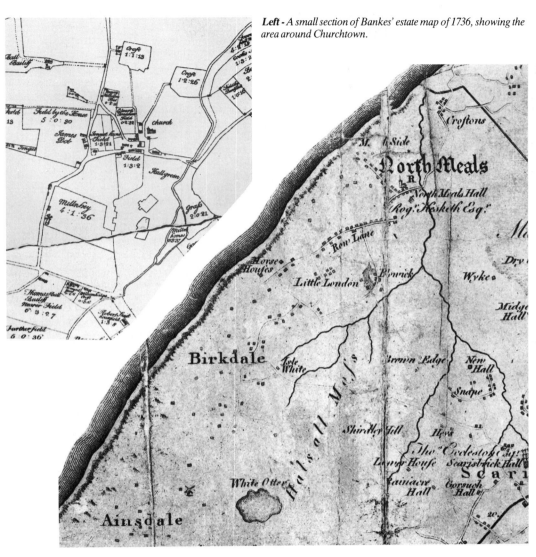

Left - A small section of Bankes' estate map of 1736, showing the area around Churchtown.

Above - A section of Yates' map of Lancashire of 1786. This map was accurately surveyed to the scale of one inch to a mile. It shows the individual houses in areas such as Marshside Road, Row (Roe) Lane, Little London, Blowick and Horse (Hawes) Houses, a few years before the beginnings of Southport.
(Reproduced by the kind permission of the County Archivist, Lancashire Record Office)

Left - Surveying techniques and quality of cartography had improved yet again by the time of the first Ordnance Survey maps in the 1840s.
(Reproduced by kind permission of the County Archivist, Lancashire Record Office)

of only five hundred souls, and it is therefore possible that the stipendiary priests were appointed for some other function which could have been anything from running a school to helping the lord of the manor with his hunting, shooting and fishing. Whatever the reason for their appointments, both priests were still assisting the rector in North Meols eight years after Sir Richard's death.

After the frictions caused during the incumbencies of Lawrence Waterward and Peter Prescot, a new, genial and expansive rector was presented by John Fleetwood in 1557. His name was Thomas Stanley and he was a son, albeit illegitimate, of Lord Monteagle who won great renown at Flodden Field. In addition to his duties in North Meols, Thomas Stanley was the Bishop of Sodor and Man, and he held the lucrative livings of Wigan and Winwick and also of Badsworth in the Diocese of York. Bishop Stanley visited North Meols seldom if at all, and during his incumbency the chancel was reported as badly in need of repair, there was no communion book in the church and not even a bible! The parishioners had to wait up to six days for baptisms and burials, until the clergy from other parishes could come to perform the office. Thomas Stanley evidently did not allow his obligations to weigh very heavily on his conscience, and when the official religion changed back again from Catholic to Protestant he took little time to adjust his views and to retain all his livings. In 1564 the Bishop of Durham wrote to his superior in York saying that 'the Bishop of Man liveth here [Durham] at his ease, as merry as Pope Joan'[9] — the impression of Thomas Stanley is that he would have made ideal material for a Shakespearian comedy.

Many of Queen Elizabeth's subjects proved very stubborn over their right to choose their own form of worship. They disliked having their religion dictated to them from London almost as much as the Londoners disliked having their religion dictated to them from Rome. By the 1580s many recusant families had become well organised, the manor houses all had their private chapels and their priest's holes. The forbidden mass was practised regularly and secret marriage ceremonies took place from time to time. When the Church authorities were seen crossing the Mersey on one of their visitations, flags were flown from various vantage points and there was usually plenty of time to hide away the priest and any incriminating evidence. But, as Lord Burghley's map of the county clearly shows, the authorities were well aware of all the furtive activity. Amongst the well known Catholic families were the Blundells of Little Crosby and of Ince, the Scarisbricks, the Southworths of Samlesbury including Sir John Southworth who was imprisoned for his faith, the Halsalls, Molyneuxs, Hoghtons, and Heskeths at both Rufford and Aughton. North of the Ribble was another Catholic stronghold with the Cliftons, Tyldesleys, Kirkhams, and Fleetwoods at Rossal and Bispham all retaining the old faith.[10]

Sir Francis Walsingham wrote to the Bishop of Chester from Greenwich Palace:

> . . . being informed of the bad disposition of the Wyfe of Bartholemew Heskyns [Hesketh], within your diocese, and howe she doeth much hurt in being at libertie to go (as she used to doe) where she will amongst recusants and the like persons.[11]

Mrs Hesketh, who was the daughter of Sir John Southworth, was living in the household of Barnaby Kitchen at Meols Hall. The letter goes on to instruct the bishop to 'apprehend the sayd wyffe of Heskins and comitt her'. She was arrested at Meols Hall and taken to the New Fleet at Salford where her father was already a prisoner.

Mrs Hesketh was influenced by a far more active recusant who was in hiding at Meols Hall in 1580. He was the Jesuit priest Edmund

Campion who, together with his colleague Parsons, landed in England from Spain and began to spread leaflets and propaganda throughout the countryside from a hidden printing press. Campion, who is said to have preached openly in Churchtown and in many other places, was reputed to be a very fine orator, and it was said that even the gentry were prepared to spend a night sleeping in a barn just to hear him preach the following morning. He defied the authorities until 1581, but events inevitably caught up with him and his body swung from the gallows at Tyburn on the first of December of that year.

Apart from the cases quoted there was surprisingly little persecution of the Catholics in Lancashire — only the very active amongst them suffered for their faith. As long as they were loyal to the crown and kept a low profile, they were generally left in peace, but some of the poorer families were badly hit when fines were introduced for those who were guilty of not attending church on a regular basis. The Queen knew that in spite of all the religious activities she need have no fear about the loyalty of these her subjects. When the Catholic King Philip II of Spain began to plan his invasion of England both John Bold and Barnaby Kitchen, who had given sanctuary to Edmund Campion when he came over from Spain, contributed the sum of twenty five pounds 'by way of a loan for the purpose of resisting to the utmost the advance of the Spanish Armada'.[12]

In North Meols the lot of the Protestants was, if anything, worse than that of the Catholics, particularly in the twelve years when the merry Bishop of Sodor and Man was the absentee rector. Very little is known about the church building at this time except that it was in a dreadful state of repair. The church seems to have had a stone foundation, probably supporting a timber-framed structure forming the nave, and an inventory from 1552 shows that it did boast a steeple and a peal of two bells, plus a hand bell which was used at funerals.[13] Peter Clayton, who had the misfortune to follow Thomas Stanley as rector, struggled on for over twenty years with the chancel falling into ruins. He left money in his will to repair the church after his death and this part of his will was apparently executed. It was not enough however, the churchyard still wanted urgent repairs and the church was still without a communion book and a bible. In 1598 it was stated that the windows were without glass and the chancel roof was ready to fall. This was during the incumbency of Robert Bamforde who resigned from his post in 1600 but continued to live in the parish.

The sorry state of the church fabric reflects the neglect of the Bold and Kitchen families during this difficult era, and for the common people of the parish the great religious conflict created a confusing dilemma, especially when many of them had lived to see the official religion of the country changed first from Catholic to Protestant, back to Catholic again, then back once more to Protestant. It is unlikely that the majority cared deeply one way or the other, or that they understood clearly the finer theological points separating the two faiths. What they did understand was that it was impossible for them to be loyal to both church and manor, and whilst to embrace the Catholic faith would put them in a favourable light with the lord of the manor this advantage was offset by the knowledge that they were acting outside the law of the land.

It is hardly surprising to find that the parish registers, which would add a lot of detail to the Elizabethan period, have not survived prior to 1594 and one wonders if they had ever been properly kept at all. The Provincial Constitution of Canterbury in 1598 required that all parish registers be kept in a parchment book and all entries from the accession of Queen Elizabeth were to be first copied into the new book. In North Meols a token attempt was made to comply with the

North Meols Tenant Farmers from 1550

This list is compiled from the dower assignment of Ellen Aughton. It is unlikely to be complete but it is valuable in listing many of the tenants in North Meols at this date.

Name	Annual Rent
Adam and Richard Abraham	7s
Edmund Abraham	21s 5d
John Abraham	12s
Nicholas Abraham	20s 8d
Gilbert Aghton	13s 4d
Nicholas Aghton	23s 8d
George Ball	16s 9d
Thomas Ball of Bankhouses, the young	14s
Robert Ball (with Richard Snape)	14s
John Blundell	9s
Thomas Blundell	?
Katherine, late wife of William Bonde	11s 4d
John Braykhyll	18d
Percival Braykhyll	?
Hugh Haychard	30s 4d
Thomas Johnson (with John Richardson)	14s
Edmund Mathew	6s
Margaret, late wife of William Mathewe, and John Mathewe	20s
John Richardson (with Thomas Johnson)	14s
Thomas Rymer of Blowyke	5s 6d
Thomas Rymer of Crossens	16s 8d
William Rymer	3s
Richard Snape (with Robert Ball)	14s
Margaret, late wife of John Wright, with Hugh Wright and Thomas Wright	14s 4d
Reginald Wright	18d

constitution and seventeen baptisms appear for the year 1595, one for the following year, and then nothing until the end of the century. Thanks to John Bold, however, the names of the families living in North Meols during the sixteenth century are well known, and in Ellen Aughton's dower assignment the names of over twenty tenant farmers are given.[14] At the inquest on Baldermeryhokes over fifty of the parish elders appeared to give testimony and most of their ages were recorded, including that of John Ball who claimed to have known seven lords of the manor and to have lived for a hundred and six years and was still living!

From the dower assignment we can estimate the population in the middle of the sixteenth century at about five hundred souls. The manor is described as containing 100 messuages, 20 cottages, one water mill, 2,000 acres of cultivated land, 500 acres of meadow, 300 acres of pasture, 20 acres of woodland, 1,000 acres of turbary, 500 acres of moor, a fishery, and 40 consolidates of rent. The estate also included property at Barton Juxta Halsall, at Thistleton on the Fylde, at Formby and at Hoole. The windmill had made its appearance to compete with water for grinding the corn. A reference to 'the oxhouse' implies that oxen still pulled the plough but, like the transition from water to wind, the changeover from ox to horse took many centuries and it is of interest to note that a reference to plough horses occurs two centuries before this time. The properties at Hall Moreton (Worcestershire) and at Nebold Comyn (Warwickshire), which were Millicent Comyn's dowry, had been sold for 20 marks in 1508.

Ellen Aughton's dower assignment gives some interesting field names, and the names of mills and water courses. Many of these add some colour to the history, and they are given here with added comments.

NORTH MEOLS FIELD NAMES 1550

Goordhay	(16 acres)
Medowhey	(7 acres. Probably a remnant of the great field called Meddehay mentioned in 1460)
Nyen Acre Field	(presumably 9 acres)
Estbankfield	(bordering on Eastbank Lane)
Brekhylhey	(farmed by the Brekhill family, near Martin Mere at Crossens)
Cokeshey	(one of the Cook's fields)
Marshhe	(marshy land, only one acre)
Cokes Croft	(a second Cook's field)
Westbankfield	(probably pairing somehow with Eastbankfield)
Cokeshey	(a third Cook's field — or was it used for cockfighting?)
Marshes	(plenty of marshland existed both seawards and towards the mere)
Rakes	(2 acres)
Baldemeyhokes	(alias the Wyke, a wonderful field name with quite a history)
New Intacke	(30 acres, this could have been recently claimed by a new sea embankment)
Awtyes Hey	(14 acres, a nickname?)
Marshe	(4 acres between Cokeshey and Cokeshey Marsh)
Bankefielde	(containing the 13th-century embankment built by the monks)
Byte of Bankefield-dych	(a byte was the corner of a field which had to be dug by hand because there was no room to turn the plough)
Ellen Acre	(probably named after John Aughton's widow)
Hyles	
Olyver Balhey	(Oliver Ball was a local worthy)

Cleyton Acre	(farmed by Hugh Haychard a variant of the name Hayward or Howard)
Howes	(100 acres. Probably sandhills, it could be the area which became South Hawes)
Watkinson Mosshay Yate	(Watkinsons were an established family)
Pyttes	(saltpits from the 13th century)
Kyrktowne Moss	(Churchtown Moss, 200 acres, mostly waste)
Crossens Common	(common land, 200 acres)
Gorseye Stynde	(around Gorsey lane)
Blowyke Stulpes	
Wennacre Grove	(now called Winacre Brow)

The northern boundary of the manor was still marked by the Snoterstone, as recorded in a document from 1547 which reads:

> . . . the said metts and boundes shall begin at a stone standing within the fflod merkes there called Snotterstone, and from thens vnto the foote of a certain poole named Walding poole . . . And it is further oderd yt none of the said parties ne enery to them belonging hereafter shall cut or delve any Turves or make any diche wthin ye space of one hundret footes vpon either side of the said meates and boundes . . .[15]

Two views showing early buildings in Churchtown. Many still survive to this day.
(E.W. Collection)

In the south, the Birkdale boundary was sometimes under dispute. Here was a stone cross standing in the sandhills. In 1533 Richard Aughton agreed with Thomas Halsall that:

> . . . Thomas Jumpe and William Rymer of Byrkedale, and John and Lawrence Ball of the Northmeles, shall set stakes on the boundary, beginning at a stake near the Carr, then to the Stone Cross in the Hawes, and on to a stake in the Hawes near highwater mark, and so on to a stake in the Warthe [beach] and so going to the South Channel and following that channel northwest to the sea . . .[16]

WATER COURSES AND OTHER FEATURES

Le Mylle Pele	(The mill stream or pill)
Le Asshurst Mylle	(A windmill)
Le Horrocks Mylle	(A second windmill in the Crossens area)
Le Polehay Dyke	(Pool Hey Dyke, Scarisbrick)
Le Wyke Dytche Mouthe	(Wyke ditch Blowick, built circa 1400 to drain the Wyke)
Le Ele Fysshyg	(The eel fishery)
Le Merton Meyre	(Martin Mere)
Le Baggmeyr	(A smaller mere, detached from the great mere)
Le Furthe	(A ford, probably over the Old Pool at Churchtown)

These details show something of the parish and the manor as it was in Tudor times. It is difficult to imagine the degree to which the countrymen were close to the land which they worked and on which they depended for their living. They watched the skies to read the weather and they followed the annual progression of the seasons by observing the changes of nature. They watched the rebirth every spring which marked the beginning of their year. They knew the Elizabethan summers when the crops were carefully tended until the corn stood high and golden in the fields, waiting for every able-bodied man, woman and child to help bring the harvest home. When autumn came the air cooled and brought with it the fogs and sea mists. As the nights closed in and the cold winter months lay ahead, the Yuletide activities gave them a welcome break from the daily routine. Then bitter winds blew from the north and the east, and the ground froze as hard as iron. Trees stood bare to the sky and fuel and food for man and beast fell low; when snow fell and covered the thatch and blew in flurries round the cottages; when the mill ground to a halt as the waters froze and hoar frost formed on the fields and the hedgerows; when the great Mere of Marton was a sheet of ice and children ran and played their chasing games on its hard surface.

The will of Alexander Hoghton of Lea Hall dated 1578 leaves musical instruments and play clothes to his brother . . .[17]

> . . . if he is minded to keep and do keep players. And if he will not keep and maintain players then it is my will that Sir Thomas Hesketh Knt [of Rufford Hall] shall have the same instruments and play clothes and I most heartily require the said Sir Thomas to be friendly unto Ffluke Gyllome and William Shakesshafte now dwelling with me and either to take them into his service or to help them to a good master.

Shakesshafte is a variant of the name Shakespeare, and many people therefore believe that William Shakespeare actually lived for a time at Rufford and knew Martin Mere in his youth.

Chapter Five

Work and Play

ATTHEW French spent his schooldays in Northamptonshire. He gained a place at Balliol College Oxford, where he took his B.A. degree at the age of seventeen. In the first year of the seventeenth century he was appointed rector of a North Country parish which was full of recusant families.

The new rector was only twenty, but when he arrived in North Meols he brought a wife with him. Elizabeth French bore him two daughters followed by a son and the parsonage at Crossens became a family house. Church life in North Meols took an immediate turn for the better. Baptisms, marriages and burials were all properly performed and the parish registers were fully kept for the first time in their history. Relations between Church and Manor also took a turn for the better, and when the official visitation came to North Meols they could find only Ellis Rimmer, 'a recusant of a long tyme', not attending church. It was noted that Rector French 'weareth the serplis verie seldom', but they acknowledged that he *did* wear his surplice on Sundays.

Matthew French created a good working relationship with the old Squire, Barnaby Kitchen. There must have been many recusants other than Ellis Rimmer in North Meols, but the squire and the rector seem to have co-operated to keep their existence from the authorities. They had known each other for only three years when the young rector received an urgent summons to go to Meols Hall. He arrived to find Squire Kitchen lying death pale on his bed. The squire asked Matthew French to write out his will, which the rector gladly agreed to do.[1] The following day (July 7th) Barnaby Kitchen died. He had been lord of the manor for 53 years and had survived his Queen by a matter of only a few months. His death marked the entry into North Meols of the Heskeths as the new manorial family, for Barnaby's daughter Alice was married to Hugh Hesketh of Rufford.

Matthew French continued with his parish duties under the new squire and under a new monarch. A few years later, in the hard winter of 1608, he had the most bitter stroke of misfortune when his wife died and he was left to manage alone with the care of his young children. It appears that Mrs French, Matthew's mother, came to live in the rectory to help with the situation, but as soon as he had recovered from his tragedy Matthew French began to look for a new wife and mother for his children. He was lucky enough to find Ellen Weardon from

An early woodcut of a shopkeeper in his shop.

Preston whom he married in the following year. Ellen bore him more children and the family atmosphere in the parsonage house was soon renewed with a vengeance.

It is possible to reconstruct some of the details of the rectory at this period from an inventory of the goods and chattels of Matthew French which was taken soon after his premature death in 1614.[2] Not only do we discover something about the rector's possessions, but the items are listed room by room so that the compilers have unwittingly given us a brief but accurate description of the rectory itself early in the seventeenth century. In order of size it was the third house in the parish, Meols Hall and Bold House being first and second.

On the ground floor was the parlour, kitchen, buttery, hall, larder, the study and a small closet. Upstairs was a room over the buttery, a room over the parlour, and a room over the hall. In most of the rooms were boards and shelving, trunks and chests, and a large number of feather beds for the family to sleep on both upstairs and downstairs. The four-poster complete with curtains, tester, and bolster must have been the bed of the rector and his wife. They slept in the room over the buttery.

In the hall could be seen a table with five large chairs and four little chairs for the smaller children. In the buttery Ellen French kept eleven tablecloths of various quality and six dozen table napkins. This was also where she kept the sheets, towels and pillowcases. In other rooms were earthen vessels and pewterware, a bed warming pan, twelve silver spoons for special occasions, chopping knives, kitchen furniture, a broken silver bowl and 'one ould watch out of order', (but still valued at £1 6s 8d). The rector had twenty yards of cloth in his house, woven by his parishioners or perhaps by his own family to supplement their income, and sixteen yards of canvas for use as sailcloth for fishing boats and windmills. It is not clear whether the little tub with fish in it stood in the larder or outside the house.

One of the most interesting parts of the inventory is the list of books in the study. Here, when he came home to read and relax at the end of his working day, Matthew French had about sixty volumes lining the shelves. Naturally enough his taste shows a strong bias towards the scriptures and we find texts on the gospels of Luke and John, Dr Abbot's text on the Book of Jonah, Dod on the Ten Commandments and Babington on the Lord's Prayer. He had at least three different bibles including a Latin version, an English Bible, and the newly authorised King James' Bible, which was then a very novel publication but destined to be the version of the bible familiar to churchgoers for centuries.

Not all the books are on theology. There was an official text on French history, the works of Horace provided a classical touch, there was a copy of Dr White's book on *Methods of Physick,* and a handsome bound volume of Maginus' *Geographie* which was much admired by his brother-in-law, Edmund Weardon.

The inventory lists the rector's corn, part of the North Meols tithes, which was stored mostly in Crossens Barn but partly in a barn at Churchtown and partly in Brekill's·Barn. He kept a horse for his own use and two riding ponies for his wife and children.

When Matthew French died in his mid-thirties he left a wife, three sons, two daughters and 'such issue sonne or daughter as my said wyffe hathe in her wombe'. The volume of Maginus' *Geographie* was left to Edmund Weardon. It is probable that his widow and children were able to remain living at the rectory because the new rector, Henry Wright, also held the living of Leyland and he chose to live there in preference to North Meols.

Henry Wright did his best to look after both his parishes but when the visitation arrived in 1625 they proved to be an extremely vigilant body and it was not possible to cover up all the recusant activities of which they disapproved.[3] The churchwardens were instructed to certify the names of noncommunicants within a fortnight after Easter every year and to fine the absentees the sum of twelve pence. Henry Wright was criticised for not wearing the surplice when he served communion.

The activities at Meols Hall were greatly frowned upon, especially the wedding ceremonies which had taken place in secret. William Hesketh, gentleman, and his 'supposed wife' were accused of 'secrett marriage', as were Richard Rimmer and William Wright and their 'supposed wives'. Thomas Rimmer had sired 'two bastards by one Rimer'. William, the son of Hugh Hesketh, 'had a bastard before marriage and married not knowne where nor by whom'! William Bradshaw and John Barnes were 'loyterers', Lawrence Ball and William Hodges 'dyd not communicate at Easter last'. Cuthbert Rimmer, the son of Ellis Rimmer, who was well known from the earlier visitation, was considered to be 'a dangerous person for seducinge of good protestants'. Gilbert Aughton and his friends Barnaby Matthew and Robert Wright were told in no uncertain terms that they were expected to be at church on Sundays and not 'draweing and sellinge drinke att service time'.

But the church authorities were not entirely without compassion and when presentations were made against Peter Rimmer and his wife Mary for 'seldome cominge to Churche and suspected recusant', they were discharged 'for ytt appeareth that he was in dette, he did not frequent the Churche soe often as he should have done and for that ytt appeareth that his wiefe was att Churche within this month and is now verie great with child'.

Legal offences were tried at the Ormskirk and Wigan Quarter Sessions. A serious case of robbery with violence came before Edward Moore JP in 1641. The offenders were Thomas Brommeley, who posed as a bailiff to the sheriff, and his motley gang of accomplices called Thomas Collier, John Smyth, James Harrock, John Hey and Jarden Warde. These six plundered their way right through the Meols demanding money from the inhabitants and threatening them with violence in they did not pay up. They told their victims they were charged to appear before the undersheriff at Bolton. The cowardly gang chose their victims carefully, deliberately picking on the elderly and the infirm.

Lawrence Watkinson, aged 'three score or thereabouts', paid them 6s 2d which was all the money he had. George Ball, aged three score and ten and almost blind, pawned a pot to William Johnson to raise the money they demanded. John Blundell, a husbandman aged fifty, claimed that they attacked him and 'beinge a poore man, & living most upon fishinge & fowlinge for his best releife maytenance: & beinge affraide of further trouble, did give them vi s vii d . . .' Edward Blundell, aged 48, appeared on behalf of his aged mother; she had borrowed two shillings from her son with which to pay them; he must have exaggerated when he gave her age as five score years. William Johnson, aged about sixty, was sick in bed when the gang came to extort money from him, and threatened that they 'would pull him out of bedd by force, & carrie him to prison'. Whereupon 'this examinant beinge very sicke, & afraid to be pulled out of his bedd, w[hi]ch might have endangered his life, for fear did give them his vis viii d & entered into bound to appeare before the saide undersherif accordinge as they directed him . . .'[4]

Another controversial side of village life is to be found in the records of the court leet and the court baron which survive for the years 1640 and 1643.[5] The attempts from the previous century to establish a court at North Meols were obviously successful and here we find the complete formal proceedings of the court, ranging from the routine items such as the scouring and cleaning out of ditches and the repair of barns and houses, to the heated disputes which sometimes arose and frequently led to verbal abuse and assault.

John Rimmer and Richard Ricson came before the court guilty of 'making a tussel the one upon the other' and were each fined six and eightpence. Hugh Hodges and Thomas Rimmer (coneyman) were found guilty of the same offence and it seems that the coneyman was not the most popular of local worthies for we find that the wife of Thomas Hughes was found guilty of striking him — whether with bare hands or broomstick we are not told but it cost her twelve pence. Peter Such of Crossens was fined two shillings for 'abusing the officer with evile words', but his picturesque speech was not recorded. Richard Rimmer was fined 3s 4d for 'Keeping a stoned horse which doeth great horte to his neighbours contrarie to the law' — a stoned horse was one which had not been gelded; it is not difficult to imagine the problems which were created when a neighbour's mare was on heat. John Brekill 'Doeth not repair his houses according to the order of the court' and he was also guilty of taking inmates against the order of the court. The court seemed hard on Blanche Knowles for it found her guilty of 'keeping a woman on childe-bead of a childe begotten in fornication'.

Some of the villagers had taken to sharpening their spades and other tools on the stones of the bridge in Churchtown. It had become a serious problem and the court agreed that 'if any man or woman shall take any stones from the church bridge or part or any, or whet any spaydes one it, for everie tyme soe offending to be fine 3s 4d'. John Wright of 'Hause' was fined twelve pence 'for stopping the water, and would not lett it kom the courses as it haith bine accustomed and would not oppene [the sluice gate] at the barliemenes appointment'.

The barleyman or burleyman, a term which is thought to be derived from 'by-law-man', was the manor official responsible for the proper upkeep of the field boundaries and the water courses. North Meols had four of these officials; William Brekill and Nicholas Wright covered the area around Churchtown, John Aughton and John Ball (Webster) covered the fields around Blowick. They were assisted by four pinders, namely Robert Wright and John Blundell for Crossens and John Bond and Richard Rimmer for 'The Wite Hill'(?). Richard Such of Crossens and Lawrence Jump were elected to serve as parish constables for 1640, Edward Wright and James Mosse were the retiring constables and were ordered to make their accounts for the year before the first of May or to pay a heavy fine of forty shillings. The jury of fifteen is thought to be a court leet feature, but the court also served as a court baron — the difference in this case being rather academic — it was a manorial court. The good men and true who sat on the jury in the 1640s were:

NORTH MEOLS JURORS 1640 AND 1643

1640		1643	
John Ball	of Blowyke	Lawrence Ball	of Lower Blowicke
Lawrence Ball	of Blowyke	John Ball	of Blowicke
James Blevin		Richard Ball	of Blowicke
John Blundell	of Hawes	Thomas Ball	of New Rowe
Richard Boonde	of Banckes	James Blevin	of Crossons
Edward Howard		Gilbert Johnson	of Blowicke
Gilbert Johnson		Lawrence Jump	
Lawrence Jumpe		James Mosse	of Crossons
James Mosse		Hugh Rymer	of Churchtown

Hugh Rymer	of Church Towne	John Rymer	of Crossons
John Rymer	of Crossons	Robert Rymer	of Bankes
Robert Rymer	of Crossons	Robert Rymer	of Crossons
Richard Such	of Crossons	Robert Rymer	of New Row
William Wattkinson		William Watkinson	of Blowicke
Robert Wright	of Rowe	Robert Wright	of Newe Rowe

In 1643 John Aughton was the clerk of the jury and Richard Wright was the overseer.

We are fortunate to have an excellent description of North Meols at about his time, written by a complete outsider. He was Dr Richard James of Corpus Christi College Oxford, who paid a visit in 1636.[6] Churchtown was then very close to the sea. Fishermen could be seen mending their nets and preparing their catch for market at the doors of their cottages in the unmade main street of the village. Around the church was a cluster of low one-roomed cottages, cruckbuilt of the traditional clamstaff and daub, and surmounted by a heavy and untidy thatch to keep the warmth in and the weather out. The sandhills, which came right up to the outskirts of Churchtown to the south, were huge. Northwards was a green swathe of seawashed turf. This was common land where sheep grazed and wandered below the high water mark when the tide receded. Boats were few but the fishing was good, and stationary nets were set to catch fish on the outgoing tide. Richard James was struck by the splendid isolation of the Meols, and he put his findings into verse:

                Let us varie sportes
        Whoe are at leasure and seek niew resortes
        For recreation. Ormeschurch and ye Meales
        Are our next journey. We direct no weales
        Of state to hinder our delight. Ye guize
        Of those chaffe sands which doe in mountains rize
(1)   On shore is pleasure to behold, which Hoes
(2)   Are called in Worold; windie tempest blowes
        Them up in heapes; 'tis past intelligence
        With me how seas do reverence
        Upon ye sands; but sands and beach and peobles are
        Cast up by rowling of ye waves a ware
        To make against their deluge, Since the larke
        And sheepe within feede lower than ye marke
        Of each high flood. Heere through ye washie Sholes
        We spye an owlde man wading for ye soles
        And flukes and rayes, which the last morning tide
        Had stayed in nets, or did at anchor ride
        Upon his hooks; him we fetch up and then
        To our goodmorrow, 'welcomme gentlemen'
        He sayed, and more, 'You gentlemen at ease
        Whoe money have and goe where ere you please
        Are never quiett; wearye of ye day
        You now come hither to drive time away;
        Must time be driven? longest day with us
        Shutts in too soon, as never tedious
        Unto our buisnesse; making mending nett
        Preparing hooks and baits wherewith to gett
        Cod, whiting, place, upon the sandie shelves
        Wherewith to feed the market and our selves'.
        Happie ould blade, who in his youth had binne
        Roving at sea, Where Essex Cales did winne
(3)   So now he lives. If any Bushell will
        Live west the world, withoute projecting skill
        Of Ermitage, he shall not need to seek
        In rocks, or Calve of Man, an ember weeke,

(1) Hoes: Hawes, the sandhills
(2) Worold : The Wirral.
(3) Bushell: A Manx hermit in the time of James I

> Heere at ye desert Meales he may, unknowne
> Bread by his own paines getting, live alone
> (4)   Without a Callott or a page to dress
> Or bring bought meate unto his holiness.
> But haste we back to Ormeskirke, least. I feare
> Our friends depart and leave us in ye reare . . .
>
> RICHARD JAMES

In this passage, not only do we see a detailed picture of the parish right down to its grazing sheep and even its fishing methods, but Dr James actually gossips with one of the locals and gives all manner of details about him.

Who was this 'happie ould blade' who made such an impression on the learned doctor from Oxford? 'Where Essex Cales did winne' refers to the action of 1596 when the Queen's favourite sailed with Raleigh into the harbour at Cadiz and tried to destroy all the shipping around him as Drake had done a generation earlier; it was one of the last piratical acts of the swashbuckling Elizabethan Navy. This aged sandgrounder had therefore served and fought in the same navy as Drake, Hawkins and Frobisher and had sailed the same swaying, rounded oaken-walled vessels. A veritable ancient mariner, complete with the gleam in his eye and ready to spin his yarns to all men, women, children and travellers who would spare the time to hear him. Perhaps he was one of the many veterans of the Spanish Armada still to be found in the coastal villages of England. Perhaps, too, as this ancient mariner had sailed under Raleigh at Cadiz, he was connected with the introduction of the potato crop into North Meols after his discharge from the Navy. The parish's one claim to fame was that it pioneered the first potato crops in England, a claim which is certainly very old but which has proved difficult to substantiate.

The old man envied the visitors their leisure, but the locals were not without time to enjoy themselves. When the week's work had been done and the duties of the parish and manor officials had been performed, there was still time for the lighter side of country life, with music, sport and dancing which had replaced the archery practice on the village greens. All the villages had their fairs and festivities and before the coming of the Civil War and the puritanical views of the Cromwellian regime they knew how to enjoy themselves. Young people would travel for miles to attend a fair or to further their courting and the parish registers show that the communities were not as inbred as some would have us believe.

William Blundell of Little Crosby looked back with nostalgia to the days before the Civil War and wrote for us 'a contry song remembring the harmless mirth of Lancashyre in peasable times'.[7] It was danced to the tune of Roger de Coverley, a great favourite in the county. He describes a gathering at Little Crosby. The dancers from North Meols are there, as are those from Formby and from Lathom and a party from Chowbent are included — Thomas Knex, the Chowbent piper, was reputed to be the finest for miles around, excelling even Lord Strange's piper who was previously held to be the best in the county.

WILLIAM BLUNDELL'S 'CONTRY SONG'[7]

Robbin and Ralph and Willy
    took Susan and Ginnett and Sisly
And Roger and Richard and Geordy
    took Mary and Peggie and Margery
And daunced a hornepype merilie
    tripped and skipped nott wearilie
Tyr'd out the Bagpype and Fidle
    with dauncing the Hornepipe and didle.

---

(4) Callot : A term for a serving maid

But Gilbert and Thomas and Harry
      whose sweethearts weare Nell Nann and Marie
Tooke sydes against Gyles James and Richard
      whose wentches were Jeane Jane and Bridgett
The wager was for a wheate cake
      they daunced till thire bones did ake
That Gilbert and Nannie and Nellie
      did swett themselves into a Jelly.

The Ladds of Chowbent weare there
      and had brought thire doggs to the Beare
But they had no tyme to play
      they daunced awaye the daye
For thither then they had brought Knex
      to play Chowbent hornepype that Nicks
Toms and Geffreyes shoone
      weare worne quit through with the tune

The ladds of Lathom did daunce
      thire Lord Strange's hornepype which once
Was held to have been the best
      and far to exceed all the rest
But now they doe hould it so sober
      and therefore will needs give it over
They call on thire Pyper then joviley
      play us brave Roger o' Coverley.

The Meales men daunced thire Copp
      and about the maypoule did hopp
Till thire shouse weare so full of sand
      that they no longer could stand stand
The Formeby trotter supply'd
      whoe though that his Breeches weare wide
Yett would he nere give it ore
      till the Pyper was ready to snore.

But Gilbert and Susan and Nannie
      with Tom Sisly and Mary
Tripped and Skipped full merily
      the music now sounding out chearily
Dick booted Nel frowted he showted
      tak't thee James Pyper of Formeby
Tak't thee, Tak't thee, Tak't thee
      tak't thee James Pyper of Formeby.

At length it was tyme to go
      alass Susan did heare the Coke crowe
The maydes might goe make up thire fyres
      els be chidd by thire Syres
Next holy day they'te daunce thire fill
      at Johnson's o'th Talke of the hill
Wheare Bell shall be brought to play
      good Lord how I longe for that day.

WILLIAM BLUNDELL

Blundell of Little Crosby
*Sable, ten billets, 4, 3, 2 and 1
argent
William de Coudray married
Amabel Blundell in 1224 and this
is probably why the families share
the same coat of arms. The
Blundells had several branches in
South Lancashire, and these are
the arms of the Little Crosby
branch which included William
Blundell, the Cavalier, and his
grandson Nicholas, the diarist.*

The best way to travel between the coastal communities of South Lancashire lay along the firm sands of the beach rather than the muddy inland farm tracks and the sandy lanes through the dunes. As the first light of the new dawn struggled through, the weary revellers began their long journey home, their figures silhouetted against the dawn sky in the early morning mist. A trail of footprints and hoofmarks lay in the smooth sand behind them. A trickle of travellers stretched out along the shore, some walking, some on horseback, some sharing a steed. Others slept exhausted in the back of a cart as the horse found its own way with the rest of the party. A pair of lovers straggled behind the main group, hand in hand, and as they pass Formby perhaps a tearful farewell and a pledge to meet again at the next gathering. On along the open sands, more farewells at Ainsdale and Birkdale until at last the spire of St Cuthbert's and the familiar stump of the

Churchtown windmill can be seen on the skyline. Perhaps it was Sunday morning, for who would have the energy to work in the fields after that night at Little Crosby? And as they took themselves off to bed, tired out, to sleep off their revelry, Henry Wright would find his Sunday congregation sadly depleted and wonder again about the problems of recusancy.

North Meols retained its annual fair but lost its market long ago in the Middle Ages. Ormskirk was the nearest market for the farmers and fishermen to carry their wares but they also travelled regularly to Croston, Liverpool and Preston, and sometimes even into East Lancashire where there was always a good market for fresh sea food.

Preston was the most frequented market after Ormskirk but the long journey of eighteen miles in each direction made for an early start and a long day. The travellers journeyed past the Snoterstone at Hundred End and came to Hesketh Bank where a bridge carried them over the little River Douglas. As the horses laboured to pull the laden carts up the riverbank they were soon overlooked by the gaunt Jacobean features of Carre House, home of the Stone family of Bretherton. They had entered the township of Hoole; it had connections with their own parish in that a small part of Hoole, like Barton and Thistleton, belonged with the North Meols estate.

The wayfarers passed by the newly rebuilt brick church of St Michael's and sometimes stopped at one of the wayside inns to catch up on news, local affairs and gossip. On one occasion they must have heard reports about the new curate. A very strange young man. He attended to his duties well enough but he seemed to have spent little time relaxing and mixing with the parishioners. It was rumoured that he spent half the night sitting at his window and gazing at the stars. He would sometimes reach for a strange tube and peer through it and frequently he pointed a cross-staff skywards and squinted along it with infinite, painstaking care. Perhaps the travellers, returning by moonlight from their long day at the market, saw him at his window peering through his curious tube at the night sky. It was rumoured that the tube was magic and filled with charmed glasses with which he hoped to bring the stars down to the earth. He could be seen writing careful notes and making calculations − if any saw his notes even the literate among them could not understand the strange mathematical symbols which he used.

A man with such an interest in the heavens must surely be an astrologer, but the curious thing about him was that he had never been known to cast a horoscope nor yet tell a fortune. What on earth was this man? Had they known that he held the preposterous belief that the sun was many times larger than the earth, and that the earth was like a tiny speck chasing round the sun, then they would certainly have dismissed him as an eccentric or worse.

This isolated stretch of coastline was a long way from the scientific world of Galileo and Kepler, yet at Hoole in 1639 there lived a man who, before the birth of Newton, before the existence of the Royal Society and before the founding of the Royal Greenwich Observatory, pushed forward the frontiers of astronomy beyond the point at which it stood after the lifelong dedication of Tycho Brahe and his pupil Kepler.

Jeremiah Horrox was born at Toxteth near Liverpool in about 1617. He was educated at Emmanuel College, Cambridge, and in 1639 he obtained employment at Hoole. Most writers have assumed that he was the curate and, bearing in mind that he was a deeply religious man and that he prepared for the Church when at Cambridge, this is a very reasonable assumption. St Michael's Church at Hoole was rebuilt by

John Stones of Carre House in 1628, but in Horrox's time it was only a chapel of ease to Croston parish church.

The inhabitants of Much Hoole and Little Hoole applied for full parish status and this was granted by Act of Parliament in 1641. Allowing for inevitable parliamentary delays, it seems certain that Jeremiah Horrox, in his capacity as curate, played some part in this development. The Church records, however, make no mention of his appointment and some have suggested that he was not a curate at all but was engaged as a private tutor to the Stone family at Carre House. His correspondence leaves no doubt that he lived at Hoole for a period from 1639 to 1640 and it was during this period that he was able to observe an extremely rare astronomical event which had never been seen before and which was not observed again until 130 years later. The observation was the transit of the planet Venus across the face of the Sun.

Using the most primitive form of instrument called a radius astronomicus, which was really little more than an elaborate version of the cross staff used by Elizabethan sailors, Horrox made the most careful measurements of the angles between the planets and the fixed stars. He found to his great consternation that the planets were not in the places predicted for them by the tables of Longomonitus from which he was working. These tables were based on the system of cycles and epicycles worked out by Ptolemy centuries ago in the ancient world.

Horrox wasted much time trying to fit his observations to the tables and to explain the small discrepancies which he naturally assumed were due to his own observational errors. Then a correspondent introduced him to the Rudolphine Tables recently published by Kepler and based on the data collected by the Danish astronomer Tycho Brahe, the last and greatest of the naked eye observers. Horrox reworked his calculations and discovered to his great satisfaction that his measured positions for the planets agreed almost exactly with the positions predicted by Kepler's Theory of Planetary Ellipses.

Almost, but not quite.

The planet Venus was not exactly where Kepler predicted, but the error was easy to explain in terms of the time which had elapsed since Tycho's observations had been made and the inevitable small errors in the original observations. To Horrox's delight, he discovered that Venus was following a course which would take it across the face of the sun in November 1639.

Horrox calculated that the transit would be visible throughout nearly the whole of Italy, France and Spain, but not for all of the transit. He discovered that the best place to view the complete transit was America, a vast new world across the Atlantic where there was probably not a single telescope — the early colonists had no time for stargazing. The astronomer lamented the wasted spectacle in verse:

Why beauteous Queen desert thy votaries here?
Ah! Why from Europe hide that face divine,
Most meet to be admired on distant climes
Why scatter riches or such splendid sights
Why waste on those who cannot prize their value?[8]

Jeremiah Horrox checked the position of Venus against the fixed stars whenever the skies allowed. He got to know the landmarks and shadows of Hoole in detail so that he could tell the time to within a few minutes from the sun and the stars. He discovered how to use his telescope lens to project an image of the sun onto a screen so that he could take measurements. He studied the sunspots to make himself familiar with any markings on the sun which were current at that time, for he did not wish to be accused of seeing a sunspot instead of Venus on the solar disc.

There was a problem. As Venus moved closer to the sun it became progressively more difficult and finally impossible to view the planet in the night sky and to plot the position against the stars. He could not be certain of the exact time of the transit. As the day came nearer he kept a day long vigil in his room, watching the image of the sun and praying that he would not miss the event.

> . . . although the corrected computation of Venus' motions which I had before prepared, and as the accuracy of which I implicitly relied, forbad me to expect anything before three o'clock in the afternoon of the 24th, yet according to the calculations of most astronomers, the conjunction should take place sooner, by some even on the 23rd, I was unwilling to depend entirely on my own opinion which was not sufficiently confirmed, lest by too much self-confidence I might endanger the observation. Anxiously intent therefore on the undertaking through the greater part of the 23rd, and the whole of the 24th, I omitted no available opportunity of observing her ingress. I watched carefully on the 24th from sunrise to nine o'clock, and from a little before ten until noon, and at one in the afternoon, being called away in the interval by business of the highest importance which, for these ornamental pursuits, I could not with propriety neglect

It was Sunday. He does not tell us what business was more important than the advancement of the frontiers of science, but it was presumably his Sabbath duties — the sun and the planets had to wait for the Hoole sermon! As he hurried back the sun was low in the sky, for the dates given are on the old style Julian Calendar and on November the 24th sunset was at 3.45 pm, about as early as it could be in these latitudes. It was also cloudy and his chances of making the observation had grown very slim indeed.

The astronomer then received proof of the blessings of his Maker:

> . . . About fifteen minutes past three in the afternoon, when I was again at liberty to continue my labours, the clouds, as if by divine interposition, were entirely dispersed, and I was once more invited to the agreeable spectacle, the object of my most sanguine wishes, a spot of unusual magnitude and of a perfectly circular shape, which had already fully entered upon the sun's disc on the left, so that the limbs of the sun and Venus precisely coincided, forming an angle of contact. Not doubting that this really was the shadow of the planet, I immediately applied myself to observe it.

Jeremiah Horrox was indeed very fortunate to have seen the event. Only 15 miles to the south his brother Jonas, watching for the event in Liverpool, did not have a clear sky all day. Horrox had no time to communicate his prediction to the rest of the scientific world and consequently only one other person saw the transit. This was his great friend and correspondent, William Crabtree, a cloth merchant from Broughton near Manchester. Crabtree too was plagued with cloudy skies, but at about 3.20 pm the clouds cleared and he saw Venus fully entered on the transit. Horrox describes the elation of his friend in a passage which shows much of the enthusiastic and sociable character of Horrox. He was ragged about his obsession with astronomy, but he enjoyed the ragging and took it all in good part.

> Rapt in contemplation, he stood for some time motionless, scarcely trusting his own senses, through excess of joy; for we astronomers have as it were a womanish disposition, and are overjoyed with trifles and such small matters as scarcely make an impression upon others, a susceptibility which those who will may deride with impunity, even in my own presence, and, if it gratify them, I too will join in the merriment'.

Horrox was one of the first true scientists. He was not taken in by the strange incantations of alchemy and astrology, and where others had clung for fifteen centuries to the Ptolemaic dogma of perfect circles, he dismissed them the moment he discovered a better system. He was the first person in England to make use of the theories of Kepler, and with the instinct of true genius he accepted the radical ideas of Copernicus and Galileo immediately because the truth in them was very natural and obvious to him.

Jeremiah Horrox was no mere stargazer; he made drawings of the projected image of Venus on the sun's disc and he took careful measurements. From these he was able to calculate more accurate values for the constants of the orbit of Venus. Furthermore, by putting his data together with that of Gassendi, who had observed a transit of Mercury in 1631, he was able to estimate a value for the parallax of the sun. The latter was a much discussed astronomical constant at the time, based on the idea that as the earth rotated on its axis it should be possible to measure the movement of the sun against the background of the fixed stars as the earth's motion carried the observer round with it. The parallax was thus related to the distance between the earth and the sun which we now call the Astronomical Unit. Horrox put the sun at a distance of 72 million miles, a crude estimate by modern standards — but it should be viewed against the previous best estimate of 20 million miles given by Kepler. His estimate was based on the idea that Mercury, Venus, Earth and Jupiter would all appear the same size when viewed from the sun — an incorrect hypothesis which explains his error in the sun's distance, but his reasoning was quite sound and not unscientific as some writers have suggested.

Why then, is the name of Jeremiah Horrox unknown outside a small circle? There are several reasons. In January 1640/1 Horrox, having returned to his native Toxteth, had arranged to travel to Broughton to meet with his friend and correspondent William Crabtree and to compare astronomical notes. The two had been looking forward to this, their first meeting for some time. On the day appointed Crabtree waited expectantly for his young friend to arrive. He waited all day in vain, for Horrox never came. There was no way in which the astronomer could keep his appointment. Jeremiah Horrox was dead.

'Thus God puts an end to all worldly affairs', wrote the dismayed Crabtree, 'And I am alas bereaved of my dearest Horrox. Irreparable loss! Hence these tears'!

Death was not the end of Horrox's misfortunes. During the Civil War a heavy-footed company of soldiers entered his father's house in Toxteth in search of plunder, and a number of his papers were looted and burned. A second portion of his work was taken to Ireland by

A mirror is aligned to pass the image of the sun into a bulky piece of photographic equipment. A scene at King George V School before the total eclipse of the sun in 1927.
(*Photo, Botanic Gardens Museum*)

his brother Jonas, the papers were lost and never recovered. A third portion, which survived for over twenty years, found their way eventually to a London book merchant called Nathaniel Brooks. They were in London in 1666, but their loss can hardly be blamed on Brooks for they perished with Old St Paul's and other pieces of our heritage in the Great Fire of London.

Thus it was not until 1672 that the Royal Society at last published what remained of the works of Horrox, and only then did they become known to other astronomers. By that time Newton's *Principia* was only 15 years in the future, and events in the scientific world had progressed so dramatically that many of his findings had been overtaken by more recent discoveries.

To judge Horrox purely on his astronomical achievements is to examine only one facet of his character and sufficient of his writings remain to show that he loved beauty as well as truth. His love of life was such that when some event moved him he would burst into poetry to express his feelings. For example, when he bought his telescope and saw for the first time that the planet Venus, as he expected, had phases like the moon:

> This prying tube too shews Venus' form
> Clad in the vestments of her borrowed light,
> While the unworthy fraud her crescent horn
> Betrays. Though bosomed in the solar beams
> And by their blaze o'erpowered, it brings to view
> Hermes and Venus from concealed retreats;
> With daring gaze it penetrates the veil
> Which shrouds the mighty ruler of the skies,
> And searches all his secret laws.

Horrox has not been forgotten by his country. He has a prestigious memorial in Westminster Abbey to add to those at his birthplace in Toxteth and his church at Hoole. But perhaps the memorial which he would have appreciated most was in the *Philosophiae Naturalis Principia Mathematica,* better known as the *Principia,* published in 1687. In it Newton showed the world how, with the help of some astonishing new developments in mathematics, all the motions of the heavens could be described by the simple law of Universal Gravitation. There amongst the names of Ptolemy, Copernicus, Kepler, Tycho Brahe, and the greatest astronomers of the past, Newton acknowledged his debt to the Lunar Theory of 'Horrocius noster' − *our* Horrox − a touching reference to the fact that Horrox was one of the author's own fellow countrymen. 'If I have seen further than others before me', said Newton, 'It is because I have stood on the shoulders of giants'. Jeremiah Horrox, the Father of English Astronomy, was one of those giants.

Chapter Six

Roundheads and Cavaliers

ND so the Civil War reached Lancashire. The county was sharply divided in its loyalties. The eastern hundreds of Blackburn and Salford declared themselves in support of Parliament, but in the hundreds of West Derby, Leyland, and Amounderness support was largely for the King. When the King raised his standard in 1642 William Hesketh, the squire's eldest son aged 27, promptly left home to become a Cavalier.

William Hesketh never returned to Meols Hall. It is assumed that he fell in battle, but the details of where and how he fell are unknown. That he was an active Royalist is beyond dispute for at the end of the war Parliament sequestered his estates for what they called Treason to the Commonwealth.

At first there was very little warlike activity and the Meols was thankful for its isolated situation. In the summer of 1642 the Royalists and Parliamentarians were becoming openly hostile to each other and there followed a scramble to get their hands on all the weapons and gunpowder they were able to find. A troop of Roundhead soldiers, under the command of Captain Geoffrey Holcroft, entered the parish and proceeded to commandeer all the firearms which they could lay their hands upon. They were able to find only 'towe fowlinge peeces and towe burdinge peeces',[1] (there was obviously some essential difference between these two types of firearm). We are left wondering just how many firearms were buried in the kitchen gardens and carefully hidden in the thatch. The owners of the firearms petitioned Colonel Moor at Ormskirk through the rector, James Starkie, for the return of their property saying that they were prepared to support either the King or Parliament:

A Civil War cavalryman

> The promises Considered yor supl[ian]ts Humble peticon is that yor good Honors would be pleased to Order that yor peticoners may have their said Armes for the service of Kinge & Parl[iam]ant (as well) for that yor supl[ian]ts beinge poore men, (as alsoe) for that Armes are verie Skant and ill to be come by, And in doeinge thereof yor peticoners (as to theire duties appertaineth) shall not onlie praye for yor good honors but shal be Readie to lay down there lyves in the said service.[1]

The chances of the owners ever seeing their fowling and birding pieces again must have been slim indeed.

From time to time groups of soldiers came seeking food and shelter and occasionally a deserter from one or other of the armies. In February

1642 two Royalists, John Maxfield and John Hunt, appeared asking for assistance to get to Cornwall. They had travelled from somewhere near Wigan and had headed for the coast where they presumably hoped to obtain a boat and to get home by sea, but the Roundheads were well organised and captured them in North Meols. Maxfield and Hunt were then escorted back to Wigan and thrown into prison. They pleaded with the Roundhead commanding officer: 'We having friends in the Meals were desirous to see them, and from thence to have gone to the Blundells of Ince, and in the Meals we were taken with your troop and brought back to Wigan where we lie in prison in great wantt'.[2]

It soon became obvious that Parliament was having the better of the exchanges. By 1644 in Lancashire only isolated pockets of resistance, such as Lathom House and Greenhalgh Castle, were still holding out for the Royalist cause. The Earl of Derby retreated to the Isle of Man and the daunting task of defending his seat at Lathom fell upon his gallant French wife Charlotte de Tremouille. For four months she resisted a siege mounted by as many as two thousand parliamentary troops.

Lathom House was situated a mere six miles from North Meols and the great siege must have had a direct effect on the parish and on all the surrounding countryside. Finding supplies for the besiegers was a constant problem and local people dreaded the appearance of armed and unpopular platoons of Roundhead soldiers with their perpetual demands for food and provisions. Crops were stolen from the fields and food was taken from the houses with a worthless promise of payment later.

It was not until the summer that news began to circulate that relief was on the way for Charlotte de Tremoille. No less a personage than Prince Rupert was advancing northwards with a royalist army. He took Stockport and advanced to storm Bolton. Amid scenes of great rejoicing he dispersed the Roundheads and relieved the Countess of Derby at Lathom House in what was one of the most romantic episodes of the whole Civil War. Royalists then began to appear from all over the county and the following month, when they were able to take Liverpool, thousands flocked to Rupert's banner. The Royalist Army swelled to 14,000. Their leaders then knew that the time had come to cross the Pennines and to go to the relief of York, which was then under a siege by a determined parliamentary force.

A pikeman

Prince Rupert's spectacular success in the North proved to be shortlived. There followed a major turning point in the Civil War when the Roundheads won their convincing victory at Marston Moor on the outskirts of York. News of this royalist defeat had hardly reached Lancashire when the people of Banks became aware of a frightening and dangerous situation which was developing to the north of them. With local knowledge and with the right state of the tide, the estuary of the Ribble could be forded at this point, and from across the river they saw a great gathering of dishevelled, mud-splattered and armed horsemen advancing towards them. Rupert's cavalry had fled from Marston Moor down the Ribble Valley and into the Fylde. Finding no sanctuary, and hotly pursued by the Roundheads, they embarked on a desperate attempt to cross the Ribble from Freckleton to North Meols.[3]

On that August day in 1644 hundreds and possibly thousands of exhausted, hungry and desperate cavalry entered North Meols on their panting weary steeds. Looting and plunder were their only means of survival. These professional soldiers with their buff coats, carbines and tattered royalist sashes were the battered remains of Rupert's once-proud cavalry — they struck terror into the hearts of the local inhabitants. On this occasion the people had the Roundheads to thank that the looting was no worse. Hot in pursuit was a contingent of Sir John Meldrum's troops who were cut off by the tide at Freckleton, but a second roundhead force under Colonel Assheton was situated at Hesketh Bank and they immediately gave chase. The Cavaliers had no time to dally. They staggered onwards and later in the same day (Aug 18th) came a second invasion of horsemen through North Meols. They were grim-faced men with swords, steel breastplates and triple barred steel helmets. They thundered through with only one objective in their minds — to hunt down their royalist quarry.

The outnumbered Cavaliers lasted for only a few more miles and made a last desperate stand on Aughton Moss. Assheton's forces were joined by Meldrum's, who had advanced through Preston, and the Roundheads won an easy victory. Reports of the skirmish differ greatly but the jubilant Roundheads claimed to have taken a thousand horse, or five hundred at the lowest estimate. The consequence was that Lathom House was soon under siege for a second time, but this time there was no Prince Rupert on his way with an army to relieve them. Lathom fell and the royalist cause in Lancashire fell with it.

Many years later, musket shot and small bore cannon balls of Civil War vintage were found during the rebuilding of some houses in Brade Street, Crossens. This evidence gave rise to a belief that the villagers set up some resistance to the Cavaliers and that a skirmish took place between villagers and soldiers in the streets of Crossens. The musket balls and cannon balls require an explanation but the story of the skirmish lacks documentary evidence.

The estates of William Hesketh, the deceased Cavalier, were sequestrated by Parliament and his heirs were therefore unable to collect the rent for many years, but William Hesketh's widow remained in residence at Meols Hall with a daughter, Ann, who subsequently married Thomas Selby from Biddeston in Northumberland. William Hesketh's premature death meant that, although he left a child, he pre-deceased his father, and because of this William's younger brother Robert Hesketh was able to make a strong claim to be the righful heir to his father's estates. A protracted legal wrangle ensued between Robert Hesketh and the Selbys. It provided plenty of material for the local gossipmongers and Rector James Starkie was overheard making a bet with a Captain Gabriel Hesketh that Robert would never get possession of Meols Hall as long as his brother's daughter (Ann Selby) was still alive. The gambling churchman eventually won his bet but not until 1667 when the said Anne Selby died without issue. William Blundell of Little Crosby (the author of the country song) noted that 'Mr Selby hath delivered for ever his "supposed right" in North Meols and Pilling to his uncle Robert Hesketh, and is now gone unto his own'.[4]

A musketeer

If William Blundell's comment is considered as typical, then the local gentry thought that Robert Hesketh had a good claim to Meols Hall. Perhaps Thomas Selby thought so too, for he surrendered Meols Hall and departed for Northumberland without even bothering to fight his case in the law courts and Roger Hesketh was at last able to get possession.

It is worth wondering why James Starkie, the Rector of North Meols, should be making bets in alehouses with military men during an era when all good churchmen were followers of Cromwell and were expected to conform to strict puritanical codes of practice. The fact is that betting was a common practice and some large sums and extraordinary stakes were wagered, the classic example from earlier in the seventeenth century is the case of Sir Cuthbert Halsall whose spending was so extravagant that he must have been a legend in his time.

In 1617 Sir Cuthbert raised a mortgage of £1,000 on his Renacres property, near Halsall, to help to pay his gambling debts. He then mortgaged his Halsall properties for £3,500, and in 1619 he borrowed £1,000 from two London moneylenders using various others properties as security. We then discover that 'the king has taken into his hands the manors of Birkedale and Aynesdale for payment of Sir Cuthbert Halsall of debt of £800'. In 1630 the Manor of Formby joined the mortgage list for £1,200. Sir Cuthbert finally borrowed another £1,000 from Robert Blundell of Ince using his already mortgaged property at Birkdale, Meandale and Ainsdale as security and died virtually penniless in 1632.[5]

Nobody could approach Sir Cuthbert when it came to the art of losing fortunes, but the Captain Gabriel Hesketh who made the bet with Rector Starkie came fairly close. He was the squire at Aughton where he held the advowson of Aughton Church (the right to appoint the rector). Squire Hesketh was a 'papist and profligate gentleman', and he therefore didn't value a protestant advowson very highly. Word got around that he had swopped the advowson for a racehorse – in fact he used it as a stake in a game of cards against a Mr Banastre of Bank. He lost!

Squire Banastre was then persuaded to sell the advowson for £100 to the Baguley family who wanted to get their hands on the living for young Alexander to fritter away. Everybody knew perfectly well that the whole business was totally illegal and that the crime of simony had been committed. They therefore concocted an incredible story pretending that the £100 had been spent on a horse. When young Baguley came to be presented to his living however, the bishop was not fooled and demanded that the new rector be presented by Gabriel Hesketh, the true patron. The whole embarrassing story was then dragged out into the open.

This was not the end of the matter, the Baguleys were still very keen to get the living of Aughton for young Alexander, and so Gabriel Hesketh let them buy him out with a bribe of twenty guineas. Young Baguley remained Rector for five years, but his appointment was still totally illegal and in 1679 the Brownswords sucessfully sued the Baguleys for simony and managed to get John Brownsword appointed to the living. The parishioners still lost on the deal, 'Brownsword hath gotten possession', wrote Oliver Heywood, 'but there's no choice, he is living as ill as the other'. The next time we hear of Gabriel Hesketh he is living in great splendour at Falcon Court in London and is known by the Londoners as the great esquire Hesketh of Lancashire. Soon afterwards we find that the great esquire has changed his London residence to an establishment called the Fleet Debtor's Prison. Having mortgaged all his estates he then sold his birthright to his younger brother Alexander who bailed him out of the Fleet for £130, Gabriel then tried to buy his birthright back again for £200![6]

The scene in Ormskirk, when the wager was laid between the cavalier, catholic Squire Gabriel Hesketh and the roundhead, puritan Rector James Starkie, sounds like a heated exchange of words which must have been quite entertaining to hear. Both were very colourful characters, and Bland describes Starkie as 'a veritable Vicar of Bray' – the parallel holds good, except that in Starkie's case 'Good King Charles' golden days' refer to Charles I and not Charles II.

James Starkie graduated from Cambridge in 1623 and was a schoolmaster at Eccleston for about two years before obtaining the post of assistant curate at the parish church in Wigan. He then became Vicar of Preston, a living which he held until his preferment to North Meols in 1639. He was an Episcopalian at the time of his institution but changed his views on Church government and became a Presbyterian when the latter gained the ascendancy. In 1648 he showed his colours by attending an assembly of Puritans in Lancaster. He held his post all through the Commonwealth years and conformed to the official Church policy at the Restoration in 1660. In 1684, the year he died, he was still at his post, and no doubt had he lived until the following year when the Catholic James II became King the indomitable octogenerian James Starkie would still have been Rector of Meols.

The start of this very long incumbency, of 45 years, began ignominiously in February 1639 when he was presented, not by the Fleetwood family who had the rights of advowson, but by the representative of the King. It may be that the reason for the intervention was the large number of recusants in the parish, for Starkie was the man to weed them out! We then find that John Fleetwood exercised his right to present the new rector on 22 March. The Crown were not too pleased about this, there followed a third presentation to a confused congregation of parishioners, again in the name of the King, on April 8th. The Crown wanted to make sure that Starkie knew that his responsibilities were to them and not to the local Catholic gentry.

Starkie seems to have cared little for the gentry, because in 1641 Ellen, the wife of Thomas Hesketh of Meols Hall, and her two sons William (the Cavalier) and Robert appear in the list of Recusants. They appear with four women — Marjorie Brekill, Elizabeth Gill, Alice and Elizabeth Wright — all fined sixteen pence. The Civil War seems to have given the commisioners more urgent things to do than to weed out people who did not attend church, and during the Commonwealth years it looked for a time as though the government might take a more lenient attitude to recusancy. A few years after the Restoration, however, Starkie seems to have been the moving force behind a longer list of Recusants, including the Selbys at Meols Hall, and again containing a high proportion of women:

RECUSANTS 1665 (11 Dec)[7]
Ralph Ainsworth
Elizabeth Aughton, widow
Alice Bankes
Jennet Blundell
Ralph Cowper
Henry Edwardson
Ellen Hesketh, widow of William Hesketh
Ellen Houlme
Elizabeth Jump
The wife of Robert Jump
Mary Lowe
Jennet, wife of Thomas Matthew
Thomas Selby Esq. and Ann his wife
Ellen, wife of Richard Wilding
George Wright
Isabel Wright spinster

The churchwardens were Robert Wright, Nicholas Rimmer and John Rimmer; they were instructed to provide a table of degrees, a book for the churchwarden's accounts, and a black hearse cloth for funerals.

The parish registers were hardly kept at all during the first twenty years of James Starkie's incumbency. We must not blame him entirely for this deficiency. The times were so dangerous during the Civil War and its aftermath that few parishes dared to keep complete registers — a record of kinship with some luckless landowner who had supported Charles I was something to be avoided if at all possible. After the Restoration, however, the North Meols registers were again properly kept and are apparently complete - the gap of only one generation remains to frustrate the family historian.

In 1678 Robert Thomason, who had been a churchwarden, took the rector to the Lancashire Quarter Sessions complaining that money due to the poor of the parish had been withheld:

> . . . James Starkey, gentleman, is indebted to the poore of the said parish in the sume of ten pounds, nineteen shillings six pence, which he keeps in his hands and deteins from the said poor. That your peticioner hath often demanded the same and the said Mr Starkey says he will pay it, but delays the payment therof.[8]

One person who suffered from the Rector's meaness was Thomas Brade of Highfield in North Meols, described as a salter:

> . . . being 100 yeares old or thereaboutes, very lame and almost blind, and incapable of the knowledg of any person unless his near neighbours by heareing them speake . . . [had formerly received poor relief of 9d per week but had received nothing for eighteen weeks] . . . [would have] . . . byn starved had he not had the releife of one Jane Lynaker his next door neighbor, who had some supply from Richard Brade his son . . . [9]

This incident shows the cantankerous side of the rector. He was quite an advanced age when this incident took place, but he had obviously been sitting on the poor money for some time and the court ordered him to pay it out immediately. In some ways he was nevertheless a dedicated man and a hard worker, for it is in his time that there is the first mention of a parish school in North Meols, and when he died in 1684 James Starkie left forty pounds in his will to put at the disposal of the North Meols Grammar School.

In 1660 is recorded the baptism of 'Elizabeth the daughter of Thomas Mather, pedagogue'. Thomas Mather was evidently the master of the village school. This school may well have been founded much earlier than 1660 and possibly, like the village school at nearby Halsall, it dated back to Tudor times, but the mention of the pedagogue is the earliest sound evidence that there was a school in North Meols.

The North Meols Grammar School had a precarious existence. The traditional classical syllabus can hardly have been popular with the farmers and fishermen of the parish, yet the school somehow managed to survive — and this was partly due to donations left by local benefactors to the school funds. James Starkie was the first recorded benefactor. He was followed by Thomas Blevin who left twenty pounds in 1690, and specified that it should be used to instruct poor children in the scriptures. Thomas Blevin also specified that he wanted to see a school in Crossens or Banks and in the eighteenth century his wish may have been realised for the parish register shows a schoolmistress at Banks and another at Birkdale — it is likely that they ran dame schools for very young children, to teach the basics of reading, writing and arithmetic before entering the Grammar School at the age of about seven.[10]

In 1692 Richard Ball left twenty pounds to the school. The wooden tablet in the church records that it was 'lost by Daniel Ambrose, made up by Lawrence Jump' — it is thus that the red face of Daniel Ambrose makes a brief appearance in our history.

In 1703 John Whitehead was master of the school. He was followed by William Dickenson, a family man whose marriage to Anne Thomasis is recorded at St Nicholas Church Liverpool in 1725. In these times the benefactors were John Aughton, a shoemaker who left ten pounds in 1719, and Hannah Woods who left the same amount in the following year. John Aughton died in Lathom but he was the son of Thomas Aughton (1630-1691) and was born in the Meols. He was an ardent Protestant who seems to have got involved with the rising of the Old Pretender in 1715.[11] Like others of the benefactors he probably received some education at the school.

In 1720 a new building was erected near the church to house the Grammar School and the building attracted the notice of the Bishop of Chester who wrote in his notes that 'here is lately built by ye two lords of this manour Bold and Hesketh a very handsome school near ye church'.[12] The Hesketh family were the main benefactors throughout the remainder of the eighteenth century.

From the Hearth Tax returns in the 1660s it is possible to estimate the population at about eight hundred, and the parish registers show a steady increase in numbers, rising to nearly a thousand by the end of the century. The Hearth Tax was raised by taxing every hearth in the kingdom, which meant that every household, except those in receipt of poor relief and those in houses valued at less tham one pound per annum, was obliged to pay a tax of two shillings per hearth. The returns for Ladyday 1664 therefore give a complete list of all the householders in the parish and there are unlikely to be any families who are not represented (see Appendix). Meols Hall had six hearths in 1664 and Bold House had four, by 1666 the numbers had increased to twelve and eight. James Starkie in the rectory at Crossens had three. This house was probably little changed since the time of Matthew French's inventory of 1614. A handful of other houses had more than one hearth. Adam Bannester of Crossens had two hearths in 1666 but by 1673 he had undertaken a bit of hasty reconstruction to get his house down to a single hearth and avoid paying the extra tax.

By the final decade of the seventeenth century Lancashire was still a mainly agricultural county, but changes were afoot and the farmers found that Liverpool was an ever growing market for their produce. Many must have seen the rapid growth of Liverpool from a fishing village to the major port and trading centre which it became by the end of the century. Daniel Defoe visited Liverpool several times during this period and noticed with interest the rapid growth of the town as it doubled in size and population with every generation. 'There is no town in England', he wrote, 'London excepted, that can equal Liverpoole for the fineness of the streetes, and the beauty of the buildings; many of the houses are of free stone, and compleatly finished; and all the rest of brick, and handsomely built as London itself . . .'

Another traveller who compared Liverpool favourably to London was Celia Fiennes who visited the town in 1698; she was no flatterer but was always frank in her observations. Miss Fiennes was no ordinary mortal but an intrepid traveller who rode side-saddle over the muddy roads of seventeenth-century England. Leaving Liverpool, to travel northwards, she found the miles very long and complained that she could have covered many more miles in the same time around London. (She was probably right, not least since the old British standard of 2428 yards was still used for the mile in the North). Eventually she passed through a 'pretty little market town' which she found was called Wigan, and she was advised to avoid the area around Martin Mere but this did not prevent her from recording the gossip of the day.

> Not going through Ormskirk I avoided going by the famous Mer call'd Martin Mer that as the proverb says has parted many a man and his mare indeed; it being nearer evening and not getting a guide I was a little afraid to go that way it being very hazardous to strangers to pass by it: so as to be able to use that mer one Mr Fleetwood has been at the expence to draine so as to be able to use the ground for tillage, having by trenches and floodgates with banks shut out the waters that still kept it a marsh and moorish ground, but it was a very great change; however it shows by what industry and some expence if gentlemen would set about it most of the waste ground, that's now a fenny moor and mostly water, might be rendered usefull and in a few years answer the first great charge on it.[13]

Yes, it was the talk of the county. Thomas Fleetwood had taken a lease of land between Crossens and Banks and had cut a channel

24 feet wide and a mile and a half long through a salt marsh to the sea. At the spring tides high water was ten feet above the level of Martin Mere and a pair of floodgates was therefore erected to be closed when the tide came in. The drainage relied solely on gravity, but if the venture suceeded then there was potentially several thousand acres available for agriculture. The contemporary view of the undertaking was cut into the marble of Thomas Fleetwood's memorial in St Cuthbert's church, translated from the Latin it read that 'having carried a sluice to the sea hard by, he converted the immense mere of Martin into firm dry land, a deed which older generations dared not attempt and the future will scarce believe'. The firm dry land was a gross exaggeration, but the works were a fine effort for a pre-industrial society and the area around the outer edges of the mere land which had been fenny pasture was drained sufficiently to be able to bear crops.

At Meols Hall the Hesketh family still adhered to their Catholic faith and after the deposition of James II they became supporters of the Jacobite movement which advocated the succession through the heirs of James. In 1694 at Manchester a number of Jacobite supporters were held in prison; amongst these were both Roger and Mary Hesketh of Meols Hall, accused of storing arms and 'war-like equipage' for distribution to Jacobite sympathisers.[14]

The Catholic support in North Meols, however, had definitely weakened at the grass roots, and there was even a swing in the reverse direction. When William and Mary came to the throne it became legal to hold Protestant Dissenters meetings provided that the meeting places were registered at the quarter sessions. A document from 1695 states that 'The dwelling houses of William Rymmer, senior, of North Meales and Thomas Brakills of the same, are intended for meeting houses for an assembly of Protestants dissenting from the Church of England and desires that they may be recorded accordingly'.[15]

The 1694 incident was the last act of defiance on the part of the Heskeths of North Meols; in the following century they did not support the risings of either the Old or the Young Pretender, for by that time they had at last embraced the Protestant faith.

Chapter Seven

Smuggler's Moon

FF the coast of North Meols there existed a relatively safe but exposed anchorage. It was an inlet from the sea about two miles long and half a mile wide, and when the tide receded it became a narrow lake known by the name of Fairclough's Lake. The depth of water was seven fathoms and vessels could approach to within half a mile of the shore, but the approaches were made hazardous by the ever changing contours of the hidden sandbanks and the anchorage provided no shelter from wind and storm.

With the thriving ports of Liverpool to the south and Preston to the north it was not an economical proposition to land cargoes on the open beaches of North Meols and hence the volume of trade through Fairclough's Lake was never great, but from 1677 until the second half of the eighteenth century North Meols boasted a customs officer. The reason seems to have been not so much because of the volume of traffic through the lake, but because of the fact that on a moonlit night in fair weather North Meols beach was found to be a highly suitable place at which to land contraband goods. Proof of this smuggling activity appears in 1688 when a case involving the brothers Barnaby and Bartholemew Hesketh reached the Ormskirk Quarter Sessions. The brothers were involved with a customs officer called William Blake who must be highly commended for his perseverance and dedication to duty.[1]

The incidents described by Blake in his statement cover a period of about two years commencing in 1686 when the ship *Mary* was anchored in Fairclough's Lake with a cargo of wine and brandy from France. On boarding the *Mary* William Blake heard the ship's master, William Benn, blaspheming at a junior customs officer who was already on board. Blake entered the cabin and rebuked Benn for his abusive language. He explained that the customs officer was only there to carry out his duty and was entitled to see all the parts of the ship. The ship's master turned and demanded to know by what authority the upstart Blake came aboard his ship, declaring that he was 'not to be called to account by every raskally fellow'! The customs officer coolly produced three warrants and placed them on the table. William Benn snatched them up 'in a hectoring manner', shouting that *he* and nobody else would be the master on his own ship.

The customs officer wisely decided to wait until William Benn cooled off but he came back the following morning, discovered six barrels of prohibited brandy and took possession of them in the name of the King. He returned to the *Mary* with some colleagues and boarded her again. This time he was greeted more civilly than on the previous day.

Bartholemew Hesketh and other gentry were present and they offered him a glass of punch and some wine. William Blake, 'suspecting them to have an evill design towards him', politely refused the offerings. The ship's cooper then tried to force a quarrel on Blake, but there were other customs men present and they intervened to prevent any violence.

Blake left the ship and remounted his horse, only to find that in his absence his whip had been broken and his saddle girth had been cut. Separated from his fellow officers, Benn's men came after him and pulled him from his horse; they chased him into the sea which was at that time approaching high tide. When Blake managed to regain his horse, he led it without the saddle girth to the sandhills, but there he was met by William Benn and Barnaby Hesketh accompanied by a gang of their supporters. The smugglers made one last effort to bribe the customs officer and passionately offered him 'considerable sums of money' for him not to measure the brandy and to keep quiet about the activities he had seen. For some reason the customs officer pulled a half-crown from his pocket and threw it to the ground, whereupon Barnaby Hesketh alighted from his horse flourishing a cane in his hand, tore the cravat from Blake's neck, and declared that Blake must fight him for the half-crown. William Benn, eager for a fight, stepped in and struck Blake several times on the head.

William Blake survived this ordeal and was subsequently able to find several casks of brandy and parcels of smuggled tobacco. He knew that there were larger quantities of brandy and tobacco in Meols Hall. He also knew that there was brandy stored in Widow Jump's house, where Barnaby Hesketh staved one of the casks and eight or nine gallons of the precious liquid ran out on the floor — two witnesses testified to this event.

In spite of all the evidence brought against the Hesketh brothers, the warrant against them was 'stayed and discharged'. The men on the bench at Ormskirk were friends and relatives of the Heskeths; they were involved in the smuggling trade themselves and considered it rather bad style for anybody to question their right to profit from it.

The anchorage at Fairclough's Lake was well known to Nicholas Blundell, the diarist and the squire of Little Crosby whose *Great Diurnal* reveals so much about country life in the early years of the eighteenth century. On 30th March 1710, he recorded that 'My wife and I went to Peter Whit[field]'s ship that lyes in Farclough's Lake, he dined with us at John Rimer's in the Meals, and after dinner he went on bord his ship the Betty with us.'[2]

We cannot ascertain from this entry whether Peter Whitfield was a bona-fide trader or a smuggler, but later entries from Nicholas Blundell's diary point to the latter. 'I mixed about eight Gallons of French brandy with water & all other ingredients', wrote Nicholas, 'and set them a running to make aqua-coelestis'. Eight gallons! A goodly supply of brandy for one household, but Nicholas had much more than eight gallons stored away — at least the customs men thought he had.

'Mr Thomas [a customs officer] serched the West Lain Hous and a deale of the outhousing at this house for brandy as he heard was conceiled here', wrote the diarist. There is no doubt that the Squire of Little Crosby was very involved with contraband brandy and it seems that Fairclough's Lake was the place where it was smuggled through the customs. Nicholas Blundell's 'Aqua-Coelestis' was a punch which he supplied to manor houses in much of the county. He tells us how to make it from brandy, water, sugar, lemons and crab vargious (a cider made from crab apples)

I scroaped 30 leomonds, the juce of them made one pint and about the fourth of a pint, I put to it one pint of brandy. I also made some shrub; the proportion was brandy two quarts, crab vargious one pint & a half, leomonds six, dubble refined sugar one pound. The proportion of mixture for my last brue of aqua coelestis was brandy two quarts, crab vargeus one pint & one fifth of a quart, lisbon sugar one pound, leomonds three and being the brandy was very good I put to it four quarts and one pint of water, the

water was first bouled, the outward rine of the leomonds was infused in
it so they were also in the shrub, but the brandy and leomond juce had not
any rine infused in it. Cozen Gelibrand of Astley lodged here. This night
I had a cargoe of 16 larg ones* brought to Whit Hall.

The reference to the Gelibrand family is of interest because Roger
Hesketh, brother of Barnaby and Bartholemew Hesketh, who were
prominent in the smuggling incident described by William Blake, married
Mary Gelibrand and was lord of the manor of North Meols at the time
of this entry in the diary.

As the eighteenth century progressed, the smuggling continued to be
a lucrative business. It expanded from brandy and tobacco to include tea
and in the summer of 1739 Thomas Aughton and his brother-in-law
Thomas Rimmer were seen to carry sixty pounds weight of tea from the
sands to be hidden somewhere in the Meols. In the same year William
Rimmer of Scarisbrick arrived in Banks with four horses and took back
with him eight half-anchors of brandy. Henry Ball, Thomas Hodgson and
William Ball were seen taking several casks on horseback to Cross Hall
and, when they had suitably concealed them in an outhouse, Mr Cross
wined and dined them for their trouble. Henry Ball announced that he
had not tasted the contents of the casks and he 'could not swear that they
contained brandy', but Lawrence Etough, who was the customs officer
for North Meols, had no doubt whatsoever about the contents and warned
him that the penalty for smuggling liquor was a hundred and forty
pounds.[3]

In this incident Henry Ball claimed that he had been bribed by the
customs men to inform against his colleagues. He had been offered a cow
by a Mr Whiteside who was the collector of revenue at Preston. Henry
Ball thoughtfully decided that a cow was too much to accept for his
information, but decided he could accept a bull calf instead. There is
another piece of evidence relating to this smuggling incident — it is a letter
from the collector of customs.

Persuant to Your Commands of the 14th instant relating to the four extra
Officers that were sent to Meals to assist Lawrence Etough, the Riding Officer
there. We beg to inform your honours that they were not sent with a view
or expectation of making seizures, but to assist him in apprehending and
taking some of the smugglers that there was warrants out against, which
we are obliged to send our own officers to execute, for the Sheriff's Officers
will not arrest any of the smugglers, as we acquainted Your Honours by
our letter of the 2nd ultimato.[4]

Here indeed was a difficult predicament for the customs men. The
Sheriff's officers refused to help them in the execution of their duties,
but when it is realised that the High Sheriff of Lancashire at this time
was Roger Hesketh, and that he was the owner of Rossall and North Meols,
then it is apparent that the smuggling situation had changed very little
since the previous century.

It is pertinent to ask if amongst all this furtive activity there is any
evidence of legal shipping through North Meols. The eighteenth century
chart of Fearon and Eyes throws some light on this question. It shows
the extent of Fairclough's Lake and the landmarks which were visible to
navigators from out at sea. They include the church spire, Meols Hall, the
Churchtown windmill and a group of cottages situated in a prominent
position on the coast exactly at the end of Fairclough's Lake as though
put there for the purpose of helping with navigation; they are called 'Sugar
Houses'. The cottages constituted a primitive sugar refinery and they are
evidence that some of the Liverpool slavers called there to unload their
sugar cane on their return from the West Indies. There is a memorial to
the captain of one of these vessels in the churchyard at St Cuthbert's:

*The 'larg ones' were large casks of brandy.

Tho' Boreas's Blasts & Neptune's Wave
Have tossed me to and fro:
In Spight of both by God's Decree
I harbour here below,
Where I do now at Anchor lie
With many of our Fleet;
Yet once again I must set sail
Our Saviour Christ to meet.

Captain Jno Grayson died Oct 18 1749.
In the 42nd Year of his Age.

The pretty epitath gives only part of the story and the burial register provides more information:

John Grayson, Capt. of the St. George, a vessel belonging to Liverpool homeward bound from Guinea and the West Indies. he was lost upon Burbo [a sandbank] Oct ye 18 the vessel and whole crew perished with him.

The *St George* had completed the first two legs of the profitable slave trade route, including the horrific middle passage from Africa to the West Indies, tossing in the Atlantic swell with a live cargo of terrified African negroes, packed tightly in filth and squalor, manacled and chained to the decks — to be sold into a life of slavery on the sugar plantations if they were still alive at the end of the voyage. Having crossed the Atlantic for a second time, and within one tide of their homes and their families, the crew found themselves floundering on the Burbo sandbank and their ship being pounded slowly to death by the heavy seas. Not a single member of the crew of the *St George* survived to tell the tale.

Churchtown was one of the coastal villages which supplied sailors for the merchant fleets of Liverpool and many local boys went to sea in search of travel and adventure. Another gravestone tells the story of Thomas Rimmer who returned to his native parish when all the world had given him up for dead: 'Here lyeth the body of Thomas Rimmer mariner who was captive in Barbary sixteen years and six months who departed this life the sixth of January in the year of our Lord 1713'.

The parish registers show occasional entries of the burials of drowned men and unidentified sailors, evidence that shipwrecks and loss of life were not uncommon events. It was not only the sailors who were at risk from the high seas, but also local fishermen and shrimpers and sometimes even those who never ventured out to sea but lived near the embankments. One of these embankments, called Nabbs Cop, was built in the seventeenth century and was named after Nicholas Abram who lived close beside it. Where Nabbs Cop ended to the south the sea defence was taken over by the sandhills, and inland the older sea defences fell into a state of disrepair as they became obsolete. Thus when Nabbs Cop was breached there existed no further defence against the sea.

Those who lived near the cop were always in danger from a high sea. Maud Bond (written as Mauddellin Bound), a widow with children to maintain, complained of an 'aggue in her lim[b]es' and pains through carrying great burdens on her head. 'Shee likewise having her house by the viollent rageing off the sea washed dowen with the foundation cleare gone upon the eleventh day of February being Shrove Tuesday last'.[5]

In 1710 Robert Abram, presumably Nabb's descendant, complained that 'a most dreadful and terrible storm of rain and westerly winds assisting the violence of the sea beat down and demolished a great part of the dwelling and outhousing . . . bordering on the banks of the sea, taking away most of his household goods, his stock of sheep, being forty six, all drowned, his corn and hay all spoiled, and himself, his wife and eight small children with great difficulty escaped their lives . . .' Robert Abram went on to describe graphically how he managed to get his wife and children into the chimney breast whilst he and his eldest son tried desperately to hold the door against the sea. It was a futile struggle. The sea broke down the door and burst into the house and the occupants were

A gravestone depicts the skull and crossbones above the names of John and Alice Sutton. Any connection with piracy seems unlikely, but the Suttons always had surprises in store.

lucky to escape with their lives.[6]

The plight of the Abrams was so bad that the Bishop of Chester allowed collections to be held in the local churches for their relief. The breach in Nabbs Cop was repaired but the lesson was not learnt and a few years later this frightening incident had almost been forgotten. Then, in 1720, Nicholas Blundell described in his diary what were probably the highest seas on the west coast during the whole of the eighteenth century: 'Dec 18. Never the like Thunder and Lightoning known at this time of the year as was this morning or rather after midnight . . .' At the end of the month he wrote: 'Till the 10th generally Raine, then to the 16th very faire, and the next four days very wet and extreamly Windy the like scarce ever known and never so high a Tide known as was these four dayes especially the 18th & 19th at the Meales & other places . . .'

Nabb's Cop had not been kept in good repair and the people watched fearfully as the high tide, driven by a gale force wind, pounded relentlessly against the sea defences. Frantic efforts to strengthen the cop must have been made at the eleventh hour, but the sea rose higher and still higher until even the oldest residents had to admit that they had never known so high a tide and, as the breakers pounded harder and ever harder against the earthen ramparts, they realised with horror that it was only a question of time before the weakest point in the embankment gave way.

The sheer horror of the sea as it broke through can only be imagined. The first tell-tale movement in the embankment was quickly followed by an angry frothing wall of salt water rushing violently through the gap in the cop. The breach, ever widening, the whole sea pouring and foaming through, the wind and the weight of the whole ocean pressing relentlessly behind it. The tidal wave came on and on. Acre after acre was engulfed by the waters which swirled round cottage after cottage and reduced them to rubble. On that December day in 1720 the floodwaters claimed over half the land area of the parish of North Meols.

More than five thousand acres were inundated, forty seven houses were destroyed and many more were completely uninhabitable. The winter stores of corn, hay and fuel were all carried away and ruined by the salt water, as were clothing and all the household goods. Nine people lost their lives, and of the livestock hardly an animal survived. The events described by Robert Abram a few years previously were repeated a hundred fold as families sat upon the rafters of the shells of their stricken homes in the cold December gales and waited to be rescued from the seas which surrounded them. A thousand acres of wheat-sown land was flooded, the bridge called 'Fine Jane's Bridge' which carried the road over the Old Pool at Churchtown was swept away,[7] and even the church and school may have been damaged, for both were rebuilt soon afterwards. For several days Martin Mere more than regained its former glory as the sea rushed forth to meet it.

When the time came to count the cost, it was obvious from the state of the land that the next year would see a very poor harvest and Christmas 1720 was the bleakest the Lancashire coast had known for generations. A petition was put forward on behalf of 135 families who had suffered most from the inundation, claiming that a hundred families were virtually ruined and homeless. The organisers of the petition were Lawrence Abram, Henry Ashcroft, Edmund Ball, Oliver Ball, Christopher Baxter, Richard Dandy, Ralph Green, William Jump, Robert Lawson, James Pratt, Oliver Rimmer, Henry Wallbank and Thomas Wignall. Oliver Rimmer's personal losses included eighty bushells of malt, for which he ruefully claimed that he had already paid the duty to the tax collectors. 'The sea had overflowed 6600 aikers of land', wrote Nicholas Blundell, when the damage had been assessed, 'washed down 157 houses and damnified 200 more; the whole loss computed to be more than £10,227.' He was quoting figures from the four worst affected parishes, as found in the inquest which took place after the inundation.

Parish	Houses Destroyed	Acres Flooded	No. Of Drowned	Estimated Cost
Cockerham	30	'Vast quantity'	'Many'	£1,736 6s 6d
Pilling	40	1500	–	£2,231
Lytham	40	'Great part'	–	£2,055
North Meols	47	5000	9	£4,205
	157			Total £10,227[8]

The inundation of 1720 was not the end of the misfortunes of that decade. In 1727 Nicholas Blundell entered another disaster in his *Great Diurnal:*

> Never so sickley a time known in Lancashire as from May till the End of this Year, abundance died but generally those above 50 years old, the Distemper was an uncommon sort of a Fever which eather took them off or ended in a violent Ague which often lasted severall Months & was scarce possible to be cuer'd and most who had these fits had them after different Mannors so that they scarce knew when to expect them.

In these decades the number of burials at St Cuthbert's was normally of the order of twenty per year. In 1727 the burials numbered 82, the following year saw 62, and the year after that 49. These figures are from a population of a little over one thousand. Nicholas Blundell clearly spoke the truth; most of Lancashire was affected by this dreadful plague but the coastal parishes seemed to suffer the worst.

It is times of great hardship which bring out the best from a close knit community and it does not seem to have taken North Meols long to recover from what were probably its worst disasters since the Black Death. Bishop Gastrell of Chester, who visited the parish in the years between the inundation and the plague, must have seen many signs of the deluge but he makes no mention of it in his notes. He divided the parish into eight parts, Churchtown, Marshside, Higher Blowick, Lower Blowick, New-Row, the Hoes-Houses, Crossens, and the Banks. Birkdale he noted as a separate township and he remarked on the system of appointing three churchwardens − one to represent the Heskeths, a second to represent the Bold family, and a third to represent Birkdale which was neither Bold nor Hesketh land and therefore required separate representation.

The Bold family were not resident in the parish and therefore they did not tend to figure as prominently as the Heskeths in local affairs, but in the 1730s Peter Bold employed a surveyor to draw a map of his estates in the Meols. The man employed was called Henry Bankes and he produced a very professional and accurate survey which showed every individual field belonging to Peter Bold.

At the southern end of the manor the surveyer, who had probably only heard the name pronounced locally, inscribed 'Bertile' on his map. Birkdale contained a few isolated settlements totalling only about forty houses and with many acres of sandhills between the settlements and the sea. Around these farmsteads were planted little copses of birch and willow. There was no church or centre of population, the families were closely related and about half of them were Rimmers.

Birkdale families made their way to church every Sunday along the old Kirkgate or Churchgate, a bridle path which ran for several miles in a straight line from Birkdale to Churchtown. It was customary to walk to church and when a death occurred in Birkdale the coffin was traditionally carried shoulder high all the way along the Churchgate. At the Birkdale boundary there was a stopping place where the coffin was placed on a large boulder whilst the bearers rested their limbs. The boulder, which also served as a boundary stone, had a hollow where rainwater collected and it was the custom to sprinkle the coffin with water from this hollow.[9] The boulder may well have been the base of the stone cross which is known to have marked the boundary in Tudor times.

North of the boundary, Henry Bankes shows a range of sandhills known as the Hawes, and seaward of the Hawes an area of 22 acres called the 'New Marsh',* covered by the sea at high tide. Inland lay South Hawes and the fields of John Ball, William Ball, William Charnley and John Rimmer. James Rimmer, coneyman, was responsible for the upkeep of the rabbit warrens and the small game on which a few depended for their living.

At the junction of Eastbank Lane with Haweside Lane is the cottage of John Ball Littleman − the extra suffix to distinguish him from the other John Balls in the parish. The suffix was usually an occupation, a personal characteristic, or a next of kin — so many individuals had the same name that the process of designating surnames frequently happened a second time in North Meols, and sometimes two extra suffices were required to identify an individual unambiguously.

Most of the cottages are shown on Bankes' map with a small enclosure or kitchen garden around them. At Little London, a place clearly shown and named by Henry Bankes, there appears to be no sign of habitation and certainly no tithebarn, although the latter is known to have stood there. A closer scrutiny shows that not all the areas on the map are covered with information; detail and blank fields are mixed in a random fashion. The survey was of the Bold estates only, and gives little detail of the Hesketh moiety. Little London, for example, may therefore be assumed to be part of the Hesketh property.

At Banks and at Blowick some fields are shown as still divided into strips of about one furlong in length and a chain in width, a legacy from the Middle Ages. Here lay some of the oldest arable land in the manor. Nine Acre Field and Ellen Acre (mentioned in 1550) are shown, and Middlehay which claims a mention from the fifteenth century. There is no field called Baldmeryhokes but Great Wyke Hey is shown near the Scarisbrick boundary with Rushy Wyke and Mary Wyke Meadow as neighbours. In Row Lane leading to Churchtown we find William Riding, John Todd, John Ball and John Rimmer, the latter farming the field called Row Hey. Other families, such as John and Ellen Aughton with their five sons and two daughters, also worked fields in the Row, but they farmed on Hesketh land and are therefore not named on the survey.

In the grounds of Meols Hall the Old Pool is shown dividing into two water courses which rejoin a furlong downstream, leaving a long island called Millers Hey. This was a relic of the watermill which stood there for several centuries. The dividing point was where the miller regulated the flow of water past the mill wheel by diverting the excess into an overflow channel. But water power had given way to wind and Bankes shows the windmill in its familiar position on Mill Lane, very close to where the water mill must have been. In the centre of Churchtown is shown the village cross, flanked by the pubs which were the centres of social life. The two largest residences, Meols Hall and Bold House, are shown near the village centre and also the school building near the parish church. The latter was in the process of being rebuilt at the time of the survey and perhaps the schoolchildren, with their master John Dickenson, gathered round the surveyor and took an interest in his work. Both the children and the surveyor must have been interested in the new building, with its spire and vaulted roof, which was taking shape near the centre of the village.

North west from Churchtown, Marshside Lane ran down to the sea at the point where the sandhills petered out. Marshside was an area where fishing communities interspersed with the smallholders. Thomas Johnson, Richard Wright, yeoman, John Johnson, Christopher Blundell, Thomas Howard, Peter Such, John Ball Bailiff, and Robert Wright, fisherman all lived there and at the junction of Baker's Lane was the field of Hugh Baker.

*The New Marsh was the site of present day Lord Street.

A section of Bankes' map of 1736, an early estate plan. The original is about 20 inches to a mile. This section shows the area around Churchtown, with the modern triangle of Manor Road, Cambridge Road and Botanic Road easily identified, as is the parish church. Note the windmill in Mill Lane and the miller's field called 'Millerhey'. On the opposite side of Meols Hall is another miller's field, on an island where the stream divides in two - this is where the water mill used to stand.

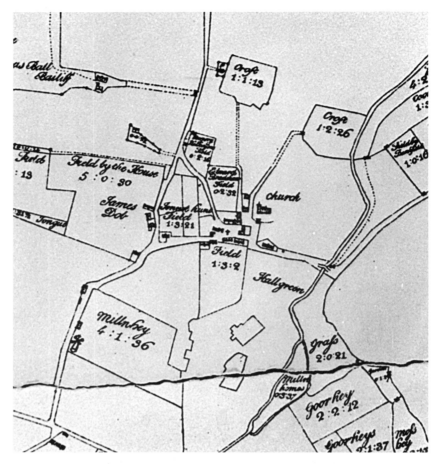

North east from Churchtown, following the remains of the earliest turf embankment, was Crossens where lived John Linaker, Robert Wright, Thomas Copeland, James Rymer farming Ball's Field, and Randolf Wignal farming the 'Field before the door'.

And on to Banks, where lay the northern boundary of the Bold estates, and of the parish, and of the hundred. Edmund Ball, Richard Dandy, Margery Riding, Richard Abram, and Thomas Brookfield farmed at Banks. It seems that there has never been a time when Banks did not have at least one Thomas Brookfield. The Snoterstone which used to mark the manor boundary lay discarded in the mud, for the surveyor clearly shows two boundary posts at the northernmost field in West Derby Hundred, farmed by Oliver Rimmer.

When he was making his survey, Henry Bankes must have met the rector looking over the rebuilding of the church, or riding astride his horse to visit his scattered parishioners. The rector's name was Edward Shakespeare – yes, North Meols had its Shakespeare in those days! Edward may well have claimed some kinship to his Stratford namesake, for he was born in Rugby and was educated at Clare College, Cambridge. The country clergy frequently suffered from mild forms of eccentricity, and Edward Shakespeare was no exception. He kept a pet canary bird called Jessey. He was so fond of his feathered friend that he 'address'd a delicate song' to it,[10] but this little-known work of Shakespeare's has unfortunately been lost to posterity.

By 1739 the rebuilding of the church was complete. At the west end was the tower housing the new clock of immaculate Wigan workmanship and surmounted by a spire rising to sixty feet. Along the south wall were five plain windows with rounded arches and above the altar in the east wall was a Venetian style window with three lights, a design very typical of the period. The building was faced with stone ashlar. Inside, the dimensions of nave and chancel together were only seventy feet by twenty. A three-decker pulpit stood about half way along the south wall and next to it the squire's pew, for, as we have seen, the Hesketh family had become Protestants. The other pews all faced towards the pulpit so that those of the congregatison in the east end of the church sat facing west with their backs to the altar.[11]

In the north-west corner of the nave was the stone font with its wooden cover and a seating arrangement around three sides of a rectangle, suitable for the accommmodation of a christening party. Opposite the font was a flight of stairs curving upwards to a small gallery which was built across the west end of the nave, it was here that the musicians sat blowing into their hornpipes and scraping and tuning their fiddles.

It is not difficult to picture the church in the autumn of 1739, soon after its completion at a cost of £1,292. Rector Shakespeare surveyed his flocks and Squire Hesketh and his lady sat in their pew. Churchwardens James Rimmer and Henry Rimmer represented the Lords of the Manor and Robert Ball represented Birkdale. The nave was filled with the families of the parish, some of whom had travelled from Hundred End in the north and others who had walked the Churchgate from Ainsdale in the south. The Rimmers, Wrights, Balls, Johnsons, Blundells, Howards, Bonds, Abrams, Hodges, Jacksons, Brookfields, Aughtons, Wignalls, Watkinsons, Suttons and a score of others filled the pews. Two young men looked rather self-conscious and the young women beside them blushed as the banns of marriage were read out between Richard Charnley and Mary Rymer and between John Blundell and Anne Threlfall. Children turned their heads to stare and there were coy looks from some of the congregation.

The harvest was safely gathered in by their own hands and by the sweat of nearly every brow in church. There were farmers with the soil of North Meols still on their boots. There were fishermen with the salt of the Irish Sea in their beards. There were tradesmen from Churchtown, shoemakers, websters, wheelwrights and blacksmiths. The new church was to these people what the new St Pauls was to London after the great fire. The adults still remembered and told their children, some lived to tell their grandchildren and some even lived to tell their great grandchildren, about the terrible plague of the previous decade and of the day when the sea broke through Nabbs Cop.

The sound of shrill piping from the gallery, accompanied by the scraping noise of horsehair on catgut, announced to Rector Shakespeare's flock that they must stand and sing. Male and female, young and old, they raised themselves to their feet and they lifted their rustic voices to the Lord as they looked forward to an unknown but hopeful future.

Chapter Eight

Winds of Change

I N 1733 Roger Hesketh of North Meols married Margaret Fleetwood of Rossall. When Margaret's father, Edward Fleetwood, died, she inherited his extensive estates on the Fylde and Roger Hesketh decided to leave Meols Hall and live with his wife at Rossall. His marriage had made him one of the largest landowners in the county and in 1740 he became High Sheriff of Lancashire. Roger Hesketh was widowed in 1752, he subsequently married Sarah Winckley of Preston and he then moved to live at Tulketh Hall near Preston where he stayed until his death in 1791. He chose to be buried in the place of his birth and a fine memorial by the sculptor Nollenkens can be seen in St Cuthbert's church. On it are displayed books, a globe and a telescope showing his interest in scientific pursuits.

When the Heskeths left for Rossall, Meols Hall took an inevitable drop in status. It came to be used as a farm house, often housing several families at the same time. Some of the building was demolished and the bricks were used to build barns and other outbuildings for the farm. From about 1780 the Linaker family were occupants and they were given an official status as agents to the absentee lords of the manor. The Bolds were also non-resident landlords until the moiety descended to a spinster, Miss Anna Maria Bold, and she took up residence at Bold House, the old family house in Churchtown. Miss Bold was a formidable but kindly old lady, whose name appears in an account written many years later which relates to the introduction of cotton weaving into North Meols.

The traditional craft of weaving had been practised for many generations in the parish. There had always been a local woollen industry and there are records of flax and hemp being grown. Nicholas Blundell regularly purchased fabric for his windmill sails from North Meols and the locally made canvas and sailcloth had a good reputation. In the 1790s the cotton industry was growing to dominate the towns and valleys on the Pennine side of the county and cotton rapidly became an essential part of the national economy and one of the spearheads of the Industrial Revolution. Cotton weaving started as a cottage industry, however, and it is not surprising to find that it was practised in North Meols at about this time.

John Hooton was the man credited with the introduction of cotton weaving into the parish. He was said by some to come from Patricroft. It is quite probable that he spent some time at Patricroft to gain experience, but his baptism appears in the parish register and he was clearly from the established local family of the same name. The account given of the introduction of cotton weaving is taken from a nineteenth-century newspaper account:[1]

> Cotton weaving at that time [the 1790s] was an excellent business, and it was soon perceived by his neighbours that honest John was doing much better than any of them. He was therefore requested to teach this profitable art: and it was very amusing to hear the old man tell what great alarm was excited among the farmers and others when a considerable number of his friends and acquaintances were preparing for looms. It was said that all the inhabitants of the parish would be weavers in a short time and the farmers would have none to assist them in seed or harvest; moreover it was affirmed by those who owned cottages (at that time built of clay and wood, the latter frequently from wrecks on the coast), that they would be thrown down by the working of these shaking noisy looms!

> These fears became so general that they reached Bold Hall, the residence of Miss Bold, one of the principal landowners in the parish at that period, and the Hero of the Loom was summoned to that noble mansion to give some account of these dangerous rumours. John stated to that benevolent lady (always styled 'Lady Bold' at North Meols) that most of the people in the parish were in great want of profitable labour; that during a considerable part of their time they were employed in spinning coarse yarn used for sail cloths, and that few could earn more than sixpence a day; he likewise most repectfully assured her ladyship that there was no real danger of injuring the cottages (and here he could speak as positively as any of his neighbours, for he was a Jack of all trades and had helped to build some of them), and when he or any of his friends had been confined in their cottages for a time at the weaving trade, they would be glad to help the farmers as they had been wont to do.

The account has obviously been put together for the benefit of a bourgeois readership but the essential points mentioning the spinning of the coarse yarn and making of sailcloth are authentic, as is the report of the fears and trepidations of the local people towards the introduction of a new industry. The account then goes on in such a patronising fashion that it begins to lose credence as an historical record, but the description is certainly that of a real event:

> When that worthy lady heard this rustic's statement she told him she was perfectly satisfied, and was glad that weaving had been introduced among the poor of the parish. John was then supplied with the good things of that hospitable mansion, and sent away with a present in money far beyond what he had ever received as a gift in any former period of his life.

> Let the reader imagine with what anxiety John would be expected by his family and neighbours from Bold Hall, and the pleasure and gratitude which would be felt when it was made known that Lady Bold was not against poor people learning to weave.

John Hooton was remembered as a man of great ingenuity and kindness. His wife Ellen lived to be 92 and it is reputed that on her death bed she claimed to die happy because she was leaving behind her 'descendants exactly the same in number as those of Jacob who accompanied the patriarch into Egypt'.[2] Reach for your bibles, ye of little faith!

The national average weekly wage of the handloom weaver was sixteen shillings a week in the 1790s, far better than the sixpence a day for making sailcloth if we are to believe the improbable figure given in the article. Wages rose to a maximum of twenty shillings a week by 1800, but then proceeded to drop steadily year by year until by 1820 the handloom weavers were fortunate to earn eight shillings a week. The decline in wages reflected the degree of mechanisation in the towns where the factory system took hold and the weavers sometimes had to choose between a job in the factory and living on the breadline. Those who depended entirely on handweaving for their income were to suffer great financial hardship, for there was no way for them to compete with the machines:

HANDLOOM v POWERLOOM

Come all you cotton weavers, your looms you may pull down;
You must get employed in factories, in country or in town,

Opposite
The memorial to Roger Hesketh (1711–1791) by the sculptor Nollenkins. He was born and buried at North Meols, but lived much of his life at Rossall and Tulketh. He became high sheriff of Lancashire in 1740. The carvings of globe, books and telescope display his interest in science.

For our cotton masters have a wonderful new scheme,
   These calico goods now wove by hand, they're going to weave by steam.

In comes the gruff o'erlooker, or the master will attend;
   It's 'You must find another shop, or quickly you must mend;
Such work as this will never do; so now I'll tell you plain,
   We must have good pincop-spinning, or we ne'er can weave by steam.'

There's sow-makers and dressers, and some are making warps;
   These poor pin-sop spinners they must mind their flats and sharps,
For if an end slips under, as sometimes perchance it may,
   They'll daub you down in black and white, and you've a shilling to pay.

In comes the surly winder, her cops they are all marred;
   They are all snarls and soft bad ends: for I've rove off many a yard;
I'm sure I'll tell the master, or the joss when he comes in:
   They'll daub you down, and you must pay; − so money comes rolling in.

The weavers turn will next come on, for they must not escape,
   To enlarge the master's fortunes they are fined in every shape.
For thin places, or bad edges, a go, or else a float,
   They'll daub you down, and you must pay, threepence, or else a groat.

If you go into a loom-shop, where there's three or four pairs of looms,
   They are all standing empty, a cluttering up the rooms;
And if you ask the reason why, t'ould mother will tell you plain,
   My daughters have forsaken them, and gone to weave by steam.

So, come all you cotton-weavers, you must rise up very soon,
   For you must work in factories from morning until noon:
You musn't walk in your garden for two or three hours a day,
   For you must stand at their command, and keep your shuttles in play.

              TRADITIONAL LANCASHIRE SONG

The factories were mainly in East Lancashire and a few weavers from North Meols left their homes to find employment there. Some stayed on as weavers and were able to change from cotton to silk weaving, because the mechanisation of silk had not progressed as rapidly as that of cotton. Many families had income from other, more traditional sources as well as weaving. Some may have thought that the inland parishes were fortunate to have the factories and regular employment but they little knew that new and unexpected sources of employment were to appear and in fact North Meols was destined to become what many people thought was the most fortunate of all the parishes in Lancashire.

Early in the nineteenth century Thomas Glazebrook, a Warrington man, came to gossip to local people and to collect information for a book which he was writing. Although he hailed from only 20 miles away, Glazebrook had some difficulty when he first encountered the outlandish dialect spoken by the natives of North Meols; he described it as 'a mixture of the well known Lancashire dialect and an idiomatic phraseology of their own'. He tells us the story of Thomas Wright, Richard Wright and William Johnson. These three had been partners for over fifty years, going regularly to market at Preston, usually travelling at night. They had an arrangement with an inn called the 'Golden Ball' at Longton where the landlord rose at 3am every Wednesday and Saturday morning and prepared a glass of gin for each of them. The landlord collected only eighteen pence, but they were the most regular of regular customers and over 27 years he calculated that they had spent £199 16s 0d. Thomas Wright claimed to have been born on the same day as the King George III (4 June 1738), and he claimed that the total number of his children, grandchildren, and great grandchildren was one hundred and ten.[3]

Another local described by Glazebrook was an old man whom he described as an 'extraordinary character' called Richard Aughton, better known by his nickname of 'Cockle Dick'. Dick's family originally intended that he should learn a trade and become a shoemaker but it appears that he had no great enthusiasm for an indoor life. He left the shoemaker's shop and for fourteen years he worked for one of the Wright family. During this early part of his life Dick was frequently employed in shrimping and cockle gathering.

> In procuring these [wrote Glazebrook] he was more expert than any of his competitors, and, on that account, obtained the title 'King of the Cocklers'. His wife, who was born in the same year and month as he was, attended Preston and Ormskirk market with fish, three or four times a week, regularly. They resided on a small farm of their own in Marsh-Side, and were well known in the surrounding neighbourhood. When about sixty or seventy years old 'Cockle Dick', as he was familiarly called, had a severe rheumatic attack brought on by carrying heavy burdens of cockles etc. and he became very crooked. Richard was originally intended for a shoemaker, but this was not to be, and he died at the head of the profession he had chosen.

In old age Dick claimed to be 'ninety-nine, nearly', but in fact a close scrutiny of the parish registers shows him to have reached a mere 94. He was born in 1729 and his life therefore belongs mainly to the eighteenth century. In October 1753 he married Isabel Blundell and, reading between the lines of Glazebrook's account, they were probably childhood sweethearts. The first of their children did not survive but they later produced a daughter Alice and a son called John. It is interesting to note that he was both fisherman and farmer. It was not uncommon for local people to follow two or more occupations. In his bent old age people sometimes called him 'Crooked Back Dick', but we learn that this was not good for his blood pressure and used to 'enrage him very much'. He is remembered by the lane where he and his wife worked their small farm in Marshside — it became known as Cockle Dick's Lane.[4]

The Shorlicars of Birkdale were another aged couple, Robert Shorlicar was a rabbit skin dealer and travelled miles to sell his wares. He claimed to be 101, his epitath in St Cuthbert's churchyard is simple and moving:

> I lodged have in many a town
> And travelled many a year;
> But age and death have brought me down
> To my last lodging here.

Robert's wife Esther Shorlicor claimed to be 99, but both the Shorlicars exaggerated, their true ages being 94 and 84. Here, for the first time, we have the mixed blessing of the data with which to destroy the cherished notions of the great ages claimed by certain Sandgrounders. Hannah Johnson of South Hawes (103) remains unchallenged, as does Gilbert Rymer (91), but Betty Sutton and Ann Such, claiming to be 95 and 93 respectively, were both 91 according to the baptisimal registers.

In 1826 the following statistics were published on the age distribution of the elderly in North Meols:[5]

Above 85 years of age 8 people
Above 80 years of age 18   ,,
Above 75 years of age 18   ,,
Above 70 years of age 59   ,,
Above 65 years of age 36   ,,
Above 60 years of age 87   ,,

This sample of 226 was taken from a population which could have been as high as 4000. If the ages could be corrected for the exaggeration factor, and if figures for the national average in the 1820s could be found with similar corrections, then it might well be possible to show a significantly high proportion of over sixties in the parish. There were certainly people around who were convinced that the Sandgrounders did live to a ripe old age.

A man who did a great deal for North Meols during his working life was John Silcock, the village schoolmaster. He was appointed in 1779 and held his post until his death in 1811. In 1780 his salary was quoted as a mere £7-10s per annum. It is difficult to see how he could possibly have lived on this pittance without some private means and it therefore seems likely that the figure quoted might have been a supplementary salary for

These cottages on Roe Lane probably existed in the 17th century. They are shown on Bankes' map of 1736 when Richard Boond was the tenant. Like many other cottages, their structure has been added to and modified, the half timbering being a later addition.

Thatched cottages in Botanic Road, Churchtown.
(E.W. Collection)

A modern view showing just how much of old Churchtown still survives today.

his duties in the Sunday School (The church accounts for 1813 show a salary of £8-8s for the master of the Sunday School). In January 1793 John Silcock married a local girl, Ann Bond, who was nine years his junior and might possibly have been one of his first pupils, and they set up house in Row Lane. The schoolmaster kept a diary which cannot now be traced, but an extract was copied and published by Edward Bland and shows the extent to which the independent churches were a growing influence in Churchtown during Silcock's time there:

> In the process of time a Mr ———, a Methodist Preacher, came to our Town, and preached at the house where I lived, but he did not come for long, for I was persuaded to write him a letter that his doctrines would no more be allowed by the ruling powers in North Meols, so that he came no more; his preaching I liked to hear, but it did not reach my heart, so that I was nothing bettered by it. After this came first one preacher and then another, of different persuations, in the bathing season, and gave us an exhortation or sermon while they stayed in town; but the most useful during his short stay with us was one Wm Bamber; the seed which he sowed in time sprang up and brought forth precious fruit.

> In some time after this the Calvanist Preachers introduced themselves and Preached regularly in the Township, after which a place was fitted up for them in Church Town, and different Preachers of that persuation visited us. Some of these held forth the doctrine of Election and Reprobation, which was not relished by some of the more enlightened part of the congregation, in consequence of which and by the persuation of some Methodist Preachers, who happened to visit the town, a division of the congregation took place, and a Methodist Missionary, H S Hopwood came and officiated in the Chapel. This was in the year 1806.[6]

One of the preachers to whom John Silcock refers was the Rev George Greatbatch, who set up the first independent mission in Churchtown in about 1805. At one time George Greatbatch had harboured ambitions of becoming a missionary among the heathen, but having arrived in North Meols he declared himself to be 'quite satisfied with the field of labour now before him, and he had no conception, until brought to the western part of Lancashire, that there was any part of his native land which corresponded as much with the ideas he had formed of a missionary station on some foreign shore.'

George Greatbatch established a school in Churchtown specifically to help educate the poorer children of the parish, and the school did a very worthwhile job. The Rev. Greatbatch, however, became so fond of telling the public what a marvellous job he had done that he began to believe that he alone was responsible for the introduction of the written word into the parish. He re-iterated his theme so many times that he eventually drew an angry response from an old boy of the North Meols Grammar School who wrote from an address in the Lake District.

'If this was the first occasion on which such twaddle had been uttered I could pass it by in silence', wrote the Sandgrounder.[7] He challenged the Greatbatch school to produce some statistics to support their case. 'A North Meols man has come down from his eyrie at Hawkeshead', the Rev John Millsom replied loftily on behalf of George Greatbatch. 'Have they selected him for their champion? He hides his identity behind a mask. Trusting your correspondent will take time to clear his eyes, and poise his wings, before he next swoops from Hawkeshead in order to strike his prey'. This was an open invitation and the North Meols man accepted the challenge. He announced himself to be Samuel Twist. 'Figures of speech are of no value when used instead of arithmetic', he declared, and went on to say that English and Latin were taught in North Meols a hundred years before Mr Greatbatch came into the parish. Taken literally, this refers to the early years of the eighteenth century when John Whitehead was master — Samuel Twist seemed well informed about his old school and he went on to describe the master and some of his fellow pupils. He had been taught by John Silcock, whom he described as a pious,

God-fearing man, devoted to his work. 'The bible was the daily lesson book and, amongst other subjects, practical mathematics was better taught than in any other parish for miles around, indeed better than they have been taught in any part of the parish since'. Mr Twist had specimens of writing, geometrical drawing, and calculations in higher mathematics done by John Silcock's pupils. He wrote of a colleague's grandfather, educated in Churchtown in the middle of the eighteenth century, who constructed a telescope twenty feet long!

He went on to mention a number of families educated at the local grammar school, including the Gregsons, Blundells, Hunts, several branches of the Wrights, Rimmers and Balls, Howards, Hodges, Hootons, Jacksons, the Linakers of Meols Hall and others. James Blundell became master of Leigh Grammar School and later the Rector of Croyland; Robert Wright was a mathematician and a navigator; James Twist was a calculator and a navigator, his brother John was an arithmetician and an astronomer. To everybody's amazement the North Meols Grammar School really had found a champion in Samuel Twist.

In addition to the telescope maker, who unfortunately is not mentioned by name, we find a wealth of amateur astronomers in North Meols. James Twist had prepared tables of the new and full moon for publication, navigational tables showing the motion of the sun and the moon, and drawings of both lunar and solar eclipses. He was described as one of the most able arithmeticians and practical astronomers in the county. Another man with a reputation for astronomy and connected with the North Meols Grammar School was Peter Aughton, who is better known for his watercolour of St Cuthbert's church which he painted in 1803. These scientific activities, which seem to originate in the eighteenth century, may well have been sponsored and encouraged by Roger Hesketh who, as we have seen, included a globe and a telescope on his memorial. Roger Hesketh does not appear as a benefactor to the school but his widow Sarah Hesketh left a hundred pounds in the year 1800.

No register of the Grammar School survives but a register of the Sunday School exists from 1814 and includes the names of John Silcock's children who, regrettably, were orphans at this time:[8]

BOYS		GIRLS		YOUNGER CHILDREN	
Henry	Ball	Ellen	Ball	John	Barton
James	Ball	Ellen	Barton	Margaret	Barton
John	Ball	Ellen	Blundell	John	Blundell
Richard	Barton	Margaret	Blundell	Miles	Blundell
Miles	Blundell	Alice	Brade	Miles	Gregson
Edward	Bolton	Margaret	Cropper	Peter	Halsall
Thomas	Bolton	Ann	Halsall	Robert	Halsall
James	Halsall	Mary	Halsall	William	Howard
Peter	Halsall	Cathrin	Hodge	John	Meadow
Robert	Halsall	Elizabeth	Jackson	Alice	Rymer
William	Howard	Elizabeth	Johnson	Harriet	Rymer
James	Johnson	Margaret	Johnson	John	Rymer
Richard	Johnson	Ellen	Linaker	James	Silcock
Thomas	Johnson	Ann	Meadow	Robert	Todd
James	Jump	Ann	Robinson	Sarah	Tomlinson
Richard	Jump	Cathrine	Rimmer	John	Wright
Henry	Meadow	Ann	Silcock		
Thomas	Rimmer	Mary	Such		
Thomas	Rimmer	Ann	Wright		
Richard	Spencer	Ellen	Wright		
James	Todd				
Thomas	Todd				
Richard	Wright				
Total of P.B. 23		Total of G.B. 20			

The children in the first two columns had the symbol 'P.1' against their names, with the exception of William Howard and Edward Bolton who had the symbol 'B.1'; these children had probably been issued with prayer books and bibles respectively. The list was accompanied by a short covering letter, slightly wanting in King's English:

> Rev Sir,
> I have put down the children's names which is instructed on the Lord's Day by me John Moss.

The 'Rev Sir' was Gilbert Ford, who had been rector since 1793 when a Bristol merchant called John Ford bought the advowson and appointed his son to the living. On his arrival in North Meols, Gilbert Ford took one look at the delapidated old parsonage house in Crossens and decided that it was quite unfit for human habitation. He obtained permission to live in Ormskirk and for 33 years he executed his duties from there. In 1826, when a new rectory was built in Roe Lane, Rector Ford at last moved to live in his parish; he died there in 1835.

The church accounts for 1813 show that a large number of prayer books were purchased in that year, at a cost of £2 2s 6d. They also show that the master of the Sunday School, presumably John Moss, recieved £8 8s 0d at Easter. Expensive items shown in the accounts were for the purchase and carriage of sand and lime and the wages of the workmen for this task. Stephen Gregson was paid two sums of 6s 6d for repairs to the church gate, 7s 6d was spent on painting the gate and a further shilling on a lock. Eleven baskets of coal to heat the church cost 16s 6d, and Thomas Hunt's wife was paid 5s for 'washing the serpels'[9].

It was traditional to supply ale for the singers and the bell ringers. Ale for the ringers on the fifth of November cost 7s, but the singers were either more numerous or more thirsty, for their ale consumption on Good Friday cost £1 18s 0d. The ringers were active again on June 4th when they rang the bells for His Majesty's birthday, but, if the dubious measure of ale consumption is taken as a guide, this was deemed a lesser occasion than the time when the bells rang out 'at the defeate of Bonaparty', recorded under November 10th 1813. The date of the account is months later than the actual event, but it seems certain that this entry is a record of the news of Napoleon's retreat from Moscow arriving in Churchtown. We can only guess at what the ale consumption must have been two years later when news arrived of Wellington's victory at Waterloo!

Churchtown at this time was thus still a rural community. The North Meols Grammar School had been supplemented by Sunday schools of various denominations so that a slightly more literate population was emerging. The influence of independent ministers like George Greatbatch was drawing some away from the traditional church, but the community was still very rural and the economy was very dependent on farming, fishing and handloom weaving.

The 1811 census shows the population of the parish to be 2,496. Churchtown was still the largest centre of population in the Meols, but near the Birkdale boundary at South Hawes a new village had appeared in the sandhills. It was populated by some who had formed the notion that North Meols was a healthy place in which to live and it was growing at a surprising rate. To discover something about the origins of this village it is necessary to meet another of Thomas Glazebrook's characters. We must retrace our steps by a few years and pay a call on the landlord of the *Black Bull* in Churchtown.

Chapter Nine

The Old Duke

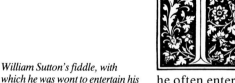

I N the evenings of the 1790s when the day's work was over, the two Churchtown pubs, the *Black Bull* and the *Griffin,* became popular places of resort. The landlord of the *Black Bull* was one of the most colourful characters in the community. He was a goodnatured, jovial fellow fond of sport and of company. He sometimes played the strings in the church gallery and styled himself a 'musicioner'; he often entertained his regulars and his guests with a piece on his fiddle. His gradely name was William Sutton but everybody called him 'Duke Sutton' or 'Old Duke'. He was in his element as the landlord of a country pub.

William Sutton's fiddle, with which he was wont to entertain his guests. In 1776, when William Sutton married local girl Jane Gregson, he described himself as a 'musicioner'; he was obviously proud of his musical talents.

(Photo, Botanic Gardens Museum)

The origin of his nickname is confused. Some say he was styled the 'Duke' because of his love of fine clothes, his black velvet coat, soft billycock hat, and his knee breeches with pearl buttons and gaiters which he loved to wear. Others said 'they styled him the Duke out of conceit', because he was constantly harping on the occasion when he had met the Duke of York. Yet others claimed that he obtained his nickname when he lost his favourite gamecock and exclaimed that 'neither Duke nor Devil shall have it!'

At this time, amongst the well-to-do, the fashion of taking the waters was rapidly changing from that of swallowing the obnoxious mineral waters of the inland spa towns to the daring feat of total immersion in the salt waters of the fishing villages around the coast. In Lancashire some of the country people had created their own variant of the new fashion by turning the annual Churchtown Fair into a sea-bathing festival. The fair took place on the Sunday after the sixteenth of August, which became known as 'Big Bathing Sunday'. It attracted people from up to twenty miles away. It was followed a fortnight later by 'Little Bathing Sunday', which was organised by Birkdale and included a rushbearing ceremony. It would be interesting to learn more about these two festivals. It seems certain that for the Birkdale rushbearing a traditional North Country rush-cart would be pulled along the Churchgate with a string of revellers, accompanied by the morris dance and the performance of ancient fertility rites. The rushes were then strewn on the floor of the church, a ceremony dating back to the Middle Ages when the rushes were used to carpet the church and the cottages.

Neither Big Bathing Sunday nor Little Bathing Sunday could be described as a very civilised occasion. Large quantities of alcohol were consumed and Rector Gilbert Ford objected strongly to the drunken scenes of saturnalia and debauchery which were enacted on the Sabbath Day.

Other ministers supported Gilbert Ford, notably the Rev George Greatbatch who must have nearly had apoplexy when he first witnessed Big Bathing Sunday.

At the *Black Bull,* however, a different category of visitor began to appear during the summer months when the middle classes began to stay at the inn so that they could bathe in the sea. It seemed a curious fashion, but there was no accounting for taste and Duke Sutton soon became aware that there was some potential in this new trade. The nearest point on the coast was at the end of Marshside Lane, where fishermen moored their boats in the rapidly silting anchorage at the end of Fairclough's Lake, but a couple of miles to the south were fine open beaches with firm sand and golden sandhills — a much more pleasant spot to bathe. The landlord took his patrons along the beach to South Hawes where they could enjoy a vast open sandy beach which was practically deserted.

In 1792 the Old Duke built a bathing house at South Hawes. It was built merely to provide some kind of shelter and changing facilities for the bathers. It seems that he did not bother to apply for a lease to build there; the land was regarded as waste and was of no value agriculturally. The lords of the manor raised no objections to the bathing house and sometimes used it as a shooting lodge outside the bathing season. The locals ragged the Old Duke for spending his money on this extravagance but the trickle of visitors continued to come and soon William Sutton built an assembly room in Churchtown and entertained his guests with balls and banquets. In 1794 the *Black Bull* was full, he needed more accommodation and he leased some extra cottages nearby.[1]

In 1797 came a development which surprised even William Sutton, for in that year a widow from the Wigan area, who must at one time have been one of his patrons, built a cottage near the bathing house. She called it 'Belle Vue Cottage' and the Old Duke discovered that Mrs Sarah Walmesley planned to take lodgers during the bathing season. He lost no time in catching up with Mrs Walmesley; he took out an official lease of six acres around the bathing house and built there a new inn. Trade was remarkably good and the next summer William Sutton decided to live at the new inn and to let his daughter Margaret run the *Black Bull* with the help of her fiancé Robert Linaker of Meols Hall. William Sutton gave his new hostelry the rather grand name of the 'South Port Hotel' but the rest of the community referred to it as the 'Duke's Folly'.

According to local tradition there had once been a deep bay of water within half a mile of the shore where vessels occasionally lay at anchor and the place had actually been a port in the true sense of the word. This description of a bay fits Fairclough's Lake very closely which, as we have seen, did support a little shipping earlier in the eighteenth century. There was possibly a 'North Port' at the Marshside end of Fairclough's Lake where the Sugar Houses once stood, and the 'South Port' was probably known to William Sutton and other local people as another place where cargoes albeit of largely contraband goods were unloaded.

Among the first patrons of the South Port Hotel were Dr Joseph Brandreth and Dr Miles Barton, two rather eccentric medical practitioners — both of whom were continually telling their patients about the health giving properties of the salubrious air of North Meols. Dr Brandreth (1744-1815) practised in Ormskirk. He was from a well known family of Liverpudlian eccentrics spanning several generations.

Dr Miles Barton (1725-1810) also practised for a time in Ormskirk and was the inventor of a concoction called the 'Ormskirk' Medicine which he claimed was a sovereign remedy against the bite of a mad dog. Sea bathing was also claimed as a remedy against the bite of a mad dog, so that the good doctor may simply have filled his bottles with little more than salt water and sold them to his wealthy patrons as an insurance against all the mad dogs which he imagined might be waiting round the next corner to attack them.

Duke's Folly

ike all 'firsts', the claim that this was the first house in Southport needs to be qualified. William Sutton built the bathing house in 1792; it was apparently a wooden structure which was occasionally used as a hostel but it was uninhabited and was erected without any building licence. The South Port Hotel was built in 1798 and was certainly inhabited by William Sutton, but Mrs Sarah Walmesley built Belle Vue Cottage a year earlier and she was certainly living there before William Sutton moved from Churchtown. The pictures show the Duke's Folly during the mid-nineteenth century, although parts of the original structure can still be seen. Herdman's watercolour shows how delapidated the building had become by the 1850s. Considering its prime position, obstructing traffic at the end of Lord Street, and considering how out of keeping it was with Victorian ideas of elegance, it is not surprising to find that it was demolished in April 1854.

Above - The Original Hotel, painted by W. G. Herdman, as it appeared in about 1845. It was also known variously as the South Port Hotel, the Duke's Folly and the Royal Hotel.
(Photo, Botanic Gardens Museum)

Right - This popular view of the Duke's Folly appears to show the original bathing house on the right. In fact, the engraving dates from the latter half of the nineteenth century and is very unlikely to be a true likeness.
(Botanic Gardens Museum)

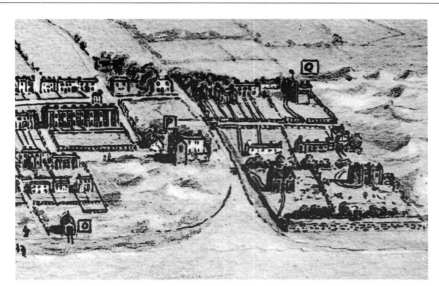

Left - *A detail from a 'Birds Eye View' of Southport drawn in 1849. The Original Hotel can be seen in the centre of this picture. Also visible are several other very early houses, including Belmont Castle (Q), Nile Cottage and Wellington Terrace. Note the straight development line along the Birkdale boundary on the right and the sandhills beyond.*
(Photo, Southport Library)

Left - *Two sketch plans, taken from Walker's plan of 1834 and the Ordnance Survey Map of 1849, show the ground plan of the Original Hotel at those dates.*
Below - *A section of Leigh's plan of Southport, drawn even earlier, in 1824. Note the early houses, the sandhills, the mouth of the River Nile and the little bridge shown in Herdman's picture.*
Bottom - *Another of Herdman's impressions of the Duke's Folly, this time in watercolours. This picture has an air of authenticity, although it is difficult to be certain about the likeness, particularly as all the early maps show a different ground plan.*
(Botanic Gardens Museum)

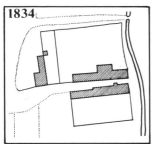

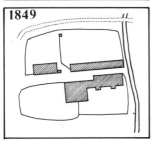

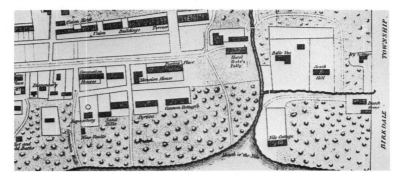

Dr Barton was present at the opening ceremony of Duke Sutton's hotel and, according to Thomas Glazebrook, 'The village received its present appelation, from the late Mr Barton, at an entertainment given by Mr Sutton, on the opening of his new Inn. The Doctor, during the evening, took a bottle of wine, and dashing the contents about him, emphatically said, ''This place shall be called Southport''.'[2]

The image of the portly Dr Barton, no doubt accompanied by his fellow practitioner Dr Brandreth, intoxicated by the wine and the sense of the occasion, seems to be authentic. He might well have made this casual remark, but the name of the hotel was most likely already decided. What Glazebrook is suggesting is that the patrons wanted to extend the place name of the inn to include the area around it and to differentiate it from the older cottages, in the same area, known as South Hawes.

The following year, Miles Barton built a residence called Nile Cottage between Mrs Walmesley's Belle View Cottage and the sea — he became the next occupant of South Port. Nile Cottage was soon joined by Willow Cottage, then Belmont Cottage, South Hill, Beach Grove, and another inn called the *Union Hotel* — a little village began to spring up in the sandhills and stargrass. Between the Folly and Belle View Cottage ran a small stream which was christened the Nile, although the only resemblance to its illustrious namesake in Egypt was the fact that it was surrounded by sand. The number of residents and visitors continued to grow and the very first people to live in Southport were Miss Bromley, Miss Leigh, Mrs Moneypenny, Miss Johnson and Mrs Halsall, these good ladies being joined by Messrs Hilton and Leadbetter who took over the lease on the South Port Hotel, and by a Mr Nevill and a Mr Tenant.

One of the earliest visitors to the bathing village in the Meols was Miss Ellen Weeton from Upholland near Wigan. She must have known the village very early in the nineteenth century because in 1808 she was able to write of the place that:

> It is becoming a famous bathing place, and is undoubtedly much superior for that purpose than the baths at Liverpool. There is no river water at the Meols, but a fine open sea, spacious shore to walk on, composed of a firm, smooth, sand, and, what suits me exceedingly, I can ramble for miles along the shore when in a humour for being alone, entirely unobserved and without the least dread of danger.

In the above passage she refers to the place as the 'Meols', but the following year she uses a different name:

> Great alterations are made at South Port. A number of houses are built of various sizes for the accommodation of families; and a new inn. Many people of some consequence and fashion, I have been told, have resorted there in the past two years. It is becoming a fashionable watering place.[3]

North Meols a fashionable watering place! Surely the good Miss Weeton must be mistaken? But others seemed to get the same strange notion and the *Liverpool Courier* actually published a list of fashionable arrivals for the year 1809.

A topological description of South Port appeared in Cook's *Modern British Traveller,* volume XX, published in about 1805. It refers to the mildness of the air, the longevity of the inhabitants, the firm beach, the trawl boat and a handsome pleasure boat. Several neat houses have been built near the inn, reads the guide, commanding a beautiful view of the sea, for the benefit of those who wish to apply for private lodgings in so delightful and healthful a situation. A more valuable and down to earth account was written by a Yorkshireman, Richard Holden, who claimed that few of the cottages had a sea view. He left Rotherham in 1808 with his wife, his daughter, his manservant and 'a little cabriolet with our own horses and a little dickey box fastened on behind'. Holden was intrigued by the octogenerian Doctor Barton. His journal consists of notes with tantalising gaps between them. On 24 May he dined at the *Wheat Sheaf* in Ormskirk:

W.G. Herdman's impression of the area around Lord Street West, known by the name of Nile Square, in about 1850.
(Painting, Botanic Gardens Museum)

The Willows. Willow Cottage was built in about 1800 and the first occupant was Mrs Moneypenny. The original was extended to the beautiful home which we see today. The Willows still captures the atmosphere of early Southport when the village consisted mainly of the beautifully individualistic 'marine villas' of the citizens.
(Photo, C. Greenwood)

afterwds went to South Port the last 2 miles deep Sand so as to be in some degree alarming − this place is of some Resort in the summer − many Cottages built to let to Strangers for £2 or 2 Gns. a Week several built by persons who have retired thither − but few of these have any Prospect of the Sea, that being entirely obstructed by Sandhills − however they are all near enough to enjoy the full benefit of the fine sands − two pretty good Hotels the old one the better − the Company not good in general − very prejudicing at first sight but improved afterwds − Dr Barton's House curious, as well as himself − Many Catholics here − the Chambermds Sister converted − she said they had bled all the protestant blood out of her − Story of her entertaining Miss Allison − Miss there is going to be a fight I can persuade them to go on to the Green where you may see them purely − Two fishing Boats go out at High Water trawl till the next Tide when they catch Flooks, Gurnett − Soles, some Turbot − black mouth − Cod ray − We had our choice − It was a little Interest to see the boats come in meet them on the beach with their Fish to see what they had got − a dangerous occupation − they continue to go in old boats after they are unfit − are often blown off by stress of Weather to Ireland, the Isle of Man, Isle of Walney.[4]

The remarks about the fight suggest a prize fight on the green of the village when, before the days of the Queensberry Rules, the combatants fought it out with bare fists to the bitter end. William Sutton would have been pleased at his remark of two pretty good Hotels, but the older hotel, which Holden preferred, was not the one run by the Old Duke at this time. It is strange that it was Nile Cottage and not the Duke's Folly which Richard Holden described as curious. Sarah Walmesley at Belle Vue Cottage and Mary Leigh at Belmont Cottage were both Roman Catholics, but his decription does not fit Miss Leigh − she was known to be very tolerant and offered her house to the Protestant Dissenters as a place to hold their meetings. Holden obviously did not stay at Nile Cottage, the house of Miles Barton, for the doctor was a Protestant and both his son and grandson became rectors of Hoole. The Yorkshireman was not impressed by the salubrious air of North Meols. Having been a fortnight without any benefit, on June 6th he moved on to Liverpool.

We are fortunate to have a fascinating description of early Southport from the pen of a walker, Richard Ayton, whose ambition was to travel all the way round the coast of Britain. Travelling north from Formby Point he describes a scene which at first seems more like the deserts of Arabia than the North of England:

> The sands are very hard and even, so that a pedestrian in spite of the dreariness of the prospect, may have some satisfaction, at least, in the smoothness of his path, though the miles are extremely tedious, and seem to be lengthened out to more than double their lawful extent. Distant objects appear most fallaciously near to the sight on this flat shore and one walks in wonder and impatience for an hour, without gaining a point which the eye had assured him was to be reached in less than half the time.

> I did at length arrive at some bathing machines, which I had for some time suspected of retreating as I advanced, and paused for rest at Southport, where an exhibition of human taste and art burst upon my view, that in

A section of the Birds Eye View of 1849, showing the Promenade and part of Lord Street behind. Numerous bathing machines congregate around the Promenade Lodge.
(Photo, Southport Library)

The beach and promenade in 1848.
(Photo, Botanic Gardens Museum)

so desolate a scene of nature had an extraordinary effect. Amidst a waste of sandhills, here are planted about a dozen houses, all fitted up in that peculiar style of natural and simple embellishment, which we sometimes see, but more often read of, in the villa of a citizen, within a morning's walk of his shop in town. The sand does not encourage anything to grow; but here are little gardens, marked out with white and green palings, which, instead of flowers and shrubs, are ornamented with spoils from wrecks, pieces of carved and painted work, figureheads, huge Neptunes and Tritons, which, inclosed in these small spaces, remind one of Gulliver in Lilliput. Nothing that paint can give of splendour and diversity of appearance has been spared on the outsides of these houses, and there are few windows not latticed, or not opening into a balcony, in which one person at least may stand at a time, and at his ease, to see the sand.[5]

As Ayton continues his narrative we discover the true nature of the grandiosely named River Nile:

The place was founded exclusively for the accommodation of bathers, and as far as was compatible with the ruggedness of the ground, everything has been made pretty to please the company. A small drain, which I hopped over when quitting the shore, I found was called the Nile, and was made, I believe, on purpose to be so called. Everything, in short, that could reasonably be expected, has been provided for the indulgence of visitors who come hither with fine taste and romantic feeling; and if a contrivance could be discovered, as the host of the inn observed, to make the sand look green and keep it out of the parlours, a person might travel very far indeed without seeing anything like Southport.

Richard Ayton was obviously very taken with the bathing village. At the time of his visit William Sutton had leased out the *South Port Hotel* but was landlord of the *Union Hotel,* the innkeeper with whom he chatted could therefore have been the Old Duke himself and it is a great shame that Ayton did not extend his stay in Southport, for had he done so we would almost certainly have learnt more about the character of William Sutton.

At this early stage in Southport's history many of the basic facilities were lacking and the traveller found that he had only two options by which to continue his journey — either esconced in the back of a humble country cart or to depart as he had arrived, on foot — there was not even a horse for hire. His next passages reveal that the English summer excelled itself in 1814:

The situation is as disagreeable as possible; a windy day smothering you with sand, and a calm one suffocating you with heat. I never felt heat so oppressive, I think, as here. When out of doors there is no quarter; all is open and exposed, without a tree or bush to fly to for shade or to look at and think of it: the eye has nothing to select and discriminate, but dwells by force, dazzled and strained, on an unvaried stretch of sea, sun, and sand.

I could procure no chaise, nor horse, nor any kind of conveyance here to help me on my journey, except a cart, and this did not travel in the course I wished to persue. The visitors are trundled away from hence in this humble vehicle to the Wigan Canal, where they meet a packet boat to take them to Wigan or Liverpool; and if a man be not bound to either of these places, he must walk or stay unless he fortunately wishes to be ferried over the Ribble, and is not, as I was, just ten minutes behind the proper time of tide.

Resolving not to stay, I renewed my expedition. ploughing my way for several miles up to the knees in hot sand; the thermometer, I had no doubt, almost high enough to drive a man mad. At the village of Churchtown, near the mouth of the Ribble, I was relieved by a paved road, which made my journey less burthensome . . .

The early residents of South Port went to great lengths to beautify their houses. Parterres of flowers formed a prominent feature in the gardens fronting the houses, with jasmine, woodbine, convolvuluses or wild grapes adorning the verandahs and providing shade as well as ornament — some of the verandahs were decorated with foliated crocket work. 'Building is still going on', wrote Thomas Glazebrook. 'For some time, uniformity of line and plan, seemed to be the principal object, but, latterly,

Belmont Castle in 1888, shortly before it was demolished.
'The castellated towers of
　Belmont frown
On what, or whom? The
　thrifty sons of trade
Who hold abode in
　Wellington Parade.'
The home of the indefatigable Robert Holt, it was built in 1820 and was a well known feature of early Southport. It was demolished in 1890.
(Photo, Botanic Gardens Museum)

considerable taste has been displayed, and the residences are really ornamental. Martindale Lodge is magnificent. On the opposite side, some new houses, with verandahs in front, are particularly neat.'

As the bathing village grew it acquired more permanent buildings, including some fine examples of Regency architecture such as Wellington Buildings (variously known as Wellington Parade and Wellington Terrace) and The Willows, also some astonishing fantasies in a mixture of architectural styles. In the latter category was Belmont Castle, a large stone building with a classical pillared portico and pointed gothic windows, the whole surmounted by square towers and castellated all the way round. Four tall chimneys protruded above and a flagstaff was mounted on top of the highest tower, it looked far more a folly than the *South Port Hotel*. It was the seat of Robert Holt.

In 1820 a shady Italian hotel-keeper called Majocchi was brought forward as a witness in a case of scandal against Queen Caroline. Many British patriots were shocked by the idea of foreigners bringing scandal against the Royal Family, and it was a great relief for them when the bill was dropped in November. Certain of the Southport residents were intensely patriotic and some just loved an excuse for a show of extravagance. Robert Holt of Belmont Castle belonged to both these categories and was the chief organiser behind a grand gala in honour of Queen Caroline.

The surrounding sandhills sprouted an array of white flags. A large banner flew from the turret of Belmont Castle on which could be read the words 'MAY THE PEACE OF OLD ENGLAND NEVER BE DISTURBED BY FOREIGN INTERFERENCE'. Proceedings commenced with a salute from six field guns and a cavalcade of patriotically attired residents processed from Robert Holt's residence to the main street of the village. All the assembly led by Mr Robert Holt sang 'God save the Queen'. An effigy of the infamous Majocchi, mounted on an ass and preceded by six butchers with bright axes, brought up the rear and was ceremoniously burned on a large bonfire. The company then sat down to an Old English dinner, the chair being most ably occupied by Robert Holt Esq.. Queen Caroline herself was unable to be present but an elegant effigy of her sat at the centre of the table. Constitutional toasts and songs followed the meal and the field guns roared another salute which signalled an illumination of the village. The most conspicuous building for its brilliance was Belmont Castle.[6]

The following year a temporary theatre was built of wood, and an

A painting of Christ Church in 1850, showing the vertical sundial on the south wall and a view of the sandhills in Chapel Street. Behind the church can be seen the school, the first in the village of Southport, with the school house to the left.

(Photo, Botanic Gardens Museum)

amateur performance of Tobin's comedy *The Honey Moon* was staged to a crowded audience. Mr Robert Holt, in the course of the evening, gave a rendering of the song *Old Commodore* in excellent style, and was rapturously encored. Perhaps it is only fair to mention that there were some who did not applaud but they wisely kept their distance. Low entertainments like the theatre did not meet with approval in all circles of Regency Society and Robert Holt knew that his performance risked a blasting from the pulpit by the Rev George Greatbatch.

In describing the deeds and character of Southport's earliest inhabitants it is necessary to mention the benevolent institutions which they created, all of which indicate a concern for the sick and the needy. The 'Stranger's Charity' was created as early as 1806, and rule four of the charity explains its purpose:

> As the sole object of the charity is the relief of the poor sick persons, to whose recovery sea air or bathing may be conducive, all patients must bring a recommendation from a subscriber, and a certificate from a regular medical practicioner, stating their complaint, and that in his opinion, they will be benefitted by sea air, or bathing.[7]

In 1816 a 'Marine Fund' was established with a view to saving lives at sea. The object was to reward fishermen and others who risked their boats and their lives by saving others. A third benevolence was the Local Dispensary, set up for the benefit of the poor of North Meols and its vicinity. Medicines were provided free to any who could not afford to pay. Standards of hygiene were appalling - patients were expected to bring their own bottle or gallipot and to return any medicine which they did not use.

Much of our knowledge of the early years of the town is due to Thomas Kirkland Glazebrook, from whom we have already quoted. He was a manufacturer of flint glass from Warrington. It was he who, in 1809, published a *Guide to South-Port, North Meoles, in the County of Lancaster.* The guide was a great success and it encouraged Thomas Glazebrook to collect more information and a second and larger edition was published in 1826.

Those who bought Glazebrook's guide certainly got good value for their money. In it he describes the approaches to the bathing village. He shows excellent but eccentric taste by choosing Aughton Church as the place from which to start for Southport, and he makes a diversion to tell his readers about the efforts of the Ormskirk campanologists and the changes rung on the Ormskirk bells. He indulges in a little mathematics and calculates twelve factorial quite correctly as 479,001,600. He uses this figure to arrive at the interesting but singularly useless piece of information that it would take the Ormskirk bell ringers 75 years 10 months and 10 days to ring all the possible changes on twelve bells. The diversion is characteristic of Glazebrook. He then returns to the main theme and describes the origins of Southport, including some of the history of North Meols. He gives a useful directory of accommodation and trades people, information on travelling arrangements, local gossip, and a very valuable account of shipwrecks along the coast with interesting details which cover several pages.

When he comes to the section on places of worship he describes the newly built Christ Church on Lord Street and he cannot resist giving an accurate and detailed account of the air conditioning system.

He feels it necessary to explain to his readers something about the sea. Here Glazebrook is in his element and he gives a treatise of several pages explaining the action of the sun and the moon to produce the tides. He refers to Professor Vince's *Four Discourses in the Confutation of Atheism from the Laws and Constitution of the Heavenly Bodies,* and he also quotes from another scientific writer of the time, Sir Richard Phillips, who:

> supposes the Earth and Moon to be united by a fixed gaseous medium, which forms as perfect a lever as a rod of iron or platina . . . they move around a common centre or fulchram in the medium of space, the arms or distances of the gaseous lever being in the inverse duplicate ratio of their distance and of their quantities of matter.

Yes, didn't Newton say something to that effect? But, says Glazebrook's guide, 'after duly studying and reading this paper, every judicious person will be sensible that it is wholly unnecessary to resort to the legerdemain power of attraction to account for the tides!!!' Then, having thoroughly confused all of his readers, just as he appears about to overthrow the Theory of Universal Gravitation in a seaside guidebook, Glazebrook admits that the mysterious 'gaseous lever' is just another term for the force of gravity.

Having first overcome his difficulties with the North Meols dialect, he chatted to the locals and drank with them in the *Black Bull* and the *Griffin.* They willingly gave him information for his guide and in return he wrote about them with genuine warmth and affection. His favourite characters were the pilot Thomas Jackson, the boatmen William Ball and Peter Ball, the fishermen Thomas Wright, Richard Wright and William Johnson, Cockle Dick, and of course, the Old Duke.

In his inimitable manner, Glazebrook continues to entertain his readers and posterity. Other writers followed him, and in the 1830s guides appeared by Whittle, Alsop and Cocker, all of whom are entertaining, all of whom are guilty of happily plagiarising Glazebrook's stories and some of whom consistently get the names of his characters wrong. But it was Thomas Kirkland Glazebrook who first set the fashion and who collected most of the early information. He richly deserves his honoured place in local history.

Chapter Ten

Taking the Waters

N 1824 the *Liverpool Kaleidoscope* published a lengthy piece of rhyme entitled *Southport alias North Meols* by John Stanley Gregson, alias Geoffrey Gimcrack of Manchester. As a sketch of a seaside watering place early in the 1820s it is a beautiful period piece. Gimcrack obviously knew Southport well and all the details in his verses are verified by other sources. He begins with a rare description of travel by canal packet, drawn by two horses at the pedestrian speed of four miles per hour (reduced to three after allowance for locks and swing bridges). Here was a unique instance in which a seaside town chanced to be served by the canal network which had developed to serve the industrial areas. In the eighteenth century the philosophy of pioneers like James Brindley was to build the canals to follow the contours of the countryside, thereby avoiding expensive earthworks and serving more towns and villages. Thus the Leeds and Liverpool Canal meandered over the Lancashire Plain to within a few miles of Southport and brought many of the early visitors. The packet boats held their own against the stage coaches only because of the cheapness and the smoothness of the ride compared to the jolting of the stagecoach.

> In the hot months when cits incline to roam,
> Grown quite uneasy, think of quitting home,
> No sooner thought than quickly they decide,
> To throw their books, *pro tempore,* aside,
> A sacrifice requiring all their force,
> And straight to Southport steer their steady course. . .
>
> Though lock and turnbridge often cross his way
> And in his 'north-west voyage' cause delay;
> If not a steamer yet of two horse power,
> Its speedy passage — just three knots an hour,
> From morn to eve; all dread of danger past,
> At Scarisbrick bridge they safe arrive at last,
> Where, like to claiming customs on the coast,
> The hulk is boarded by a clamourous host
> Of boys and Jarvies, lords of caravans,
> Carts, coaches, cars, and shandry-dans,
> Like hookers-in soliciting pell mell
> To drive you to BARLOW'S or to CLARE'S hotel.[1]

Having completed the final part of their journey, Gimcrack describes their first impressions of the bathing village:

> And strangers for a time express surprise
> When naught but sand-hills meet their wond'ring eyes;

Anon the church the carriage heaves in sight
The Hesketh Arms, the playhouse on the right
At further end of what is termed 'the town',
The castellated towers of Belmont frown
On what, on whom? the thrifty sons of trade
Who hold abound in Wellington Parade . . .

On fine summer evenings the lodging house keepers stood in little groups at the centre of the street awaiting the arrival of the first conveyances from the canal at Scarisbrick. When the first coach appeared, a long and rather ancient nautical telescope was brought to bear on it, to determine whether or not there were people riding on the top. Debates followed in the middle of the street as to whether or not there was a goodly number of visitors arriving. The second coach turned the corner and if that too had people riding outside or on top then a great cheer echoed around the sandhills. It signified that the remaining coaches would be full.

Gimcrack's holidaymakers, having found their overnight accommodation, wait for the next day to get to grips with the serious business of taking the waters. This was a very elaborate procedure. It involved the correct form of dress and naturally required a bathing machine in which to change and from which to bathe with the assistance of a dipper. At Southport, contrary to the normal practice, the dippers were traditionally male; the job had certain attractions and the ladies had certain favourites:

The night pass'd o'er, at morn behold a band
Of lovely damsels troop along the sand,
Clad in flannel dress of blue or red
And oil-case cap, as covering for the head;
With joy they hasten to the blue marine,
And patient wait their turn for a machine,
And, it is said, those they prefer to call
Of 'Handsome John' and eke 'Sweet William Ball'
Like to the Naiads, as we read at school,
They quick descend and trouble well the pool;
Heedless of bathing seen by vulgar men,
They dash and splash, and splash and dash again;
And though these feats the grinning beaux discern,
They scorn to show a symptom of concern.

The writer then finds it necessary to give a conditional apology for this open admiration of the fair sex:

No further we pursue this luscious strain,
Lest we at least by some be deemed profane;
Though true it is, as almost all agree,
The men in sailing boats are worse than we —
These navigators bold are most to blame
Who tack, and re-tack, without sense of shame;
'Keep within compass' not their maxim here,
The ladies' eyes the stars by which they steer!

We knew it was the morning, and that the newcomers were eager to take to the water, but we now discover that all this activity has taken place before breakfast!

Now, as retires the health-conducing wave,
The beaux depart to breakfast or to shave;
Meanwhile these sea-nymphs, or the glowing fair,
Haste to the toilet to arrange their hair;
Apres déjeuner, early yet the day,
Only appear in simple neglige,
And as it is the custom'd 'turn of tide'
Engage the ponies for a morning ride,
(Alas! Poor brutes, they're almost ridden to death,)
Or ramble up the sand-hills out of breath,
And then run on down without the least alarm
Or walk to Churchtown or to find 'Lost Farm';
Some to Old Harry Rimmer's pleased will go,

The Sands at Southport. An early engraving, showing the promenade. The Promenade Lodge, which dominates this scene, was built by Samuel Whiteley in about 1840. It is sometimes confused with Whiteley's Repository which stood further inland. This picture shows clearly the construction of the first Southport promenade. (Botanic Gardens Museum)

High tide at Southport. A smart turnout of day trippers, complete with long skirts, lace trimmings and hats. The clothing does not prevent the more adventurous from getting their feet wet whilst their chaperones look on apprehensively. (E.W. Collection)

The sands at Southport.

And to his fiddle point the pliant toe.

The Lost Farm was a farmstead in Birkdale which had been completely overwhelmed by blown sand. It became a regular excursion for visitors and on the return journey they would often stop at the cottage of Old Harry Rimmer (1742-1828) who, up to the age of eighty, entertained guests on his fiddle whilst they tripped up and down on the green in front of his cottage. His favourite tunes were said to be 'Buttered Peas' and 'Lads Thrashing Barley'. In the evening the dancing began in earnest.

> But lo! the evening comes, and now begin
> The sports and pastimes of the world within
> All from those outdoor games must now desist,
> As the old folk retire for rubs at whist,
> While youth and beauty, dress'd in flounce and frill,
> Haste to the ball, as they prefer quadrille;
> Some to the play, which should not be despised,
> Where th' School for Scandal is most scandalised;
> With scenes like these, diurnally they close,
> At length out-wearied, cheerful seek repose.

In its first twenty years Southport came from nowhere to become the leading seaside resort in the Northwest, easily outstripping the Fylde resorts which looked on with envy but which were less accessible and unable to compete on equal terms. Southport was particularly popular with the ladies and part of the reason was no doubt because they preferred the attentions of the male dippers to those of their own sex. But no visit to Southport was complete without a boat trip across the Ribble to Lytham where Mrs Ellen Gillett was a serious rival to Sweet William Ball

> Each day with like pursuits is occupied,
> Thus to portray them I have humbly tried,
> And hasten now to lay the pencil down,
> And, via Lytham to return to town;
> But such a rage for Meols the ladies take,
> That Blackpool, Lytham, tout-le-monde forsake,
> For such a name hath this said sandy spot,
> That both, alas are now well nigh forgot,
> And naught is left a stanza to inspire,
> Save Ellen Gillett and her red attire.
> Her hat, her lappets, oh! the jolly dame,
> She ranks the first and best of bathing fame!

At last the holiday comes to an end. Gimcrack and his colleagues take their leave of the seaside.

> Farewell, farewell! ye healthy sea-girt lands
> Of star-hills, sea-gulls, sea-shells, shrimps and sands;
> Thanks for our renovated health we pour;
> May mussels, cockles, crowd upon your shore;
> Turbot and cod, and periwinkle be
> Procur'd in plenty from the Irish sea;
> To every cottage and to every Inn
> May strangers swarm, and all be *taken in;*
> Thus adding yearly to your wealths increase,
> And to your hearths − true happiness and peace.

Southport still had a little way to go, however, to become the most popular seaside resort in Lancashire. In the first decades of the nineteenth century that title belonged to an unlikely resort on the Mersey estuary. Liverpool had prospered on the slave trade and later on the import of raw cotton and the export of manufactured goods and by the 1820s it had become the second largest city in Britain. To the north it had fine sandy beaches and Liverpolitans did not need to travel far to enjoy sea bathing. Liverpool's clientele was mainly local; her beaches steadily gave way to docklands and as Southport grew Liverpool steadily declined as a seaside resort but the latter's contribution to the development of the seaside holiday in Lancashire has consistently been ignored.

Not everybody was of the opinion that the crowded beach was the ideal and when Ellen Weeton returned for one of her regular visits in 1824 the solitude which she had known in her younger days was gone. The scene was one of earnest activity, with bathing machines trundling their occupants continually back and forth to the water.

> I like to bathe alone, and a private bath is just to my taste. I have seldom bathed but at Southport, and there it is sadly exposing, as all who resort there well know, and the modest complain much, gentlemen's and ladies' machines standing promiscuously side by side in the water! Besides, at spring tides, it is hardly possible to have a machine for one person, such crowds resort there to bathe; and there are no dressing rooms, time is positively not allowed for any one to dress in the machine before quitting it. Perpetual rappings at the door, and 'oh do come out', 'do make haste', reiterated until we are thrown into a trepidation, so as not to be able to finish dressing; and probably, on issuing forth, two or three *gentlemen,* to your utter confusion, at the door, ready to jump in! The bustle, hurry, and confusion are most extremely disagreeable; the only comfort is, that amongst such a crowd we may pass unnoticed perhaps.[2]

Ellen Weeton was not the only person to complain about the promiscuous mixed bathing. When Whittle's guide to Southport was published in 1830 he wrote:

> The beach is most fashionable, and indeed the only promenade about Southport which affords any agreeable diversity of scenery, and the time for enjoying its attraction is a rather singular one, so much so, that we are warranted in supposing that the attractions are not simply confined to the beach itself, but extend to objects of a different and less sublime nature.

The observations of earlier writers make it easy to deduce the meaning of the latter remarks. He goes on to describe a scene very similar to that described by Ellen Weeton:

> At the height of the tide every machine is in motion, carrying, indiscriminately, occupants of either sex, at no unsociable distance from each other, not provided even with screens, which are common at all continental bathing-places, but left to the uninterrupted gaze of the passing crowd, which paces the shore for the edifying purpose of gaining sympathetic health, so that it appears, in the cold eye of philosophy, like the fountain of Salamis, so famed of old for its power of conjunction.

Whittle wags a stern finger at those in authority and lapses into the royal 'we'.

> We would not contend for any hypocritical fastidiousness of delicacy, but there are certain limits of decorum, beyond which modesty, sensitive as it is, ought not to pass; and though there may be no real or moral contamination, 'tis well to observe them even for appearance sake, for it

Donkey Riding on Southport Sands, oil painting by W. Watson.
(Botanic Gardens Museum)

Built only two years after Wellington's victory at Waterloo, this Regency terrace is a fine asset to Lord Street and retains much of its original character. These private residences are mentioned in Gimcrack's verses of 1824 and in other early accounts of Southport. They are older than both Lord Street and the Promenade and were once situated on the village green and known as Wellington Parade - the first fashionable parade in Southport.
(Photo, C. Greenwood)

is not enough to avoid actual criminality, but the very semblance also.

Only a short distance along the beach, at Birkdale, it was not uncommon to find casual bathers running naked down to the sea, and similar scenes could be witnessed on Big Bathing Sunday — but nobody cared about that. The point was that Southport had become a highly fashionable place for respectable people to take the waters and it was therefore expected to maintain certain standards.

Soon afterwards, although the Victorian era was still a few years away, a new strict set of bathing regulations was introduced. The first rule stated that 'There shall be a vacant space of one hundred yards between the bathing ground appointed for ladies, and that appointed for gentlemen; which ground shall be marked out by posts, with proper inscriptions upon them'. This rather more civilised arrangement was in force when Sir George Head visited the beach some years later. He noted the conspicuous position of the boards displaying the bathing regulations and he noted also that when the ladies were bathing the pleasure boats were prohibited from approaching within a distance of thirty yards, the fine for this offence being five shillings. The new regulations did not prevent Sir George from obtaining as much pleasure as his predecessor Geoffrey Gimcrack out of watching the proceedings. The ladies' bathing costumes gave decent coverage to the ankles but the shoulders were daringly bared:

> All the old bathing women at Southport (to make use of an Hibernicism) are young men, that is to say, stout, lusty fellows under middle age. Whether the service diminishes the chilling effects of the water; whether it makes young men old, or old men young, is a point, they say, not yet determined; at all events the young ladies one and all, without hesitation, submit to their guidance, such as they are. The guide, or male personage, or what not, having taken his post in front of the door of the machine, in the usual manner, the young lady undresses within. Having dismembered herself of her apparel, she puts on a dark blue bathing dress, (in which I perceive no other differences from those commonly used, than that it was invariably fastened with strings between the ankles), and in this costume makes her appearance, 'albo sic humero nitens, ut nocturno renidet, luna mari' — her shoulder white as the clear moonbeam that glitters on the midnight sea -- on the upper step of the sanctuary. Presenting both her hands to the guide, and supported by his grasp, she then falls backwards on the wave, receiving the embraces of Old Neptune as young ladies usually do, with the accompaniments of giggling, kicking, splashing, and wincing.[3]

There was no shortage of young ladies in Southport but there was a great shortage of eligible young men and some of the latter were more interested in sport than in the opposite sex. Some of the younger ladies developed a phobia lest they turn into old maids before finding themselves a marriage partner. In 1830 they issued a plea for help in the *Liverpool Mercury:*

Gentlemen, – As I know you are friends to the fair sex, I think you would be doing the ladies of Southport a very great kindness, if you will call the attention of bachelors to their sad condition. There are in this village no fewer than four score marriageable ladies, and some of them charming ones too, but to all human appearances, the greater part of them are doomed to be, what is most dreaded by young ladies – 'old maids' – as there are only four single gentlemen in the place, and two of these are fixed down bachelors, more fond of guns, dogs, hawks, & c. than the ladies . . .[4]

The Liverpolitans were not immune to this plea from the heart and a week later the *Mercury* published a reply.

To the Ladies of Southport,
Ladies. The same kind medium which has been the instrument of laying before the public your pitiable case, will, I trust, convey to you the sympathy of one of your opposite sex, who, though in a large and populous town, has to complain that an object has not presented itself to him with whom he might mingle his ardent flame, for in truth, Ladies, I abhor the name of 'bachelor', as much as you can that of 'old maid' . . . I have only to say, that if any lady has confidence to reply to my letter, she may depend that I never will betray her candour. I shall, of course, hope to receive a real name, when mine shall be made known,. – Address to the post office, to be left till called for. EROTA.

Communications to the bathing village improved steadily, and the stagecoach arrived to compete with the canal packet for passengers to and from Manchester. The *Preston Pilot,* travelling via Wigan and Ormskirk, made three journeys every week; it formed a daily connection with the *Self Defence* which ran through Bolton and Chorley in the bathing season. Yorkshiremen and their families travelled on the *Accommodation* to Preston where it connected with a coach service to Rochdale, Halifax and Leeds. The *Amnity* provided a Sunday service as far as Ormskirk, and the *Eclipse* ran daily to and from Liverpool. Ellen Weeton travelled on the *Eclipse* when the English summer was at it worst:

The wind blew so furiously, no umbrella could be opened or carried. the coachman was very attentive to me; he gave me a stout horse rug to cover my shoulders, and another to cover my knees, and in this elegant costume I rode through Ormskirk and Liverpool to the inn there, as heedless and contented as possible, the rain soaking through all the way, and trickling in little streams down my back, so that I was literally wet to the skin.

In the 1831 season, however, many of the visitors from Manchester had given up both the laggardly canal packet and the *Preston Pilot* stagecoach. They had arrived in Southport by a more circuitous but quicker route via Liverpool. An entirely new form of transport had arrived just too late for the previous season, but in the first summer of its operations the Liverpool and Manchester Railway took through bookings from Manchester to Southport – passengers changed at Liverpool for one of Bretherton's coaches.

Soon a 'new and elegant Four-inside Patent Safety Coach' called the *Favourite* met the two o'clock train daily at Liverpool to carry passengers to Southport. Some passengers decided it was quicker to leave the railway at St Helens and travel by coach from there, and in 1835 the railway company agreed that one first class coach should be reserved for Southport passengers and would be detached from the trains at St Helens. The following year the *Manchester Guardian* advised its readers that 'the most direct, safe and expedious route to Southport is by Railway to Newton, where a superior *Light Post Chaise* waits daily to convey passengers'. The chaise was for first class passengers, but a 'Patent Safety Coach' was available to meet the second class train.

In the 1830s Mancunians travelled by rail and stage, Lancashire artisans arrived by canal packet, and Yorkshire families braved the stony jolting passes of the Pennines just to visit the bathing village in North Meols.

Chapter Eleven

The Bathing Village

THE bathing village acquired its first church in 1821 and an early account of a service in Christ Church was given by a visitor calling himself Nathantiquarii, writing in the *Liverpool Kaleidoscope*. The account was also published in Whittle's guide of 1831.

A church has lately been erected, which is a great convenience to the visitors, who were formerly obliged to go to Churchtown. It is built of brick, in a neat and unostentatious style, with a small tower. The pulpit is rather fancifully suspended over the communion, between the reading desk and clerk's pew. The service was in some measure interrupted by the continual unlocking of the seats. As for the music, 'Twas a villainous compound of bad sounds; 'twas no music of the spheres; no choir of cherubim; but the discordant harmony (the concordia discors) of mortal melody; the shrill tones of the flageolet, played by the not unpretending hand of village minstrelsy, were overpowered by the acute notes of female vocalism; and the loud bass of rustic capability of lungs overpowered the dull monotony of the hoarse bassoon: there was no sympathy of intonation — no combination of melodious sounds; but all was the struggling of discordant rivalry:

The writer adds that the performance was so ridiculous 'as to render necessary no little effort to preserve a due gravity of decorum'. On the first reading there appears a remarkable resemblance, even to 'the acute notes of female vocalism', to the scene described by Thomas Hardy in *Under the Greenwood Tree* when the Mellstock Quire gave their Christmas Morning performance. On a closer reading, however, we find that at Christ Church it is not the village minstrels but the vocalists who are the cause of the disharmony.

Christ Church is depicted on James Leigh's plan of 1824 which shows the extent of the bathing village at that time. The South Port Hotel is clearly labelled as the 'Duke's Folly', the Union Hotel is shown and also the new Hesketh's Arms Hotel situated opposite to the junction with East Bank Lane, and with a billiard room just behind. Lord Street was still not named, but Coronation Walk had been given its name the previous year at the Coronation of George IV. Samuel Whiteley's repository stood on Coronation Walk; this was built in 1812 and was basically 'an extensive shop, containing conchological varieties, and a well selected assortment of fancy articles, fitting for a watering place'. It also contained a warehouse 'plentifully stocked with the necessaries and luxuries of life', a small library and a news room. In Regency and Victorian society many people were avid readers of the newspapers, it being their only way of keeping up with current affairs.

An early photograph of Christ Church on Lord Street, showing the main details of the original design. The church was consecrated in 1821 and on the Sunday following Whittle tells us that 'A judicious sermon, well adapted for the occasion, was preached by the Rev William Docker from the 95th psalm and the 5th verse ... in an animated and energetic manner.'
(Photo, Botanic Gardens Museum)

Nathantiquarii describes the village in 1832:

> Southport consists principally of one long straggling street, so wide that the intermediate space is filled by gardens, or rather small fields. The general aspect possesses too much regularity to be consistent with beauty; and yet the only beauties it can boast of is in its *individual* irregularity. When viewed from a distance, the sides of the street present one long, equal monotonous line, with scarcely one house projecting beyond another; but, when more nearly approached, each cottage or at least set of cottages, exhibits its own particular feature and distinctive character, and affords an agreeable variety, which, from its minuteness, is lost in the distance.

The earliest reference to Lord Street by name is in the rates assessment book of 1831. At that time only a small part of the street was recognised as a place to promenade. This was on the south side and was known as Wellington Parade. Lord Street developed steadily throughout the 1830s, and gradually became noticed as an unusually fine thoroughfare.

In 1842 Thomas Tidmarsh, much against his will, found himself bound for Southport. Some seemingly well-informed person had assured him that Southport was a dismal place, but his doctor insisted that he make the visit for the sake of his health. The morning dew was still on the hedgerows when Mr Tidmarsh estimated himself to be about two miles from his destination. A church came into view:

> . . . and immediately afterwards I found myself in a long and beautifully picturesque street. Houses of a graceful aspect, some with grass plots before them, bloomingly gemmed with buttercups and daisies; others with gardens luxuriating in flowers, and rich in loveliness and perfume; others again half hid behind the shady retreat of their shrubberies, ever and anon peeping through the branches whose leaves were then pearled with the morning's crystal dew-drops, studded the respective sides of the street, each rivalling the others in cleanliness of appearance and architectural neatness, and forming in combination one lengthy and un-swerving line of light, beauty and proportion . . .

Why stay in dismal old Southport? He quickly decided that this was the place where he would stay. He stopped the coach and ordered the driver to put him down there and then, and he explained that he intended to stay at this place instead of going on to Southport. But the coachman, to Thomas Tidmarsh's surprise and utter astonishment, informed him that he was already in Southport!

The town's first newspaper, called The *Southport Pleasure Boat,* did not appear until 1842 and the venture only lasted for thirteen issues. It was two years later that the first issue of the *Southport Visiter* appeared; the title included what was then an acceptable alternative spelling of 'visitor'. It was originally published only in the summer months but the newspaper was destined to last for so long that in later generations the title was deemed to contain a spelling mistake. The directors bravely chose to stay with their original spelling.

> *The Southport Visiter and General Advertiser* was [wrote Frank Robinson[1]] a local newspaper dedicated wholly to serve and further the interests of the town. Very moderate expectations were entertained by the proprieter and publisher when it was established, but the signal success of the first season led him to enlarge it, and otherwise to improve its general character, on its re-appearance. There was decided proof that it had been established in the 'nick of time'. Its principal feature was intended to be a list of the visiters, but more was required; the inhabitants wished to know what events had occurred at home and abroad during the past week, the number of 'little strangers' added to the population, the fond hearts that had been united, and the names and ages of those upon whom sentence of death had been recorded; the tradesmen, necessarily unknown to the majority of the ever-changing population of visiters, required a vehicle to make known to the public the articles they vended, the 'fresh arrivals', &c.; in a few words, an organ of communication was required between the inhabitants and the visiters, − between Southport and the rest of the country. The paper is at present published during only six months, from the first Saturday in May, to the last Saturday in October, but hopes are entertained of its permanent

A rare early view of Lord Street taken in about 1860. It shows the view looking north from outside the Scarisbrick Hotel, near where the Natwest Bank now stands. None of the buildings in the foreground survive to give the modern observer a reference point.

(Photo, Botanic Gardens Museum)

Southport in 1834

Walker's plan shows Southport in 1834, before the first Promenade was built and completely surrounded by sandhills. Practically all the development was along 'Lords Street' and the long front gardens which became the boulevards can be

clearly seen. On the left can be seen the original houses clustered around the River Nile, and the planned development of the cross streets is shown. A close scrutiny will reveal several street names which no longer survive. As the 'Description' on the map indicates, this excellent map was drawn specifically for potential developers who might be interested in purchasing building land. One can see several of the planned roads, many as yet without names.

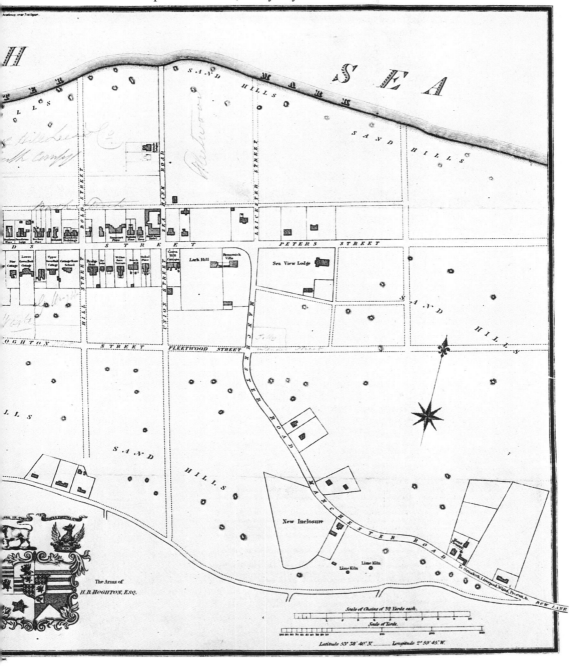

publication. That the Visiter has been of service to the town, no person laying a claim to sanity can doubt; but it is in perpetual and not partial support that the inhabitants will receive those great advantages which may be acquired by this means.

The first issue, which appeared on 4 May 1844, consisted of eight pages, of which the first and last consisted solely of advertisments. From the names of the local tradesmen on these pages, we can judge the extent to which the local families had benefited from the growth of the town:

> Richard Rimmer, a linen and woollen draper, 'Ever grateful for favours conferred, begs to inform his numerous customers that he has in stock an immense variety of goods in the above branches of business, which have been carefully selected from the first manufacturers, and are such that he can confidently recommend to his friends for their durability and cheapness. They may be *equalled by some* but *surpassed by none*.[2]

Rimmer also sold Dublin Porter, bottled or draught, and Pale India Burton Ale with his linen and woollen goods.

James Hunt, the proprieter of the Scarisbrick Arms, advertised open and closed carriages, with very superior horses, and steady drivers. He reminds us that the railway had arrived to compete with the canal and stagecoach, and he advertised coaches to and from Euxton railway station 'From whence persons may proceed to all parts of the kingdom'. He also ran an omnibus built by Cowburn of Manchester, and other conveyances, to meet the canal packet boat which still ran to Scarisbrick Bridge from Manchester.

William Ball advertised the Victoria Baths to 'all who may favour him with their support, to prove himself worthy of their confidence and patronage', but he added a note that 'No person with an offensive ailment will be allowed to bathe in these baths'. Dare we make the assumption that this man was Gimcrack's 'Sweet William Ball', favourite of the ladies' dippers in his youth? The Victoria Baths, which first opened in 1839 at a cost of £6000, stood in a central position on the promenade. Frank Robinson gives a full description:

> The facade is towards the sea, and is composed of a central portico or colonnade of Ionic order, with balustrades to the right and left, so forming a continuous covered parade. The entrance to the right leads to the ladies' baths, and that on the left to the gentlemen's. A refreshment room divides the entrances, over which is another apartment, and above that there is an open gallery. Tepid and cold swimming, hot, shower, vapour, and other baths are instantly obtainable, with every convenience, and the most civil and obliging treatment. At the end of the lobby is the engine-room, which was formerly used as a conservatory, − a singular and unusual combination of objects. Mr Clayton, the architect, took advantage of the high temperature produced by the boiler to form the conservatory, and the effect, as may readily be imagined, was really admirable. It was furnished with one hundred and fifty pots of rare and beautiful plants, and the stage was surmounted by a bust of 'The Iron Duke'.[3]

The writer goes on to say that the conservatory was regrettably (by 1848) a thing of the past, the Victoria Baths was under new management and the botanically minded engine tender had 'ceased his connection with the establishment'.

The inside pages of the first *Southport Visiter* contained plenty of national news but very little in the way of local events. It did, however, contain much of local interest in the editorial; it contained good and bad poetry, some amusing examples of early Victorian humour and an important centre page spread which listed visitors to the town at the early part of the season. These pages were the main *raison d'être* of the newspaper as well as the reason for its name. The visitors bought the paper to see their name in print and class conscious mothers, like Jane Austen's Mrs Bennet, eagerly scrutinised the pages trying to assess the relative wealth and status of the other visitors, with a view to forming the correct acquaintances for their unattached daughters. The chauvinistic 'Hints on

Matrimony' section was designed to help them:

> No woman will be likely to dispute us when we assert that marriage is her destiny. A man may possibly fill up some sort of existence without loving; but a woman with nothing to love, cherish, care for, and minister to, is an anomaly in the universe — an existence without an object . . .

Also aimed at the gentler sex was the column on 'Advice to Young Ladies':

> What a pity it is that the thousandth chance of a gentleman's becoming your lover should deprive you of the pleasure of a free, unembarrassed, intellectual intercourse with all the single men of your acquaintance! Yet such is too commonly the case with young ladies who have read a great many novels and romances, and whose heads are always running on love and lovers . . .

Those female readers who had the wealth to keep up with the latest fashions were a dazzling sight when they paraded up and down Lord Street. The 'Fashions for May' column helped them to stay in touch with the latest creations:

> CAPS: The most decidedly favourite style of cap is that made of tulle cheffonne, interspersed with clusters of heath, or any very small flowers. Those caps made entirely plain upon the forehead are now very much in vogue; a broad curtain is placed at the back, headed with a wreath of flowers or leaves, and which only just reaches to the ears on each side, where it is attached with a bunch or cluster of the same . . .

> BONNETS: The form of those for the new season is as distinguished looking as they are pretty. We have seen several of straw coloured satin, covered with crepe of the same hue, and trimmed simply with ribbons pariel to the satin, and figured with a cerise coloured stripe; the under part of the brim decorated with sprigs of geranium and the Spanish jasmine; others in white satin trimmed with lace, and fullings of tulle in the interior; or those in pink grose de Naples covered with a rice antique lace, and having for an ornament a branch of roses, intermixed with bunches of currants . . .

> DRESSES: The new cut and novel appearance of those dresses which have the corsage open in front, cause them to be adopted for almost every style of dress, at once combining elegance, ease, and comfort. The high corsages amazones and demi moutons are in great vogue, and the embroideries destined for these dresses of the present season are well worthy of attention. Les chicoree ruches, the trimmings fontagues, and the bias gothiques, are all and each of them made up with such extreme taste, that nothing can equal the invention and perfection to which they can be brought. The ceintures of robes de ville are mostly formed round, and very low on the hips, and the skirts immensely wide and very long . . . Fashionable colours for the present month are now commencing to be of the gayest tints, such as pale pink, bordering or cerise, blue lilacs, and greens of every shade, straw colour, peach, and shots and shaded tints.

If the ladies were to promenade around the town in these high fashions, then Southport needed to get involved with more down to earth matters such as the paving of the streets, street lighting, drainage and sewage disposal. The administrative machinery of the North Meols Parish Council was quite inadequate to meet the exacting requirements of the town which had grown in its midst. In 1846, Southport obtained the right through an act of Parliament to set up its own local government, to manage its own affairs and to levy a rate to raise money for improvements. This move was therefore an important event in the development of the town and represented the inevitable breakaway from the inadequate administration of the parish and manor officials of North Meols. A committee called The Improvement Commissioners was set up to deal with local matters. The first committee consisted of five Reverends including the Lord of the Manor, several doctors, and local tradesmen; the Balls and the Wrights still had to be differentiated by profession.

THE IMPROVEMENT COMMISSIONERS 1846[4]

William Ball (Brewer)	Richard Lewis
William Ball (Captain)	William Linaker

The Promenade

he first promenade in Southport was completed in 1839 and soon became a popular and fashionable place to walk and be seen. On the map it is shown as 'Marine Promenade' because Lord Street was, of course, an earlier promenade. As with many other seaside resorts, the Promenade became one of the focal points of the town and along its route swimming baths, leisure lakes, funfairs entertainment establishments, the Grand Pavilion and the Aquarium were built, catering for all tastes. The first Victoria Baths were erected in the same year as the Promenade itself, at its north end. The south end was marked by the Promenade Lodge and clusters of bathing machines could be found at both ends, with gentlemen's and ladies' bathing kept at a respectable distance from each other.

Above - *The wooden jetty was the forerunner of the pier and its remains now lie under the Marine Lake. Visitors were prepared to pay for the privilege of walking on its slippery planks. The circular reservoir provided sea water for the Victoria Baths. Painting by E. Vernon.* (E.W. Collection)

Below - *The outside of the Victoria Baths, 1871. The reopening of the Victoria Baths was the excuse for the gala occasion with a procession through town, ceremonial lifeboat launching and a ball at the Town Hall.*
(Engraving, Southport Library)

Below - *A section of a 'Birds Eye View' of Southport drawn in 1849.* (Photo, Southport Library)

Below - *An engraving from around 1850 of 'Southport from the sea'.*
(Botanic Gardens Museum)

Above - *The Promenade Lodge, painted in 1852, dominates the bathing machines in this scene. One machine has just entered the water.*
(Botanic Gardens Museum)

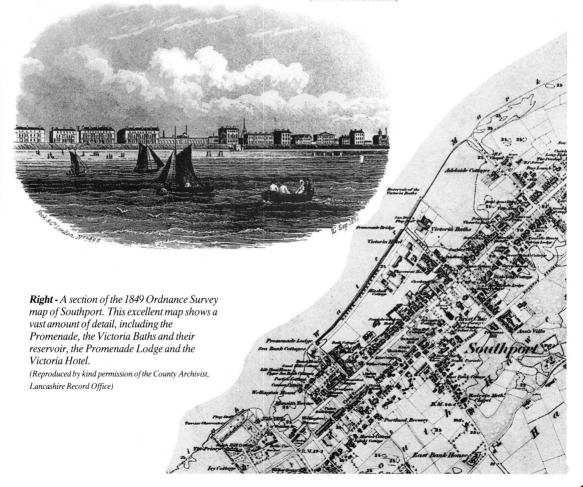

Right - *A section of the 1849 Ordnance Survey map of Southport. This excellent map shows a vast amount of detail, including the Promenade, the Victoria Baths and their reservoir, the Promenade Lodge and the Victoria Hotel.*
(Reproduced by kind permission of the County Archivist, Lancashire Record Office)

Charles Clough	James Longton
Singleton Cooper	James Mawdsley
Rev William Docker	Bennet Smith
Rev George Greatbatch	William Tyrer
William Gregson	William Wales
Rev Charles Hesketh	William Walker
Rev John Hill	Samuel Whiteley
Thomas Hulme	Richard Wright (Builder)
Rev Johnathan Jackson	Richard Wright (Land Agent)
William Jolley	

The nineteenth century was approaching the half-way mark and Southport had become a much sought after place in which to live. The number of middle-class residents was increasing very rapidly and great pride was taken in the general appearance of the town. It is one of the great qualities of Southport, however, that as the town increased in wealth and prosperity it never forgot its origins. The names of the Improvement Commissioners show that plenty of much needed new blood was mixed in with a large proportion of old — they show that local people profited by the growth of the town and that Southport was a natural child of North Meols. The townspeople were always full of concern and generous to help whenever accidents occurred to the fishermen and other local people. The Rev George Greatbatch organised a relief fund for the handloom weavers in the parish when their plight became desperate through lack of work and low wages. There were always plenty who were willing to help with Sunday schools and like activities which were the only means by which the majority of children could learn to read and write.

It was well known that the town had been founded by a local man, but Victorian society was very class conscious. It is therefore significant to find that Southport always acknowledged the contribution of the poorer classes to its history. Thomas Glazebrook must certainly be given much of the credit for this tradition. He was obviously fascinated by the locals but, when Bland's fine history appeared in 1887, many human stories were woven between the deeds of the local dignitaries. Examples are the burial in 1844 of Ann Rimmer (84), Ellen Baker (84), and William Johnson their neighbour, a fisherman; the story of Richard and Gilbert Wright (father and son) and Thomas Bond who drowned when a sudden gust of wind upset their fishing boat; of John Wright (Manty) and his son, who lost their boat and fishing tackle through fire; of Peter Ball the town's bellman who was so poor that a subscription had to be raised to bury him; and many others from the grass roots of the community.

The thing Southport desired most of all was a direct railway link, and this was not long in coming. Bills authorising the lines to both Liverpool and Manchester were given assent in 1847. The lines would put Southport at the apex of a right-angled triangle with the old Liverpool and Manchester line as a baseline. Robinson gives a popular view of the proposal:

> Upon completion of the lines of railway which have been sanctioned by the legislature, persons may leave the most remote places in the kingdom without that serious consideration which under the old system of travelling was necessary. The packet, which actually performs the passage between Manchester and Scarisbrick Bridge (Within six miles of Southport) *in one entire day,* will, it is presumed, be converted to some baser use; and the stage coaches, easy, safe, luxurious vehicles, as they have been of late years, are to be superceded by first-, second-, and third-class trains, combining the speed of lightning with the comfort of a chair in your own homes. The coachmen too, merry, tale-telling, jovial fellows, as they are, will find their occupation gone, and the whip and the reins will be to them things of recollection; and the very turnpike roads are threatened to be usurped by green grass and noxious weeds. Cooke, Howarth, and Fidler, farewell! the scream of the railway whistle is to be substituted for the sonorous 'all right' of your careful charioteers, and the progress of Southport is onward!

Construction of the Liverpool line from Crosby began in January 1848 and was completed as far as the Birkdale boundary by June of the same year. The powers of the Southport Impovement Commissioners ended abruptly at this boundary line, for Birkdale belonged to a different landowner and, until the middle of the century, Birkdale was able to retain much of its rural character; the coming of the railway, however, was destined to bring about great changes.

Thomas Weld Blundell drew up a plan for the development of Birkdale as a high class residential area − it was to be laid out by surveyors and landscape gardeners and building was to commence on the land known as Aindow's Hills, an area presumably occupied by the local family of that name. The original plans show about two hundred houses, each detached and standing in a generous plot of land. It needed extensive capital and there was much speculation as to whether the up-market properties of the proposed Birkdale Park Estate would sell, especially in view of the fact that many similar properties were springing up in neighbouring Southport. Thomas Weld Blundell's ambitious plan had no takers.

But Birkdale was ripe for development. The railway company's half-yearly receipts amounted to nearly five thousand pounds, running expenses were less than three thousand, leaving a far healthier surplus than even the most optimistic shareholders had predicted. The Liverpool merchants could easily commute by rail from Birkdale and housing development began to look a much better prospect. Within a few years Birkdale was boasting residences which were claimed to be superior even to those in Southport.

In later years the Birkdale residents took great pride in their area. For several decades they had their own local government and because of this independence they wanted to identify with their own founder. They associated the birth of Birkdale Park with a builder called John Aughton who invested some of his own money to build the first houses there. John Aughton's life is less well known than that of William Sutton but, because of the importance to Birkdale, it is worth relating here.

John Aughton was not born locally but he did have strong local family connections and his father Richard was born at Churchtown in 1789. Richard was a younger son from a large family and he left Churchtown as a young man to find work as a joiner in Preston. It was there at the parish church that he married Margaret Pilkington in 1811 and his identity is proved beyond doubt by his marriage bond which describes him as a joiner aged 22 from North Meols. We next hear of Richard in the late 1830s when Sir Peter Hesketh Fleetwood, lord of the manor of both Rossall and North Meols, began to execute his ambitious plan for a new port on the mouth of the Wyre. The town of Fleetwood was to be connected with the manufacturing area around Preston by means of a railway.

In 1850 we find that the son, John Aughton, had moved from Preston to Southport and in that year he took up one of Thomas Weld Blundell's leases and started to build in Birkdale Park. The first stones which he laid were said to be those of Lulworth House but there is a mystery surrounding this building for there is no record of its existence in the 1851 census.[5] Much better documented is Birkdale Lodge, the finest example of John Aughton's work, which was started in the same year.

John Aughton and his father both worked for the architect Decimus Burton during their time at Fleetwood, and the domestic architecture of Birkdale may therefore be said to be indirectly influenced by this London lansdcape architect. Cedric Greenwood describes some of the main features of the vernacular style:

> Not unnaturally, most of the houses John Aughton built in Birkdale are in the same style, although they are quite different in design and use segmental as well as Roman arches. And it seems that he − or his architect if he had one − unwittingly set a vernacular style of domestic architecture, for a great many of the houses built in Southport and Birkdale in the latter half of the nineteenth century have the same low roof, pediments, prominent

The wooden post-mill which ground the corn of Old Birkdale for several generations. The miller turned the whole mill to face into the wind by means of a great pole at the rear. The site was close to the Birkdale boundary, at the corner of Moseley Street and Upper Aughton Road. Peter Travis was the miller in 1845.
(Photo, Botanic Gardens Museum)

The Free Library and Town Hall, Birkdale. Birkdale retained its own local government until 1912 when it became part of Southport. It still retains a great deal of local pride and the loss of these fine civic buildings was one of the greatest local disasters in post-war planning.
(E.W. Collection)

Birkdale Lodge. This is the finest surviving example of John Aughton's work in Birkdale and is symbolic of the new residential Birkdale which first appears in the 1850s.
(Photo, C. Greenwood)

eaves, Roman and segmental arches and arched recesses that we see in
Birkdale Park. Because of this strong Italian influence, Gothic never got
a real hold on domestic architecture in Southport.[6]

Birkdale Lodge was one of the best examples of the vernacular
architecture. Greenwood gives us a detailed description:

> At first sight it looks like a Victorian Gothic villa but this is only because
> of the steep pitch of the spire on the tower. The hood mouldings, smartly
> picked out in black against the white walls, also smack of Gothic. But if
> the pitch of the spire was as low as the pitch of the roof, Birkdale Lodge
> would be a classical Italianate villa, what with its prominent overhanging
> eaves and forming pediments, its Roman arches and its shallow, arched
> recesses in the west wall . . .

> There is a surprise in store for anyone entering it for the first time. Right
> in the centre of the house is a great oak hall, like the hall of a Tudor mansion
> house, rising the full height of the house. It is panelled and half-timbered
> with a magnificent carved oak fireplace, stained glass windows on the
> staircase and a galleried landing. It's like the set for a period play: because
> of its central position in the house the doors of all the rooms open onto
> the hall. One door, in the corner of the hall, leads into a pleasant cast-iron
> and glass conservatory . . .

The builder was, on his own admission, a restless spirit and in 1854,
when he had built up an excellent local reputation, he was persuaded by
Samuel Bidder to leave Birkdale for Canada and to undertake a contract
on the Grand Canadian Trunk Railway. On 6th February, James Hunt
and other of his friends organised a farewell dinner to be held at the
Victoria Hotel on the Southport Promenade. The Victorians certainly knew
how to give a send off — the festivities began in mid-afternoon and
continued until the small hours of the morning. There were speeches,
toasts, dinner, a presentation, and a party of glee singers to provide
entertainment. The *Southport Visiter,* which had grown substantially in
the first ten years of its existence, had become a paper with excellent
coverage of local events; the proceedings and the speeches were reported
with admirable Victorian thoroughness. John Aughton and his wife were
presented with a silver tea service and he was obliged to stand and make
a speech.

> I came to Southport, as Mr Hunt justly observed, about four years ago.
> I had capital to invest somewhere. I did not desire to travel far from my
> native town or the sphere of my childhood. I came here on the earnest
> solicitations of one individual by whom it was no doubt intended that I
> should serve some party purpose, which I have ever been opposed to. That
> individual is not here tonight and his absence, I assure you, gives me greater
> pleasure than his presence.[7]

We are not told the name of the politically motivated individual, but
everybody present seemed to be in on the secret, for this part of the speech
was greeted with loud laughter.

> This testimonial comes from parties, all of whom at that time I was totally
> ignorant of, which speaks tenfold in my breast towards you, gentlemen,
> who subscribed towards it. (Cheering) Those whom I did expect to be my
> friends when I came, have proved not so; and I am not afraid to tell them
> so. Their promises have remained unfulfilled, their professed friendship
> illusory and inconstant, and why I speak of it thus publicly is to show that
> many whom you may look on as friends may not always prove so . . .

> I have said that I came to make an investment of capital, I began at
> Southport, and a short time afterwards I threw my efforts into the
> neighbouring village or town of Birkdale. You have there before you
> monuments of what my intentions were — to do good to both this place
> and that. In doing good to Birkdale I felt I was doing good to Southport,
> and if that should prove to be the case, I can only say that my best wishes
> have been realised to the greatest extent. There is no doubt that sometime
> Southport and Birkdale will become one important town — that they will
> form one of the first watering places in the country.

The amalgamation of the two towns was evidently a topic under
discussion and, because of their very close proximity, it remained a topic

for discussion long after this time, but Birkdale resisted takeover by Southport until well into the twentieth century.

> The truth is that I never gathered much by stopping at home. What money I have made has been by leaving home especially under the auspices of the esteemed friend (Mr Bidder) whom I am now going to join in Canada. The very man who first invited me to leave my native town, and whose inducements and promises were fully and satisfactorily fulfilled . . .
>
> I can assure you that nothing will give me greater pleasure when leaving the world than to hand it (the tea service) down to my children to show that their father in Southport was thought worthy to receive so handsome a tribute at your hands . . .

The vice chairman, Mr James Hunt, who was the proprieter of the Scarisbrick Hotel on Lord Street, then proposed the health of Mrs John Aughton and the Lancashire Witches — this was evidently a family joke and was greeted with loud cheering. The toast was followed by a party of glee singers led by a distant cousin Linnaeus* who gave a rendering of *Non Nobis Domine,* and the chairman then proceeded to make his own speech:

> Thirteen or fourteen years ago, Mr Aughton and his father were connected with laying out and building another important town, that of Fleetwood on Wyre, and although that place had not turned out in the prosperous manner that had been anticipated, the time would come when it would take its place amongst the towns and cities of this country and perhaps Birkdale too would ultimately find a place on the map of England.

The speeches were followed by more toasts, sentiments and songs. The festivities continued into the night and in the small hours most of the company were still prolonging the occasion. When John Aughton left for the new world, one of his last sights in England was Brunel's iron steamship the *Great Britain* which was anchored in the mouth of the Mersey, but as he departed and watched his native coastline recede below the horizon, Birkdale had not seen the last of him.

The first *Southport Visiter* of 1857 contained an announcement of his arrival, complete with family, on Christmas Eve 1856 — a date which happened to be his eleventh wedding anniversary. According to the newspaper his wife Elizabeth and children had travelled over hundreds of miles of 'inhospitable and frozen regions' to join him in Canada where the railway was opening up new frontiers. With the press in full attendance and with full masonic ceremonies Elizabeth laid the foundation stone of their new home; it was in the road named after him. After this ceremony some Victorian drawing room entertainment was provided which included 'sweet tones of music from Miss Aughton, a promising young lady nearly deserting her teens'. (She was his daughter by an earlier marriage). We are left guessing as to whether his daughter was a singer, pianist, or other musical performer.

---

*Linnaeus was the son of Henry Aughton, one of the many North Meols weavers who had found alternative employment in Southport. Henry had become a well known donkey carriage driver and would entertain his clients with a commentary on every botanical specimen they met on their journey. He became an ardent admirer of the Linnaean system of classification, and insisted on naming his firstborn after the Swedish scientist. But young Linnaeus grew weary of following his father from sandhill to sandhill and was drawn away from the paths of pure science by the lure of the arts.

Chapter Twelve

An American Visitor

T was in the 1850s that the American writer Nathaniel Hawthorne was appointed American Consul in Liverpool. When his wife Sophia and his three children arrived from America to join him he acquired lodgings with Miss Bramwell at Brunswick Terrace on the Southport Promenade. He described his landlady as a 'tall, thin, muscular, dark, shrewd and shabby looking mistress' (shabby was his favourite adjective); she charged him ten and ninepence for each bed and twelve and sixpence for the parlour, with the option of a better parlour at the weekend.

Hawthorne's *English Notebooks* are a valuable record of the English scene in the 1850s. He had a sharp eye for detail and was often able to see faults which the English were unable to see in themselves. His attitude implies that he must have read Mrs Trollop's snobbish account of America, a handy little volume which introduced a new word into the American language and which probably did more than the war of 1812 to harm Anglo-American relationships.

Like all good Americans, Nathanial Hawthorne expected England to be populated mainly by the peerage and, on reading through the list of arrivals in the *Southport Visiter,* he was disappointed to find them mostly of the middle classes, with the name of only one nobleman and three baronets listed. His longing to meet the aristocracy did not seem to correlate with his opinion of the Royal Family. Miss Bramwell had patriotically attempted to brighten up the living room with a pair of coloured prints, one of Queen Victoria and the other of her beloved Albert. Nathaniel examined his new quarters critically:

> I suppose our parlor deserves description, as a fair specimen of what lodging-house parlors generally are, in England. Fifteen feet square, covered with an old carpet, which has a patched covering of drugget in the middle; a square center-table; half a dozen chairs, two of which purport to be easy-chairs, but turn out not to be hospitable or kindly, when you sit down in them; a sofa, shabby and not very soft, but long and broad, and good to recline upon; a beaufet, in which we keep some of our household affairs, and a little bit of cupboard, in which we put our bottle of wine, both under lock and key. On the mantle-piece are two little glass vases, and over it a looking glass (not flattering to the in-looker); and above hangs a colored view of some lake, or seashore; and, on each side, a cheap colored print of Prince Albert, and one of Queen Victoria; and really I have seen no picture, bust or statue of Her Majesty, which I feel so certain to be as good a likeness, as this cheap print. You see the whole line of Guelphs in it — fair haired, blue-eyed, shallow-brained, common-place, yet with a simple kind of

heartiness and truth, that makes one somewhat good-natured towards them.[1]

His brilliant description of the Southport Promenade in high summer captures the seaside atmosphere from the 1850s in a way which has seldom been equalled. The sting in the tail is pure Hawthorne:

> The town has its amusements; in the first place, the day long and perennial one of donkey-riding along the sands, large parties of men and girls pottering along together; the Flying Dutchman (a great clumsy boat on wheels) trundles hither and thither, when there is breeze enough; an archery man sets up his targets on the beach; the bathing houses stand by scores and fifties along the shore and likewise on the bank of the Ribble, a mile to seaward; the hotels have their billiard rooms; there is a theatre every evening; from morn till night, comes a succession of organ grinders playing interminably under your window; a man with a bassoon, and a monkey, who takes your pennies and pulls off his cap in acknowledgement; and wandering minstrels, with guitar and voice; and a highland bagpiper, squealing out a tangled skein of discord, together with a highland maid who dances a hornpipe; and a Punch and Judy show; in a word, we have specimens of all manner of vagrancy that infest England.

> In these long days, and warm and pleasant ones, the promenade is at its liveliest at about nine o'clock, which is but just after sundown; and our Rosebud [his little daughter] finds it difficult to go to sleep amid so much music as comes to her ears from bassoon, bag-pipe, organ, guitar, and now and then a military band.

Some of Hawthorne's frustration was understandable when we realise that he wanted to see the great cathedrals, the Shakespeare country, the capital and the historic towns which were too distant to be of easy access when his job held him to one location. He was obviously unfortunate to choose lodgings in the noisiest part of Southport but he made no attempt to move and Sophia Hawthorne and the children seemed happy enough with their dark shrewd landlady. In October, when the holiday season ended, little Rosebud no longer had the distractions to keep her awake

A photograph, of the Flying Dutchman, taken in the 1870s outside Victoria Baths. Sand-yachts first appeared in the 1840s and came into their own on the open beach. The early sand yachts were clumsy and difficult to manoeuvre; in fact they were banned after one of them collided with a bathing machine and a child was killed. They were eventually reinstated in 1852.
(E.W. Collection)

at night and they had the house to themselves. Hawthorne commuted daily to Liverpool and the family stayed on through November and December. When Christmas came some local children arrived at his door to wassail him this was something unexpected which he seems to have enjoyed, but he did not record any details which might throw some light on any local variations of this very old Anglo-Saxon custom. On the night of 18th of February (1857), something quite unexpected happened. The house was burgled!

It might be expected that he would be very annoyed at this turn of events, but Nathaniel Hawthorne was a very complex character and he privately admitted that he was very amused by the incident. It did, after all, confirm his opinion that England was infested with all kinds of vagrancy! He described how he reported the robbery to the police. The police station was situated in the basement of the chaste, white Town Hall, newly built on Lord Street.

> We gave information to the Police; and an inspector and a constable soon came to make investigations, making a list of the missing articles, and informing themselves as to all the particulars that could be known. I did not expect ever to hear any more of the stolen property; but, on Sunday, a constable came to request my presence at the Police-Office, to identify some stolen property. The thieves had been caught in Liverpool, and some of the property found upon them. The Police Office is a small, dark room, in the basement storey of the Town Hall of Southport; and over the mantlepiece, hanging one upon the other, there are innumerable advertisements of robberies in houses, or on the highway — murders too, I suppose — garrotings, and offences of all sorts; not only in this district but wide away, and forwarded from other police stations. Being thus aggregated, one realises that there are a great many more offences than the public generally takes note. Most of the advertisements were in pen and ink, with minute lists of the articles stolen, but the more important ones were in print; and there, too, I saw printed advertisements of our own robbery, not for public circulation, but to be handed out privately among police-officers and pawn-brokers.

He goes on to give the police force a back-handed compliment and follows with some interesting comments about Peel's custodians of law and order. He is secretly impressed with the police force, to such an extent that at one stage he even drops his guard and refers to '*our* Southport inspector':

> A rogue has a very poor chance in England, the police being so numerous and their system so well organised.

> In a corner of the police-office stood a contrivance for precisely measuring

The Town Hall was designed by the architect Thomas Withnell and the foundation stone was laid in 1852. This very early view shows the original layout of the entrance steps and the gardens in front of the building. The entrance to the police court was on the extreme left. The gun is a Russian 18 pounder from the Crimean War; it was later moved to Hesketh Park where it remained until 1940 when it was melted down for scrap as part of the war effort.
(Botanic Gardens Museum)

the height of prisoners; and I took occasion to measure Julian [his son], and found him four feet, seven and a half inches high. A set of rules for the self-government of police-officers was nailed or pasted on the door, between twenty and thirty in number, and composing a system of constabulary ethics. The rules would be good for men in almost any walk of life; and I rather think the police officers conform to them with tolerable strictness. They appear to be subordinated to one another on the military plan; the ordinary constable does not sit down in the presence of an Inspector, and this latter seems to be half a gentleman; – at least such is the bearing of our Southport inspector, who wears a handsome uniform of green and silver, and salutes the principal inhabitants, on meeting them in the street, with an air of something like equality . . .

A few days later the thieves were brought before the magistrates in the Town Hall. The court room was crowded with people who had come to witness the drama. Nathaniel Hawthorne was present to observe this carriage of English justice but he was not required to give evidence. Also present was Miss Bramwell wearing a bright new crimson bonnet with a pointed pheasant feather at the side[2] (an item from the newspaper which clashes sharply with the American's shabby description of his landlady).

The accused were two brothers called James and John MacDonald. They were referred to as 'prisoner James' and 'prisoner John' to avoid confusion. They had tried to pawn Hawthorne's coat in Liverpool and had been apprehended with most of the stolen goods still upon them. In fact, one of them was still wearing the American's boots, yet they protested their innocence and were quite unabashed by the growing mountain of evidence which accumulated against them. Hawthorne described them as two young men, seemingly not much over twenty, terribly shabby, dirty, jail-bird like in appearance, but intelligent of aspect and one of them quite handsome. They were characters more out of Dickens than Hawthorne; judging by their sharp wit, they might have been the Artful Dodger and Sam Weller. They were already well known to the police.

The stolen goods were produced. In addition to the coat and the boots there was a rosewood box containing three pairs of gold earrings, a coloured feather fan, a bone painted fan, a bone needle case, a copper twopenny piece, a guard fastener in the shape of a hand, a large sized common pin, and a number of letters all from the same correspondent. Nothing, with the possible exception of the earrings, was of any great value.

A thimble and a pencil case were produced; they had been given to Mary Sumner, one of the housemaids,[3] by Mrs Hawthorne – a fact which makes us suspect that Sophia Hawthorne was a better ambassador than her husband. Mary Sumner described what she remembered about the night of the robbery. On the night of the 18th of February she locked the door of the front hall and the side door as usual. At about four in the morning she had heard a rummaging noise in the lower part of the house – she decided to go as far as the top of the stairs to investigate but, hearing nothing more, she had gone back to bed again. She and Emily Hearne, a second housemaid, described the scene which they found in the morning. The kitchen door was wide open, all the drawers had been pulled out and the cupboard door was open, the whole room had been turned inside-out.

Little Rosebud's workbox had been ransacked and Sophia Hawthorne's workbox had been moved to a shelf near the door. The side window was found to be open with the centre bottom square of the sash broken, and the master's hat was found outside lying on the windowsill.

Mary Sumner recognised the thimble and the pencil case in the courtroom. On being questioned about it prisoner James glibly replied that he had bought a dozen thimbles for twopence-ha'penny each, and he had bought the pencil case for four shillings.

Emily Hearne recognised a plaid scarf which she had seen many times in the house. 'Oh yes. You may swear to a lamp post by seeing it many times, if you swear only by appearances', declared Prisoner James.

Peter Pickup, a greengrocer, was brought to give evidence. He recognised the two men because they had spoken to him asking after lodgings in the town. 'Did ye hear me speak', interjected one of the prisoners. 'Yes', replied the greengrocer. 'And your speech now betrays you'. 'Ye ought to be a philosopher to tell a man by his speech', came the ready response. George Bernard Shaw's Professor Higgins had been anticipated by about two generations.

At this the courtroom audience were beginning to enjoy the proceedings and they began to titter. The prisoner complained that it was a shame to make a laughing stock out of innocent men, and to make them stand in a degraded position for what 'they had honestly bought' — the magistrate gave him a caution. The prisoner recovered some of his composure and proceeded to entertain the court with a long tale about where he had bought the various articles found upon him. The boots which looked so much like Mr Hawthorne's had been bought for him in London by his sister who, it appears, was housekeeper to the Earl of Shrewsbury. He claimed that they could produce a respectable gentleman 'in the Protestant line' to prove that they were in bed when the burglary was committed. The Protestant gentleman could not be found and his sister had most inconveniently left for the continent six months previously and could not be contacted.

To the amusement of the courtroom audience, the brothers dug themselves deeper and deeper into the pit which they had created and they were committed for trial at the next Liverpool assizes. Nathanial Hawthorne enjoyed the proceedings as much as anybody but the rogues with their sharp wit and glib tongues had made an impression on him and he was characteristically moved to record that he 'rather wished them to escape'.

Nathaniel Hawthorne and his family remained at their lodgings on the promenade through the spring and into the summer. In July they departed by train to see the Art Treasures of Britain exhibition which was being staged in Manchester. The family remained in Manchester for about six weeks, after which time Nathaniel resigned the American Consulship in Liverpool.

In the 1850s the seaside holiday was undergoing rapid changes. In earlier days visitors had happily sailed in the fishing smacks to Lytham for a day's excursion, but by the time the second edition of Glazebrook appeared in 1826 the resort boasted seven pleasure boats, all capable of accommodating forty people. In 1835, Sir George Head described the scene when the pleasure boats loaded their patrons:

> To get some half dozen ladies on board was part of the day's adventure for as the tide was not yet sufficiently high it was indispensible that they should be carried in men's arms for some distance towards the boat. The young gentlemen of the party very gallantly proffered their assistance.

He tells us that the excursion cost sixpence. He obviously enjoyed the female company and after returning from Lytham he accompanied the ladies on a donkey ride to sample the fare at the Isle of Wight and the Ash Tree Inn at Birkdale.

In the 1840s boats plied to Blackpool, Liverpool and sometimes further afield. In 1850 a small wooden jetty was built by the fishermen and the pleasure of carrying the ladies out to the boats became a thing of the past. 'During the winter gales and high tides large portions of the jetty were generally carried away', wrote Bland. But visitors were drawn to it and would actually pay just to walk its length. 'A penny or halfpenny used to be charged to anyone not going by the boats for the privilege of walking upon its slippery planks'.

By this time pleasure steamers had appeared in many resorts and it was obvious that something more than a wooden jetty was required to keep

Southport Pier

outhport pier was not as early as the famous chain pier at Brighton or Telford's long wooden landing stage at Herne Bay, but historically it is as important as any pier in England. It has the strongest claim to be the first seaside pleasure pier, and it was the longest in the country for many years. By 1862 it boasted the first powered pier tramway with open 'knifeboard' seating and white-knuckled passengers were whisked from end to end in 3 minutes by a stationary engine. Nearly 130 years have passed since the pier was planned and a substantial length now never gets its feet wet, but inspired planning by our great grandparents ensures that the shore end never gets its feet dry.

Right - *The Promenade in 1864. An early view looking north, showing the first Victoria Baths, the original plain entrance to the pier (as it was in the 1860s before the Oriental style of pavilions became the fashion) and the Fernley drinking fountain.* (Engraving, Botanic Gardens Museum)

Below - *Holidaymakers with straw hats and parasoles outside the entrance to the pier; even the children are wearing hats. A picture taken soon after the opening of the Pier Pavilion in 1902.* (Valentine Collection, St. Andrews University Library)

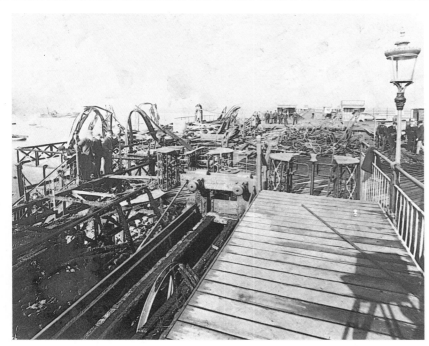

Left - *Surprisingly, perhaps, fire was a greater danger to the pier than storm damage. There were fires in 1897, 1933 and 1959. This picture shows the grotesque tangle of twisted iron girders and the charred planking after the fire of 1897.*
(Photo, Botanic Gardens Museum)

Centre left - *The pier train, the Belle, with driver Dick Ball in 1955.* *(E.W. Collection)*

Centre right - *A view of the pier extension in the late nineteenth century, showing a paddle steamer departing and a few promenaders taking the sea air.*
(St. Andrews University Library)

Bottom - *A panoramic view of the pier entrance showing the pier stretching to the horizon. The Marine Lakes, Pleasureland, Princes Park and the sea bathing lake can be seen in the background.*
(E.W. Collection)

Southport in the forefront of seaside development. In 1852 a committee was formed to promote a pier. The Pier Company, instigated by Samuel Boothroyd, was formed in 1859, and as visitors seemed to enjoy taking the air from a slippery and exposed wooden jetty, the pier was planned from the outset with the promenaders in mind. The first pile was driven on August 14th of that year.

James Brunlees, an experienced railway engineer, proved to be the right man for the design. The construction of the pier was by a novel method of 'jetting' which Brunlees perfected. This involved pumping water down a pipe to the foot of the pile, thus making the sand at the bottom fluid enough to rotate the pile and sink it. It was the best part of a year before the pier was completed, and the opening was considered a great event. The *Illustrated London News* showed a picture of the opening ceremony, with banners proclaiming 'Welcome Strangers' and 'Success to the Pier Company' strung to the flagpoles at the entrance, and surrounded by people in top hats, crinolenes, bonnets and parasoles. The programme for the opening day, which referred to the new attraction as The New Iron Pier, stated that several eminent scientific noblemen and gentlemen the mayors of the principal provincial towns had been invited to attend.

Local traders were asked to close shop on the great day, so that their employees could join in the procession. Music was provided by the band of the 3rd Royal Lancashire Militia and by the Fife and Drum Band of the 13th Lancashire Rifles. An opening address was delivered, the company sang three verses of God Save the Queen, and a first class steamer arrived from Liverpool.

The new iron pier was certainly something to be proud of — nothing quite like it had ever been seen before! Earlier piers existed in the south of England but they were designed purely on practical grounds to serve the shipping. Southport Pier, too, was very obviously constructed to serve the shipping, but it was also designed for promenading and pleasure purposes, and on this account it has the strongest claim to be the first pleasure pier in the country. It was also an incredible length of 1200 yards, and radical innovations like a pier tramway had therefore to be built to enable those with a willing spirit but weak in the flesh to reach the far end. The first pier tramway opened in May 1863 and ran right down the centre of the deck, greatly to the detriment of the promenaders. When the season was over the Pier Company decided to widen the deck and to rebuild the tramway at one side.[4]

The Pier Company had invested £8000 in their venture, and they were

Nine very imposing NCOs from the 13th Lancashire Rifle Volunteers find time to pose for a photograph in 1860. These veterans of the Crimean War could handle swords as well as rifles and it was their band which played at the opening of the new iron pier.
(Photo, Botanic Gardens Museum)

delighted with their financial success. Even Lord Street for a time took second place as young and old wanted to promenade along the pier. In November 1860 a dissatisfied customer wrote to the *Southport Visiter* complaining that the 'turnstiles are extremely inconvenient, for elderly ladies especially, the amplitude of dress rendering it impossible to pass through them without much unpleasantness.' Crinolenes and immensely wide skirts were still very much the fashion, but the Pier Company were on to such a good thing that the secretary was able to give the pompous reply that such ladies could buy tickets, valid for a month or more, which would allow them as contractors to use the gates instead of the turnstiles!

Other resorts quickly followed Southport, and the 1860s saw a great spate of pier building all around the coast. The piers grew pavilions, pagodas, some amazing and extravagant adornments and a whole architecture of their own. Things had moved on since the fishermen ferried the visitors across the Ribble. The age of the paddle ship had arrived and Southport Pier serviced these pleasure steamers for over sixty years.

An earlier scheme for a purely commercial pier fortunately came to nothing. It involved running a railway from Manchester right through the middle of the town and onto the pier, so that manufactured goods could be exported from Southport. The railway to Manchester did become a reality in 1855. The pomp and ceremony attached to the opening of this branch line was very typical of such an event in the mid-nineteenth century, and is therefore worthy of description.

At about one o'clock on Saturday the 7th of April, a gaily decorated train, heralded by detonating signals along the line and loaded with directors and officials of the railway, puffed briskly into the station. The train was greeted by the strains of the Churchtown Brass Band. Half an hour later it was followed by a longer train of fifteen carriages, carrying another four hundred invited guests who were obviously of inferior status to those on the earlier train. The railway company had inadvertently managed to offend many of the local socialites by not inviting them to the Director's Dinner. This was only one of their mistakes. Even worse was that they refused admission to the gentlemen of the press, so that many people who prided themselves on knowing everything of moment that happened in the town found themselves missing out on this latest action. A correspondent calling himself 'Veritas' referred to the event in very offended tones:

> A train arrived, its approach being intimated by some very modest reports of cannon − of the value of at least a shilling each. Some fat, well-fed, good sousy-looking directors stepped from the carriages, accompanied by some cormorant lawyers. They distributed themselves over the village to sharpen their appetites − they sat down cosily at an hotel − they ate − they drank − they spoke (I suppose) − they departed −doubtless taking with them the good wishes of the people of Southport.[5]

The train left for the return journey to 'vociferous cheering of crowds of persons who had congregated to see them off, and who seemed well satisfied with this, the only part they were allowed to take in the proceedings'. These were the ordinary mortals who had turned out *en masse* to witness the opening ceremony. When the train was leaving the station the locomotive gave an ungainly lurch and promptly left the rails. We are not told of the crowd's reaction to this latest piece of drama but they were evidently better pleased with the spectacle than the hungry social climbers who had not been invited to dinner.

Southport thus became directly connected by rail to the cotton towns of East Lancashire and for the first time it was an easy day trip for the millworkers to enjoy a day at this seaside resort. On the 7th of June in the same year, which happened to be Whit Week, the *Visiter* reported that 'The railways from the manufacturing districts poured in their thousands daily, who flowed through the streets in one vast living stream, and swarmed on the wide expanse of the shore like a newly disturbed ant-hill'.

The East Lancashire Railway claimed to have carried 22,120 arrivals and in the same week the Lancashire and Yorkshire Railway carried 19,235. The railway companies were delighted. Those engaged in the holiday trade were delighted. But not everybody was delighted with the massive influx of visitors. Those who had come to live in Southport did not quite know what to make of it all. The ratepayers of Birkdale Park increased their resolve not to merge with Southport. Ellen Weeton would have turned in her grave!

Before the advent of the railways, the seaside holiday was the privilege of a fortunate minority. Simply getting to the coast took time and money and, once there, the holidaymaker stayed for weeks, months, or sometimes for the whole season; some of them even decided to live there permanently. Southport began life as a seaside variant of the Regency Spa Town with elaborate bathing procedures, the Grand Promenade, galas and balls, whist and quadrille in the evenings. Partly through good planning and partly due to sheer good fortune, the legacy of the early days had given rise to Lord Street, which was rapidly becoming one of the finest thoroughfares in the kingdom.

But Nathaniel Hawthorne's picture of Southport in 1856 was radically different to Geoffrey Gimcrack's description written a generation earlier. In the middle of the nineteenth century the seaside holiday was in a great state of flux. The railway made the day trip possible and at much the same time the Victorian working classes had at last found their hard won freedom and were able to combine the excitement of a ride on the train with a day by the sea for themselves and their families.

The newcomers did not have their names recorded in the *Southport Visiter,* but it soon became apparent that there was money to be made from this new class of holidaymaker because of their sheer numbers, and Southport was in an excellent position to profit from it. Whit Week was

exceptional, but at the height of the season the number of visitors was quoted as between eight and ten thousand at a time when Blackpool could only muster between fifteen hundred and two thousand.[6]

In the first half of the century Blackpool had tried hard to emulate Southport as a middle-class resort but, even with the advantage of a much more accessible sea, Blackpool's efforts, without the wide streets and boulevards of its rival, met with little success. In the 1850s Blackpool recognised the potential of the working-class holiday, the resort abandoned its middle-class pretensions, and openly advertised Sea Bathing for the Working Classes.[7]

Following the success of the pier at Southport, Blackpool Pier was opened in 1863 with the object of providing 'greater promenading space of the most invigorating kind'. Blackpool's first pier (which became known as the North Pier when Central Pier opened in 1868) was a fine example of the early work of Eugenius Birch, and it brought a touch of style and decorum to the promenaders with their top hats and silk parasoles. The pier was a great success, but not quite in the way it had been envisaged; within a few years it was bursting at the seams with Lancashire millhands. Blackpool's first pier was the final attempt to emulate Southport, and the Fylde resort thereafter created its own unique seaside atmosphere.

Southport too profited greatly from the day trippers and many new attractions and amusements were provided, but Southport always put the traditional clientele first and only deigned to provide new amusements as long as the character of the town remained unchanged. Southport had a clear choice to make: to compete with Blackpool for the title of the most popular resort in the region, or to retain the title of the most fashionable resort in the north of England. Southport was still the North's most popular resort until late in the nineteenth century, but the days when the town could aspire to both these titles were numbered, and it soon became very evident that it was the fashionable title which was valued more highly.

Many in Lancashire had witnessed the influx of the Irish into Liverpool after the great potato famines of the 1840s, and they had seen areas like Everton and Kirkdale fall from fine residential areas to depressing slums in less than a decade. Southport's decision was based on pride rather than altruism, but Lancashire badly needed better residential areas, and with the advantage of hindsight we can now see that any other decision would have been a total disaster for the region as a whole.

Opposite
Top left - *The Prince of Wales Hotel was built in 1876/7 when the Union Hotel, which had been on that site since 1805, was demolished. It is one of the most impressive buildings on Lord Street and it became one of the first RAC approved hotels early this century.*
(Photo, C. Greenwood)
Top right - *When the Original Hotel was finally demolished in 1854 the licence was transferred to the Royal Hotel on the promenade. An extension was built in 1865 and it can be identified by the conical tower and the different architectural styles. The Royal Hotel is an excellent example of early Victorian architecture in Southport and its preservation has become all the more important since the demolition of the Victoria Hotel.*
(E.W. Collection)
Bottom left - *The Palace was the largest and finest hotel in Birkdale. It was opened with great ceremony in 1866, with Edward Bisserot as the first manager. It had a railway station and at one time even an aviation landing strip with regular flights to Blackpool. Sadly, the hotel was demolished in 1969.*
(E.W. Collection)
Bottom right - *The Victoria Hotel opened in 1842 and occupied a prime site on the promenade. John Salthouse was the first proprietor and he retained it for 20 years. A magnificent cast iron portico was added to the main entrance in 1903, but when the hotel was demolished in 1971 the portico had decayed so badly that local preservationists were unable to save it.*
(E.W. Collection)

Chapter Thirteen

Warriors of the Sea

HE stretch of coastline between the Mersey and the Ribble appears harmless enough to the eyes of the landsman. There are no cliffs, no islands, no jagged rocks to tear the bottom out of a vessel, nothing but soft yellow sand. Yet, in the proud heyday of sail, there was a time when it claimed as many victims as virtually any stretch of coastline in the British Isles.

The reasons were threefold. Firstly, it was a westerly shore, with prevailing winds always driving the ships onto the sands. Secondly, hidden under the shallow waters were treacherous sandbanks which acquired names like Burbo, Packington, and Mad Wharf. Thirdly, the ever growing volume of shipping in and out of the Mersey made it one of the world's busiest sea routes. Vessels from all over the globe, many of which were navigating in unknown waters, tried to negotiate the treacherous Formby Channel to gain the safety of the Mersey estuary. It was an easy enough task in fine weather with daylight, a pilot boat, and buoys to mark the channel, but at night with a storm brewing, using outdated and badly copied charts and with visibility down to a few yards it was an entirely different matter. As early as 1776 the Port of Liverpool financed a boat at Formby Point for the purpose of assisting vessels in distress, a move which gives Formby a claim to be Britain's first lifeboat station.[1]

In the eighteenth century and well into the nineteenth, the shipping magnates in Liverpool had little respect for the natives of their neighbouring coastal parishes. They were all branded as smugglers and wreckers – and not without just cause. There is no evidence in North Meols of the practice of setting false lights deliberately to mislead a ship but the smuggling was indisputable, and it was true enough that if any vessel was unfortunate enough to be stranded on the coast of North Meols then the natives would pick it clean of anything of value within an astonishingly short time – even a mast or a spar would end up as the ridgepole of a farm labourer's cottage.

When the *Ann E Hooper* of Baltimore was wrecked in 1862, about 1500 barrels of flour were washed ashore and saved, but an equal number of damaged barrels remained on the beach. Local people wanted the dry flour in the centre of the barrels but the wreck officers prevented them from taking it. 'Tobacco, bacon, and clockworks might have been found in all quarters', wrote Bland. 'The tobacco was consumed, but the bacon went bad through being buried in the sand whilst wet. Twenty-five years after clockworks could have been found in the thatch of old cottages in Birkdale.'

Thomas Glazebrook published a list of 48 vessels wrecked and 43 vessels 'saved' off the North Meols coast, covering the period between 1790 and 1824. The list was compiled by Thomas Jackson, Richard Ball and Peter Ball who put their heads together and pooled their memories; it is, therefore, unlikely to be complete.

The fishermen always kept an eye open for vessels in distress and they knew well enough if one of them was in danger of striking a sandbank. They were always prepared to give assistance but they expected to be rewarded for their efforts. In 1811 a Portuguese brig from Lisbon was in distress. She fired her guns all morning and hoisted a jack calling for a pilot to help her. Thomas Jackson, who was the pilot, answered the call. He informed the captain of their whereabouts and gave him sailing instructions. The Portuguese captain hoved round and sailed off leaving a very dismayed Thomas Jackson staring after him – he made off 'without making the boatman the slightest remuneration.'

Other interesting entries include the loss of some of the Duke of Wellington's supplies for the Peninsular Wars:

1810: A brig, laden with provisions for the army in Spain. Vessel totally lost. One man drowned, the rest saved. this was a dreadful case. One of the Southport boatmen was drowned. Pilot Jackson and two others clung to the mast which fell overboard, and their preservation was miraculous.

1814: The ship TOM. General cargoe, machinery etc., for Demerera. Vessel totally lost. Fourteen of the crew saved: - four saved on a raft on which all had got. It sunk, when the fourteen above named were taken up by the Southport boatman, and rescued from their perilous situation.

1823: A brigatine. The MORNING STAR, owner Mr Taylor, from Africa to Liverpool. Laden with elephant's teeth, gold dust, beeswax, etc. Struck on the banks, was taken first to Lytham and afterwards to Liverpool.

Some of Glazebrook's entries provide sufficient action for a whole 'Boy's Own' story:

1822: The brig WILLIAM, stuck on the banks. Was got off and piloted to Liverpool. She had been a pirate vessel, and was taken to Malta where the crew suffered. They had scuttled the brig ANN at sea, staved their boats, took their compasses, and nailed the hatches on the crew, whom they had placed in the forecastle. A cook's axe having been accidently left below, the crew forced the hatches open, repaired one of their boats with canvas, and escaped.

In 1816 a Marine Fund was set up to try to provide a lifeboat and a boat was actually purchased but it proved to be so unseaworthy that the boatmen refused to put to sea in it even on a calm day. Rescues continued to be made on a private enterprise system by the local fishermen until 1840 when a new fund was established and a lifeboat again purchased. The new lifeboat was constructed along the lines of a whaling ship; it was named the *Rescue,* and Richard Rimmer was the first coxwain. Lieutenant H. G. Kellock was appointed to take charge of the lifeboat operations. Kellock was an excellent man for the job; he was a veteran of Nelson's navy and had served aboard the *Royal Sovereign,* she of a hundred guns, the sister ship of the *Victory* which led the lee column into battle at Trafalgar.

Another ex-naval man who had served on a British man o' war joined the lifeboat crew and became coxwain in 1846. He was William Rockliffe and one of his earliest actions was described by Lt. Kellock in a letter to Lloyds head office in London:[2]

22 Nov 1846
At daylight yesterday we discovered a vessel sunk at the break of the Horse-bank with a signal of distress flying, at the time blowing hard from the S W with a heavy sea. At 11.30 am we succeeded in floating our boat. She crossed the Horse-bank through a very rough sea and at 12.45 reached the mast, then about nine feet above the water, and found the master wrapped in the gaff-topsail, very much exhausted; they succeeded in taking him off, and landed safe about 2.30pm, when I found that the crew, too, had broken

Southport lifeboatman John Jackson, wearing his cork life jacket, probably photographed after the Mexico disaster of 1886.
(Photo, Botanic Gardens Museum)

Above - *William Rockliffe served in the Navy on a British Man o' War. He was one of the most respected of the Southport lifeboatmen and a very popular character. During his career as coxwain from 1846 to 1873 he helped save no fewer than 367 lives and many vessels.*
(Photo, Botanic Gardens Museum)

Above right - *William Rockliffe's cottage in Eastbank Street, Southport, in 1850. These cottages occupied the present site of the fish market. Rockliffe was also the District Receiver of Wreck and the green in front of the houses was often cluttered with wreckage. The seagull in the picture frightened off both children and adults who dared to enter the garden.*
(E.W. Collection)

adrift from her in their own boat, the sea being so heavy they could not regain the vessel. I had much doubt as to their safety.

At 9pm I despatched the lifeboat to find if they had landed on the Lytham side, which they did, to the great astonishment of all in this place, and our boat brought the two men here today at 2.30pm through the heaviest sea I have ever seen a boat afloat in on this coast. About twenty minutes before landing, to give you an idea of the weather, her tug-sail, a small one, single reefed, blew nearly out of the bolt-rope, so much shattered that it is past repair. I assure you that the conduct of the crew is such that justly merits a handsome reward, and my best endeavours shall be used to obtain it for them.

Kellock seems to have missed out a key point. From his letter it seems that there was no reason for the boat to leave Lytham in the heaviest seas he had ever seen navigated on this coast. But the competence of William Rockliffe was beyond dispute; he was coxwain for 27 years, during which time he saved many lives and never lost a single crew member. Local pride in the lifeboat ran high and the newspapers usually gave good and accurate coverage to the rescues, but the Southport lifeboat was not the only one serving the area and it was not uncommon for the Lytham boat to get to a ship first and steal the honours. Pride would not allow the editor of the *Southport Visiter* to admit that Lytham too had a fine lifeboat crew and in 1859 the newspaper criticised William Rockliffe for not reaching a vessel in distress before the Lytham lifeboat. The coxwain was justly annoyed with the editor's comments and wrote to the newspaper:

Dear Sir,
Having seen in the SOUTHPORT VISITER, for December 22nd and 29th, statements respecting the Lifeboat, in which you express a desire for better information and ask certain questions, I have pleasure in giving you the following. In the Visiter of the 22nd you state that on Tuesday a vessel was seen in distress on the Horse-bank, but for some reason or other those in charge of the lifeboat obtained no definite information respecting her, and that on Wednesday morning the Lytham boat was launched and succeeded in saving the poor fellows. I beg to say that on Tuesday we boarded the above vessel and the same day sent a telegraph message to Liverpool, stating that the schooner Pilgrim, laden with turnips, was sunk off Southport abandoned by her crew. In the Southport Visiter of the 29th, after mentioning the rescue by the Lytham lifeboat of a ship's crew, the statement: – 'The Southport crew are never reported as accomplishing the same results.' I beg to state in reply to this grave charge, that the Southport crew have been the means of saving upwards of 200 lives, many instances of which have appeared in the columns of the Visiter, and for the above services I have been awarded the Medal of the R.N.L.I. for the preservation of life from shipwreck.

The only other statement that I wish to reply to is 'that vessels one after another have been in distress, and the Southport boat has been inactive or unsuccessful.' Justice requires me to say that no crew has been in distress off Southport but that every exertion has been made to rescue them by the

The crew of the ill-fated Eliza
Fernley pose smartly with their
oars at the vertical.
(Photo, Botanic Gardens Museum)

volunteer crews of the lifeboat, often in peril of their lives, and every such
effort has been successful. In closing I desire to say that no information
was asked of me respecting the above, but whenever such information is
asked for I shall be most happy to give it.

Signed, Wm. Rockliffe.

It appears from this letter that the newspaper did not even attempt to find
out the facts before decrying the efforts of the lifeboatmen and the editor
eventually had to apologise. Honours between the Southport and Lytham
lifeboats ran about even; the Lytham boat nearly always had more water
to cover but she could usually make good headway under sail and
eventually the Lytham boat was launched with the aid of a steam tug.
At Southport launching was a problem because of the shallow shore and
the lifeboat was usually drawn along the beach on its carriage by a team
of horses and launched at the nearest point to the distressed vessel. The
horses baulked and shied away from the breakers, and launching into a
breaking sea was a difficult operation. Once in the water it was usually
necessary to row the whole distance into the wind.

In 1863 Rockliffe was the coxwain of the *Jessie Knowles* when she went
to the assistance of the Norwegian barque *Tamworth,* bound from
Liverpool to Havannah with coal, salt and ironmongery. The crew of
seventeen were rescued. The King of Sweden and Norway sent the lifeboat
men two pounds each and awarded William Rockliffe the 'silver medal
of civic achievements'.

Another fine rescue was in 1873 when a French brig called *Zoe* was
wrecked on the horsebank. On this occasion it appears that the regular
lifeboat was being serviced and a boat called the *Marco Polo* went to the
rescue. The Frenchmen were seen struggling to get away in a small boat
of their own and when the *Marco Polo* threw them a hawser they refused
to accept it thinking they were under attack by pirates! The rescuers turned
for home, but the confused sailors shouted for them to come back again.
It was fortunate that they did, since shortly afterwards the *Zoe* sank to
the bottom and only the French ensign at the masthead remained visible.
She broke into pieces on the next tide.

There was one occasion when William Rockliffe refused to launch the
lifeboat. The date was 28th September 1873 when the *Nazerine,* which
had apparently been fighting against heavy seas for six days to get out
of Liverpool, was grounded on the Burbo bank. Knowing that she was
in distress the New Brighton and Liverpool lifeboats were launched but
the weather was so bad they couldn't even find the *Nazerine.* The Formby
lifeboat was launched but the sea was so ferocious that it could make no

headway at all. William Rockliffe, for the only time in his life, declared that it was impossible to reach the vessel and refused to risk his crew. All sixteen of the crew of the *Nazerine* were drowned and three exhaustive enquiries followed. Rockliffe's decision must have been the most difficult he had ever made, but after the enquiries it was found to be fully justified.

The lifeboat always figured prominently in the processions and pageantry which the Victorians loved so much. Mrs Catherine Winters, an Irish barrister and writer, described one such occasion when the excuse for the procession was the re-opening of the Victoria Baths on the Promenade. The appearance of the lifeboat *Jessie Knowles* was heralded by the band of the Lancashire Hussars, the Bacup Prize Band, the Band of the Boy's Refuge, and the Dewsbury Prize Band. A hot-air balloon ascended from the sands, then the *Jessie Knowles* was ceremoniously launched from the vicinity of the pier. A large and enthusiastic July crowd packed the Promenade which was one bright display of flags and banners. The President of the Southport branch of the Lifeboat Association was Lord Skelmersdale. He was noted in the evening for his great gallantry when, 'to make himself agreeable, [he] not only danced with everyone, but with every one twice over, as gentlemen were scarce.'[3]

A privileged family watches the lifeboat approaching London Square from Lord Street at about the turn of the century. The spire of Christ Church and the clock tower of the Cambridge Hall can clearly be seen beyond the trees.
(Botanic Gardens Museum)

A wreck washed up on Southport beach - testimony to the treacherous nature of that apparently harmless coastline.
(E.W. Collection)

In its lifeboat history Southport had only seven boats and six coxwains before the R.N.L.I. closed down the lifeboat station in 1926. Many must have known all seven of the boats and all the coxwains. In 86 years nearly four hundred lives were saved:[4]

	LIFEBOAT	LIVES SAVED
1840	*The Rescue*	176
1861	*Jessie Knowles*	80
1875	*Eliza Fernley*	46
1886	*Mary Anna*	7
1888	*Edith and Annie*	12
1902	*Three Brothers*	(No record)
1904	*John Harling*	at least 63

COXWAINS
Richard Rimmer 1840-46
William Rockliffe 1846-73
Charles Hodge 1873-86
William Robinson 1887-99
Richard Robinson 1899-1920
Richard Wright 1920- 25

C. HODGE. Coxwain.

A cameo photograph of Charles Hodge who was coxwain of the Eliza Fernley when she was lost during the rescue of the Mexico.
(E.W. Collection)

There were some occasions when lives were lost and the lifeboat was unable to render any assistance. In 1848 fourteen bodies were washed ashore from a vessel called the *Ocean Monarch* which had caught fire out at sea. The number of local catastrophies, too, was very high and indicates the degree of danger to which fishermen were subjected in the normal course of earning their livings. Bland records several fishermen drowned in 1833 when the Rev. William Alexander adopted one of the fishermen's orphaned daughters; in 1849 the fishing boat *New Ann* was run down at sea, three men and a boy were drowned; and in 1851 Richard Alty and Peter Rimmer died when their boat, the *Joseph and Mary,* was wrecked. The townspeople on every occasion raised a subscription for dependent relatives.

In January 1869 a local catastrophe occurred when seven shrimpers were

A striking painting of the Mexico, showing the barque grounded on Birkdale beach in 1886, with only her mizzen mast standing. Stores are being unloaded before the attempt was made to refloat her.
(Botanic Gardens Museum)

drowned. The shrimpers worked from horse drawn carts at low tide and on this occasion they were caught by a very sudden and dense fog. They were unable to sit out the fog as a fishing boat might have done, and in trying to regain the shore they lost all sense of direction and were caught by the incoming tide. There was little the lifeboat could have done on this occasion and a fog bell was erected at Marshside to try and prevent a similar catastrophe from happening again. The following year saw another similar accident when Edward Hunt was drowned in a fog whilst shrimping, but generally speaking the fog bell did serve the purpose for which it was designed.

On the ninth of December 1886 a ball was in progress in the Town Hall when the proceedings were hushed by the boom of the lifeboat gun. All the town knew that somewhere out to sea there was a vessel in distress. The ship was an iron barque called the *Mexico*. She had been built on the Tyne shipyards at Sunderland but belonged to the Port of Hamburg; after leaving Liverpool the heavy seas had driven her towards the coast and she had floundered on a sandbank between Spencer's Brow and the Horse Bank.

The night was very rough and cold, with a gale blowing from the south-west and registering force seven on the Beaufort scale. There were frequent squalls of rain which, according to some reports, were accompanied by outbursts of hail. It was a dark, cold and miserable night on which to put out to sea, but three lifeboats answered the *Mexico's* distress call. The first to launch was the Lytham boat, the *Charles Biggs* which took to the water at 10pm. She was a new lifeboat incorporating some of the latest design technology; the crew had spent two weeks in practice but this was her first call in anger. 'The sea ran mountains high and the breaking water was fearful', said William Clarkson, the Lytham cox, describing the scene as they got underway.

For a time they lost sight of the lights of the *Mexico* altogether but, after pulling at the oars for a mile and a half, they managed to set a sail and to find their bearings again. It took them a further two hours to reach the *Mexico*. As they got nearer they had to get the sail down and make the final approach with the oars. A tremendous sea caught the boat with such force that four of the oars were broken, but the *Charles Biggs* stuck to her task and managed to heave to at the fore side of the mizzen mast. One of the crewmen threw a lifeline to the *Mexico*.

The crew had assembled near the mizzen mast where they had lashed themselves to the rigging. The captain of the *Mexico* threw down a box about a foot square, but it missed the boat altogether and he let out a great oath shouting 'There go the ship's papers'. Then came a heavy swell which broke the line. The lifeboat crew managed to get a second line aboard. The first of the *Mexico's* crew slipped down the rope as the ship began to sink. One poor sailor fell between the ship and the lifeboat and was nearly crushed to death, but luckily a second crewman caught him by the legs. A third crewman jumped and landed safely in the lifeboat. The line broke again. A third line was thrown and secured with difficulty. A crew member jumped and landed painfully across the oarlocks. Then came the mate, and finally the captain with the rope tied round his waist. The lifeboat turned for home.[5]

Lytham was not without its lifeboat tragedies and the disaster of 1852 was still remembered when eight men drowned in practice as the lifeboat capsized, but the *Mexico* was a fine rescue and the *Charles Biggs* had proudly accomplished her first mission. As she made back for home the crew saw no signs of any other lifeboats in the area.

At St Annes the launching was a similar scene to the one at Lytham. A crowd had assembled to see the lifeboat on its way. She was the *Laura Janet,* built in 1881. The cox, William Johnson, had been suffering from consumption but there was no question in his mind of not answering the distress call. The *Laura Janet* was launched at about 10.25pm and proceeded under oars for about five hundred yards before making sail and crossing the Salthouse Bank where only the previous week she had rescued the crew of the steamer *Yan Yean*. Fishermen's wives and kin watched her as long as they could, straining their eyes out to sea as she made to cross the Ribble estuary. She disappeared in the darkness but they still waited in the hope of a last glimpse. Then a freak gap appeared in the clouds and the *Laura Janet* could be seen well on her way, illuminated by a cold beam of white moonlight, slowly tossing and dipping in the waves far out to sea. The cloud cover formed again and that was the last they saw of her. They waited.

At Southport the distress signals were seen at about 9.30 pm and the crew was assembled by ten o'clock. Doctor Pilkington rushed out from the town hall to join the crew, but he was too late and by the time he arrived the boat was already overmanned. A crowd ran down to the beach as the lifeboat *Eliza Fernley,* with its carriage wheels churning the wet sand, was hauled along by a team of straining shire horses. They were whipped into a clumsy gallop along the beach for three or four miles, and in the howling wind and the dark of the night the lifeboat crew were followed by a running stream of humanity — wives, sweethearts, neighbours, friends, children, young boys whose only ambition was to be in the lifeboat crew when they grew up, and a couple of excited barking dogs.

The lifeboat was launched with difficulty into the teeth of the gale. The tide was at half ebb and the breakers were enormous. The frightened horses reared up and shied away from the breakers. The onlookers cheered and the lifeboat crew cheered back as the *Eliza Fernley* got under way. All they could see of the *Mexico* was a faint lantern on her mizzen mast; the mainmast and the foremast had been carried away by the storm. For more than two long hours the crew strained at the oars through the heavy seas. They were beaten back so many times that it was one o'clock in the morning and they were close to exhaustion before getting anywhere near the stricken barque. At last the *Eliza Fernley* gained a position thirty yards to the west of the starboard bow. At this moment the rowers caught a glimpse of the St Anne's lifeboat on the other side of the vessel, travelling under sail at a great speed, but further out to sea. This convinced them that they were the first to reach the *Mexico.*

'Get the anchor right', yelled Charles Hodge, the coxwain, above the storm. They were now so near that one of the Jackson brothers made ready to throw a line and the cox prepared to turn the lifeboat broadside on for the final approach. Just as the *Eliza Fernley* was turning a huge wave began to appear from the sea. It continued to rise and rise until it became an horrific towering wall of falling water glinting grey green in the light of the lanterns. It was what the seamen called a green-back advancing towards them. The wall of water caught the lifeboat in the worst possible position, broadside on just as she was turning. The gigantic wave sucked the boat sideways into itself and carried her right over. The next thing the crew were aware of was that their lifeboat had capsized and they were clinging for life to an upturned boat in the cold December seas, caught in the mountainous breakers and the fiercest storm for a generation.

'A great green-back struck the *Eliza Fernley* at the quarter, with the force of a rock', said Henry Robinson. 'You'd a' thought a mountain had thrown itself at you. The boat capsized like a cork'. Some were trapped under the boat, others clutched desperately for the oars and the gunwales. John Jackson described his predicament:

After capsizing I found myself in the water, having fast hold of an oar.
Me and Richard Robinson got hold of the oar. The oar was fast to the boat.
I managed to get hold of the lifeline. Sometimes I was at the bottom of
the boat, sometimes alongside, and sometimes the sea washed me underneath.
I had my belt on. After capsizing I found Richard Robinson and his brother

Henry Robinson (1860-1938) was a survivor of the Mexico disaster and he lived to recount his memories fifty years after the event. He always maintained that if only the circumstances had been known sooner many more lives would have been saved.

(Photo, Botanic Gardens Museum)

ELIZA FERNLEY

Charles Hodge (60) Cox
Ralph Peters (60)
John Ball (27)
Henry Hodge (43)
Peter Jackson (52)
Thomas Jackson (27)
Benjamin Peters (24)
Harry Rigby (27)
Thomas Rigby (62)
Timothy Rigby (27)
John Robinson (18)
Richard Robinson (25)
Thomas Spencer (48)
Peter Wright (24)

Survivors:
Henry Robinson
John Jackson

John along side me. The boat lay like a log. It had capsized in three fathoms of water. Her side rose once as the sea left her, but she came down again bottom upwards.

The lanterns had gone out, the men could not see each other properly in the darkness and they could only communicate by shouting loudly above the noise of the storm. John Jackson heard voices and banged on the side of the upturned lifeboat. 'Where are you', he shouted. 'We're inside', came the reply.

He thought he could see his brother Peter Jackson who was clinging tightly to the stern. 'Peter. Aren't you trying to get away?' 'I don't think I can', was the reply. 'I'm cramped'.

John Jackson tried to keep his limbs moving to fight off the cramp from the penetrating cold water. 'I think she'll never be righted', said a voice. It sounded like Richard Robinson voicing the worst fears of the men, and his words were all too true. John Jackson felt somebody leaning heavily on his arm, it was Richard Robinson pleading 'Jack. Will tha' help me'. He managed to raise his friend's head a little but the sea swept him clean away and he never saw Richard Robinson again. The *Eliza Fernley* made several attempts to right herself but, hampered by the anchor cable and the weight of the men clinging to the gunwales, each time she failed.

On both sides of the Ribble, as the night wore on, friends and relatives waited expectantly for the return of their lifeboats. The truth did not dawn until about three in the morning when, to their horror, the *Eliza Fernley* was discovered on Birkdale beach with her bottom upwards. As the tide receded somebody thought to look underneath her. They found three dead bodies.

John Robinson was found on the shore about 300 yards from the wreck. He was laid on the starr grass of the sandhills and a coat was wrapped around him. He died in the arms of Thomas Rimmer at 3.30 pm. Peter Jackson was found just alive and was carried to a plate layer's hut on the railway. A fire was lit and two doctors applied artificial respiration for two hours. He died at 4.45 am. John Ball was discovered standing dazed and semi-conscious in a pool of water. In the small hours of the morning a horse drawn cab clattered over the wet cobbles of the empty streets on its mission of mercy. John Ball was still alive when the cab reached the infirmary but he died there the next day. They claimed that Ralph Peters was still alive when they found him, but he only lived for another five minutes. Henry Robinson and John Jackson somehow managed to struggle ashore half drowned and they staggered home to their families. As the dawn came closer more bodies were washed ashore.

At St Annes the lifeboat had still not returned when daylight broke and the storm abated. St Annes summoned the services of the lifeboats from Lytham and Blackpool to search for the *Laura Janet*. Some were confident that they would find her riding out the storm in the Ribble estuary, but the lifeboats returned emptyhanded. It was nearly noon before Edward Bland, with the aid of his telescope, saw the white bottom of a capsized boat on Ainsdale Beach. The boat was the *Laura Janet* which had also come so close to the *Mexico*. Three bodies were found under her. The watch on one of the men had stopped at 2.20am, but nobody knew exactly what had happened at that time, because nobody from the *Laura Janet* lived to tell the tale.

Two lifeboats were lost. Only two lifeboatmen survived from the *Eliza Fernley* and the entire crew of the *Laura Janet* was drowned. The bodies of the lifeboat crews were laid out side by side in the empty splendour of the Birkdale Palace Hotel.

The next day news of the tragedy spread rapidly through a stunned nation. A hundred years later families on both sides of the Ribble proudly claimed kinship to those who answered the distress call of the *Mexico* on the night of December the ninth, eighteen hundred and eighty-six.

THE WARRIORS OF THE SEA[6]

Up goes the Lytham signal St. Anne's has summoned hands!
Knee deep in surf the Life-Boat's launched abreast of Southport sands!
Half deafened by the screaming wind: half blinded by the rain,
Three crews await their coxwains, and face the hurricane!
The stakes are death or duty! No man has answered 'No'!
Lives must be saved out yonder on the doomed ship Mexico!
Did ever night look blacker? Did sea so hiss before?
Did ever women's voices wail more piteous on the shore?
Out from three ports of Lancashire that night went Life-Boats three,
To fight a splendid battle, manned by Warriors of the Sea!

Along the sands of Southport, brave women held their breath,
For they knew that those who loved them, were fighting hard with death,
A cheer went out from Lytham! The tempest tossed it back,
As the gallant lads of Lancashire bent to the waves' attack;
And girls who dwelt about St. Anne's, with faces white with fright
Pray'd God would still the tempest, that dark December night.
Sons, husbands, lovers, brothers, they'd all given up their all,
These noble English women heart-sick at duty's call;
But not a cheer, or tear, or prayer, from those who bent the knee,
Came out across the waves to nerve those Warriors of the Sea!

Three boats went out from Lancashire, but one came back to tell,
The story of the hurricane, the tale of ocean's hell!
All safely reached the Mexico, their trysting-place to keep,
For one there was the rescue, the others in the deep
Fell in the arms of victory! Dropped to their lonely grave,
Their passing bell the tempest, their requiem the wave!
They clung to life like sailors, they fell to death like men,
Where, in our roll of heroes? When in our story? When?
Have Englishmen been braver, or fought more loyally,
With death that comes by duty to the Warriors of the Sea!

One boat came back to Lytham! its noble duty done,
But at St. Anne's and Southport, the prize of death was won!
Won by those gallant fellows, who went men's lives to save,
And died there crowned with glory! Enthroned upon the wave!
Within a rope's throw of the wreck, the English sailors fell,
A blessing on their faithful lips, when ocean rang their knell.
Weep not for them dear women! Cease wringing of your hands!
Go out to meet your heroes across the Southport sands!
Grim death for them is stingless! The Grave has victory!
Cross oars and bear them nobly home! Brave warriors of the sea!

When in dark nights of winter, fierce storms of wind and rain,
Howl round the cosy homestead, and lash the window-pane,
When over hill and tree-top, we hear the tempests roar,
And hurricanes go sweeping on, from valley to the shore,
When nature seems to stand at bay, and silent terror comes,
And those we love on earth the best are gathered in our homes!
Think of the sailors round the coast, who braving sleet or snow,
Leave sweethearts, wives, and little ones, when duty bids them go!
Think of our sea-girt island! A harbour, where alone,
No Englishman to save a life has failed to risk his own!
Then when the storm howls loudest, pray of your charity,
That God will bless the Life-Boat! And warriors of the Sea!

CLEMENT SCOTT

*John Jackson, a fisherman, was
another survivor of the Mexico
disaster, though he lost his
brother. He gave his full story to
journalists on the following day,
but was unable to speak at the
inquest because he had undergone
surgery the previous day.*
(Photo, Botanic Gardens Museum)

Chapter Fourteen

Victorian Childhood

NE Saturday night, when Paul Lloyd was about six years old, he was not sent off to bed at his usual early hour but he was allowed to sleep fully dressed on the settle in the living room. At about midnight the little boy was awakened by his grandmother who was holding a tallow candle lantern in one hand. She shook him and bathed his eyes with cold water; then she led him to the 'lawse box' stable — she had promised to show her grandson how all animals were born. The scene in the stable as he sat perched upon a milking stool, waiting expectantly for life to be created by the light of the lantern, was something which young Paul never forgot. A large white sow lay grunting in the straw just beneath him.[1]

After a while Granny Peet told him to look carefully and he saw a little piglet being born. It was followed by a second piglet, then a third.

> We watched and waited until the eighth and last piglet arrived and was suckling. How fascinating it was to see each little pink pig appear and immediately turn his little nose towards the sow's nipples. I noticed that each was fastened to its mother by a long red cord, and that each in turn, as it appeared, planted its little feet firmly and, his little nose twitching — pointed directly to where his breakfast was flowing over in anticipation of his arrival. He started to struggle free, just like 'Owd Doll' [the Lloyd's shire mare] when moving a heavy load. After a long pull and a strong pull, each piggy in turn broke his umbilical tube and found his place at the 'table'. And all the time the sow was doing her best to sing him a lullaby. Granny told me the little pigs could smell the overflowing milk, and that pigs seemed constantly hungry; all of which gave them the urge to pull.

Paul Lloyd was born in 1886. His parents farmed Peet's Farm in Peets Lane which they had inherited through his grandmother who actually *was* a Peet. It was many years later that he wrote down his memoirs, and they included a vivid account of his childhood in Churchtown. He remembered everything with a clarity and detail, which gives a discerning child's eye view of the scene in the 1890s.

One of Paul Lloyd's earliest memories was before he had reached his fourth birthday. The occasion was his christening which had been arranged at home and was to be shared with his cousin Hugh who was only one year old. Both the boys were washed and scrubbed and dressed in their Sunday best, Paul in a little shirt and knee length trousers and little Hugh in a girl's frock with a clean white apron. His granny, mother and aunt went to the window to look for the rector. Looking past the snowball tree and the flowering currant bush they could see his familiar figure approaching. 'Lo tho bod, he's cummin o'er 't hey', said Paul's mother.

At this young Paul sneaked out of the back door to look. A large man in black clothes was crossing the plank on the ditch and carrying something white on his arm. Paul took fright and ran. He crawled into a brick dog-kennel at the bottom of the orchard thinking that he would be well hidden. It was no use, the sharp eyes of Granny Peet spotted him and she hauled him out by his foot. His irate mother flapped around his soiled garments and tried to put them into a presentable array. The adults looked at each other and at the frightened child; they decided that the show must go on.

> . . . I was picked up by the minister and found myself higher above the floor than I had ever been before. I was not affected so much by the height as I was by apprehension concerning the ability of the Minister to sustain my weight . . . Throwing my arms tightly around the Minister's neck, I hung on for dear life and hoped for the best. Thus commenced one of the toughest battles I have ever fought; but the odds were against me. I was outclassed; I had made the mistake of tackling an opponent in a heavier class than myself and I lost. The Parson eventually loosened my grip on his neck, spoke my name, held my head and wet it and at the same time said some words (not in the dialect) which I did not understand . . .

The parson gave Paul a baleful stare. 'Th'art o' weet through, and th'art witshod!', exclaimed Paul's mother. It was true, he had perspired so much that even his feet were wet through.

Paul remembered meeting the parson again on his first day at Sunday School. He saw the churchman in an entirely different light:

> At the church there was a small group of boys about my age, and the Rev Charles Hesketh Knowlys, rector, was there to give us our first Sunday School lesson. He talked to us and told us that we and all folks were the children of God. He said that we were made in the 'image' of God and then, as we did not understand what was meant by 'image', it not being in the dialect, which was the only speech we knew, he changed it to 'likeness'. He understood the dialect but did not often use it. Then he told us that there was 'a home for little children above the bright blue sky' where everybody would go to live someday. He was very kind to us, and we thought he must be very like God and very close to Him.

Paul wandered home alone after his first Sunday School lesson, thinking all the time about what the rector had told him. Dinner was not quite ready, so he wandered off into the orchard and seated himself on a stone well cover to solve the mystery of the creation before his meal was ready:

> I worked it out this way. If I was made in God's likeness and He was the father of everybody, He must be very very old. And being old, and there being no scissors or razors in the sky, He must have long white whiskers like the oldest man in the village, because he had long white whiskers. Then as God had made everybody I tried to work it out this way; my parents made me, my grandparents made my parents, and my great grandparents Gregson who lived at Marshside made them... and that was as far as I had knowledge of.

But Paul exercised his fertile imagination as he sat on the well cover with a pose like Rodin's thinker and his little brow furrowed whilst his dinner went cold, until he arrived at the question 'But who made God?'. 'And that is where I stayed', he says, 'I could imagine no further'.

It appears that Charles Hesketh Knowlys could speak the dialect if he chose, but the speech was of course a great social divider. The rich and gutteral dialect of North Meols was still the normal speech in every rural household. It can be classified as a variant of the North Mercian dialect which was a speech pattern common to the counties from Lancashire to Shropshire. The 'thee and thou' of the second person singular was the normal form of address for small children and close friends. The dialect was rich in words which have now disappeared from our vocabulary and when properly spoken it had great charm and character.[2] Paul Lloyd must have wondered why the rector spoke 'proper' English when the Bible spoke a language which was nearer to the dialect. Everybody in North Meols understood 'English', but locals who flaunted it in preference to the dialect were looked upon as upstarts, and were said to 'talk fine'.

On one occasion the large white sow was on heat and Paul and Dick, always willing to learn more about the facts of life, were given the job of taking her along Peets Lane to Billy Prescot's in the village where the boar would be glad to do the honours. On the way they met a dignified lady from Southport who 'spoke fine'; she must have wondered why two boys were driving a pig through the village. 'What is that my little man?' she asked of the smaller of the two boys. 'Hooas an owd soo ma'am, un hooas brimmin', replied Paul. The use of the dialect in such a fine presence caused great embarrassment to brother Dick who took it upon himself to explain to the lady in English. 'He means that we are taking the soo to Mister Billy Prescot's boar becos hooas brimmin', said Dick.

We are not told the dignified lady's reaction. Possibly she was able to deduce the meaning of the dialect word. What might have surprised her was that one of the boys she was addressing was a future Mayor of Southport!

Paul Lloyd also recalled his first day at the more serious educational establishment — the day school:

When I was five my mother took me to school. I was the only boy entering that day. I recall going through the door of the Infant's school and my mother giving my name and birthday date to one of the teachers, Miss Blanch Barker. We were in a large room with many small boys and girls sitting at long low desks. There were large pictures on the walls showing the four seasons of the year with animals and crops germane to each season. But what impressed me most and completely fascinated me, was the instrument fastened to the top inside of the door through which we had entered . . . It closed the door after us!

The school at Churchtown was an L-shaped single-storey building of brick with a high slate roof. It was airy and substantially built. Inside it was fitted with moveable glazed partitions reaching from floor to ceiling. The rooms were heated by an open coal fire, and sometimes in the winter the children were so cold that they had to go to the fire to warm their hands before they could do any writing. The only elements of plumbing which the school contained were pipes to supply gas lights with a naked flame for each classroom, and pipes to supply one water tap for the boys' school and one for the girls' school. There were no flush toilets. Each school had one cloakroom and the playgrounds were surfaced with clean, bare red sand and were bounded by high brick walls to keep the children in and to separate the boys from the girls.

When Paul had been at school for about a year Miss Barker told the

Boys greatly outnumber girls in the Churchtown Council School 2nd Class of 1900, but the girls have been awarded prominent places at the front of the picture.
(Photo, Botanic Gardens Museum)

class that they were to be put in Standard One, and they would have another teacher. This was a move from infants to juniors and it was considered to be a high academic achievement. At the age of six the boys marched through the girls' school into the boys' school where they were put under the charge of Miss Catherine Gregson, a former pupil born in Churchtown:

> Here each boy eventually acquired a nick-name. There was 'Smiler', 'Miriam Tum's John', 'Tuffy's Wright', 'Quack', 'Surrey' etc. There were so many Wrights and Rimmers that they had to be numbered. Only boys local to the North Meols district were so designated. 'Foreign' or fancy names like Halliwell, Turnbull or Lovelady were allowed to stand.[3]

It was common to find children from the industrial towns of Lancashire whose families had moved into the area. These children were often surprised to find that they were allowed to attend school all day. Before moving to Churchtown some of them had been working for half the day in the factory. They called themselves 'Half-timers' — a stark reminder that in the 1890s and later many children were still employed in the cotton mills at a relatively tender age.

The school contained nearly 700 pupils. Discipline was very strict and the cane was the normal punishment for any offence:

> For really serious offences the offender was taken to the headmaster or headmistress; in these cases, when guilt was proven, the culprits were taken to the cloak room and the punishment was applied to the posterior, bare or covered according to the severity of the offence . . .

> The instrument for punishment was a length of sugar cane 5/8 inch thick and about 30 inches long with a crook at one end. Some teachers acquired considerable skill in manipulating the cane, and some of the more venturesome boys were just as adroit in their stance when receiving. The most effective place for the cane to make contact was the tips of the fingers of the hand held out, palm up. That was a real stinger. Early in the game, being sensitive to pain, I learned to extend my hand to about four inches less than the maximum and at the very last moment when the cane was about two inches above my hand I would thrust my arm out to the full extent. The sharpness of the note and the 'swish' of the cane was the guide to the velocity and striking power as well as the degree of pain generated. The effect of the cane striking the thick cushioned palm was nothing to the excruciating pain of a direct hit on the very tips of the fingers. But just as warring nations develop skills to neutralise the enemies' weapons, our teachers developed an effective technique in their field, they simply grasped the culprit's wrist with one hand and wielded the cane with the other hand . . . and they never missed a finger tip!

When a pupil was due for punishment and the cane was worn out or split, the condemned was given a penny and ordered to go to Rowbottom's shop in the village to buy his own new instrument of torture.

Every year on Shrove Tuesday the boys would all be at school before the teachers. It was barring out day or 'Poncake Toosda'. By tradition the day could not be declared a holiday unless the teachers were prevented from entering school, so the boys locked all the doors from the inside. The teachers then tried every means to enter and failed until a window was opened for one teacher to climb in. This was not the orthodox way to enter the school and a holiday was then declared and taken; the children rushed home to gorge themselves on a feast of pancakes, the ingredients of which had been prepared by their hard-working mothers the night before.

The segregation of the sexes was very strict and during playtime the older boys would give each other a leg-up to the top of the high wall which separated them from the girls. From this vantage point a whole forbidden world could be viewed and they could shout teasing remarks as they watched the girls dancing out the Morris Dance and 'Ring-a-Ring-a-Roses.' As he progressed through the standards there came a day when it was Paul's turn to sit on the wall to watch the girls, and on one occasion the

An early picture of Belle Vue Cottage. This was originally the home of Sarah Walmesley who became the first resident of the bathing village in 1797.
(Botanic Gardens Museum)

A painting of the old lock-up and pinfold, Churchtown, in 1850. The lock-up was a small stone building near the site of the present entrance to the Botanic Gardens.
(E.W. Collection)

The Black Horse on Eastbank lane in 1851. This unassuming hotel was the predecessor of the present Shakespeare Hotel and was kept by James Ball, better known by his nicknames 'Carrion Crow' or 'Old Crow'.
(E.W. Collection)

Below - *An excellent example of Herdman's work, full of character and showing a panoramic view of old Churchtown in the 1850s, slightly flawed by an inaccurate depiction of the church spire.*
(Botanic Gardens Museum)

girls challenged him to drop down on their side. He accepted the challenge and risked the cane by joining in their games, but soon the bell sounded for the end of playtime when the children had to fall into lines.

'I suggested to the girls that they help me back over the wall', he wrote, 'but instead they mobbed me and drove me through their playground and into the street which was out of bounds. I was just barely in time to line up with the boys and march into school. It was a very close call'.

Paul Lloyd escaped the cane on this occasion, but his brief contact with the opposite sex had stirred something deep inside him and that very evening after school he did not go fishing and bird-nesting with his friends; instead he carried a satchel home for a little girl whom he does not name. It was a turning point in his life and in his attitude to the opposite sex. 'To me they were not human', he said. 'They were angelic'.

Paul remained at school until after his thirteenth birthday when Mr George Vine, who had succeeded Mr Gosson as headmaster, asked him to stay on as a pupil teacher. George Vine was a Cornishman who deserves credit not only for being able to understand the North Meols dialect, but also for gaining the high respect of the children and the community. Paul accepted his first job at a salary of half a crown per week.

In Paul Lloyd's time the farmers of Marshside, Crossens and Banks still worked plots of land which were held on a lease of three lives from the lord of the manor, ancient customs and traditional ways of life were lovingly preserved and the country people retained a fierce and stubborn independence, earning a living from the soil and the sea as their ancestors had done since time immemorial.

One man who lived among these people and understood them was the Rev William Bulpit, the Vicar of Crossens. He was interested in the customs and the folklore. He was welcomed into the homes where he ate of their arvel bread and drank their braggart drink. He accepted the loaves they gave away at funerals and attributed these traditions to their Viking ancestry. When they suffered illness and could not afford a doctor he gave them his own medical concoctions – his cures owed more to the spirit than the flesh!

William Bulpit's first living in North Meols was at Banks and he never forgot the warmth of his reception there. On entering his new house he found that the parishioners had left a sack of corn, a sack of flour, some pork, eggs, and butter as a welcome to their new minister. When it was time to plough the glebe land or to set his potatoes it was done for him as boon work.

Good pictures of the suburbs are rare and the children are well aware of the camera in this winter scene taken early this century. The Southport Tramways Company Depot is just out of the picture on the right and old Churchtown can be seen in the distance.
(E.W. Collection)

*The clock on the tower of St
Cuthberts church, North Meols.*

He described some of the people he knew in Banks. There was Joseph
Todd, an horologist who repaired the church clock at Churchtown, a
hobby which he combined with that of a bonesetter. There was John Riding
who owned a barometer but who was often seen bringing it out of his
cottage to see the weather for itself because he declared that it lied. Hugh
Ball the churchwarden was a stickler for punctuality; he always wore two
watches and it was he who started a new clock fund with a five pound
note. The women too had strong characters. Mrs Ellen Linaker and Mrs
Isabella Thompson were both women farmers; the former aspired to being
a poetess and the latter steadfastly refused to ride on the newfangled
railway. Old Mrs Lowe had the toothiest smile in Banks for she had never
shed her first set of teeth!

Amongst Bulpit's older acquaintances were his churchwardens, William
Rimmer and John Brade, Thomas Ball and Richard Brade, Guardian Hugh
Ainscough, Yeoman John Brade and Overseer John Linaker. He
remembered the hospitality of Mrs Henry Ball of Bonney Barn where he
sat in the inglenook by a peat fire one winter's night surrounded by four
generations of her family, with the firelight glinting from the polished
brassware. It was a local custom to give twenty ounces to a pound of butter.

Henry Rimmer the organist loved a practical joke and at Christmas when
his father John Rimmer put a pot on the fire for the carol singers to have
some hot refreshment, young Henry substituted a stone for the meat.
Another practical joker was William Ball, but the locals were wise to him
and on one occasion they got their own back — he was defeated at an
election in Churchtown when the Marshside fishermen voted by passing
through a door. They unconstitutionally re-entered by a back door and
voted again.

There was rivalry between the fishing communities at Marshside and
Banks but in Crossens the people were mostly employed in agriculture
and thought that any community which reeked of fish was inferior to their
own. Marshside had boat builders' yards and workshops with sailmakers,
net braiders, basket weavers, shrimp shillers and potters. Like Banks it
was a tightknit community with a lot of intermarriage and a strong sense
of identity. Local news was transmitted by John Wright (Degwin) who
was the Marshside bellman. On May Day a pole constructed from three
boat's masts lashed together and topped by a green bush served as a
maypole.[4]

William Bulpit even went out fishing with some of his parishioners, and
on one occasion returned red-faced after unwittingly eating two women's

*Little Ireland was mentioned in
the Southport Directory of 1876
as consisting of 47 households
and a school. This photograph
was taken around 1890. Most of
the residents were descendants of
families driven out of Ireland by
the potato famines of the 1840s.
Little Ireland was described as 'a
low squalid-looking place,
destitute of all sanitary
arrangements'. They were an
unfortunate small community
who were unable to integrate with
other local people; their village
was demolished in 1904.*
(Photo, Botanic Gardens Museum)

dinners whilst they went without. He took a great interest in local families and he loved local history. He was always searching for relics of the past and brought back two limestone boulders to the churchyard at Crossens. He found the remains of a dug-out canoe which had once sailed the waters of Martin Mere. Most important of all he wrote down and published an account of his activities and the people he knew.

Bulpit knew that in the Middle Ages the boundary of North Meols parish had been marked by the Snoterstone which stood on the mudflats somewhere near the hamlet of Hundred End and the Wilding Brook which flowed nearby. He made enquiries from local people and discovered that the stone had been seen within living memory. He determined to try and find it and to establish the line of the medieval boundary.

> . . . the Snoterstone was looked upon as a boundary stone of the West Derby Hundred and of North Meols from the time of the conqueror, even if not from an earlier date. So I was anxious to investigate concerning it, for it had been covered up by silt by the sea and not seen for a generation. However, on digging down we did not find it. Then it was determined to examine the ground by means of steel probes, eight feet long, and four men worked systematically for two months trying the ground. At length, after a number of false alarms, the stone was found. A fisherman said to me that when the Snoterstone was found a 'Half stake, with his family mark upon it', would also be found. This came to pass, and the position of the stone having been verified, the oaze was allowed to cover it up. The discovery of the Snoterstone proved that the boundary of North Meols had been moved southwards, and now both the Snoterstone and the Walding (Wilding) Brook are within the Hesketh liberties instead of forming a boundary line . . .[5]

All the churches held traditional annual festivals, one of which is described in detail by Paul Lloyd who gives an account of the Churchtown festival. Every year in the month of May the schoolchildren held a pageant of 'Merrie England' and crowned their May Queen. Boys and girls were chosen to represent historical and folklore characters in the pageant. Queen Victoria was represented, the Lord Chamberlain, John Bull, Robin Hood and his merry men; there were soldiers and sailors, athletes, morris dancers and maypole dancers, even Robinson Crusoe and his Man Friday were not forgotten. Those selected for the parts were trained and rehearsed long before the great day and, when at last it arrived, they assembled in Churchtown and were taken by horse drawn tram along Mill Lane to the Rookery on Roe Lane which was the residence of Mrs Anna Maria Alice Hesketh, the lady of the manor.

Old Mrs Hesketh, who was in her eighties, loved to see the children

All local churches held annual festivals with processions which paraded along the village streets, a spectacle of costume and colour. Churchtown Festival would have looked very similar to that of nearby Crossens which is shown here around the turn of the century.
(E.W. Collection)

The Rev Charles Hesketh (1804–76) was very influential in the growth and planning of Victorian Southport. He served as rector of North Meols from 1835 and he donated land for the Botanic Gardens in 1875. His concern for Southport was equalled by his great grandson, Roger Hesketh, in the more difficult times of the 20th century.

perform and she was given a private showing of the Morris Dance in the grounds of her home — it was a dress rehearsal before the real event. The Morris Dance in North Meols had become the prerogative of young girls and, unlike most parts of England, after the 1890s it was seldom performed by men. The girls wore brightly coloured dresses and carried tambourines or sticks with bells and coloured streamers. A well-trained troupe in full flight, high stepping in unison, with bells jingling and tambourines waving was a dazzling and heart-warming spectacle.

From the Rookery the children remounted the tram floats and progressed to the centre of Southport. Here the Morris Dancers had the honour of leading the procession along Lord Street and they were joined by the lifeboat *Edith and Annie* on its launching carriage drawn by a handsome groomed team of powerful shire horses. The lifeboat crew was a makeshift one for the day, consisting of grinning boys who had been allowed to wear the coveted cork jackets — the sons of the lifeboat crew were given priority for these highly valued positions.

The climax of the May Day festivities came later in the day. The procession returned by horse tram to Churchtown and all the players dismounted for the pageant. At the iron entrance gates to the Botanic Gardens a milk white pony, immaculately groomed and ready harnessed, waited patiently, held by the proud father of the Queen-elect. She descended from her float and mounted the pony, the entourage then progressed through the gardens to a large field where a throne and a maypole were set up in readiness for the coronation ceremony. There followed the blowing of a great horn and a juvenile herald shouted in a loud voice 'Oyez, Oyez Oyez. The Queen proclaims an ancient holiday with rustic games'.

It was then the turn of the maypole dancers to do their piece. Girls of uniform height were chosen for the part; wearing crisp frilly dresses they formed up in a large circle around the maypole. From the top of the pole were suspended a large number of coloured ribbons and the performers, each holding a ribbon in one hand, commenced their dance. Half the dancers circulated clockwise, the other half progressed anti-clockwise, each weaving right and left of the dancers moving the other way. Excitement amongst the children mounted and teachers held their breath as each rotation brought the dancers closer and closer to the base of the pole, for one false step could leave the ribbons in an almighty tangle. At last the whole pole was neatly pleated with coloured ribbon and the dancers stood in a tight circle. There followed a calculated pause, each dancer turned about, the dance was repeated as the ribbons unwound. The watchers called for an encore and the whole process was repeated several times.

The boys, waiting impatiently to be allowed their part in the proceedings, were then given the stage. They put on a tableau of Robin Hood and Sherwood Forest, with Friar Tuck, Little John, Will Scarlett and Maid Marion all making appearances. Other tableaux followed, then games and races where the boys were once more allowed to show their prowess. All the proceedings were watched by relatives and parents straining to catch a glimpse of their offspring, and by all the village worthies. But the most appreciative were not the children or the parents; they were the older generation of grandparents and village elders who stood leaning on their sticks and nodding sagely throughout. As the sun sank low in the sky and the great day came to an end they remembered their own youth when they too had been a part of the May Day Pageant. And there must have been a tear in the eye of more than one old lady who remembered the day, many long years ago, when she too had ridden a milk-white pony through the Strawberry Gardens and sat on a wooden throne with a cardboard crown upon her head.

Chapter Fifteen

Coming of Age

THE Improvement Commissioners continued to levy the rates and to administer local affairs until 1867 when a charter was obtained which gave Southport county borough status. The area of the new borough was identical to that covered by the Improvement Act of 1865. Four wards, called West, Craven, Talbot and East, were created, each with six councillors and two aldermen. The first municipal election was held on the first of June 1867. It was a non-political election, but not without a touch of drama when the returning officers for West Ward declared that many voting papers were invalid simply because the word Southport did not appear after the names of the candidates. After a careful scrutiny of the votes the following councillors were duly elected:

MUNICIPAL ELECTIONS 1867

WEST WARD	CRAVEN WARD
Richard Ball Brewer	Edwin W Stocker
Richard Ball Albion	Thomas Fisher
James Scott	Thomas Marshall
Amos Gregson	Isaac Beswick
Seth Rimmer	James Whitehead
Samuel Boothroyd	William H Talbot

TALBOT WARD	EAST WARD
Henry Robinson	John Holt
John A Robinson	Gilbert Harrison
William Sutton Senr.	Peter Wood M.D.
William Sutton Junr.	George B Barron
William Smallshaw	Thomas Houghton
Thomas Bond	Taylor R Stephenson

Messrs Boothroyd, Gregson, Harrison, Holt, Stephenson, Talbot, Wood, and Sutton senior were elected aldermen and the honour of being the first mayor went by unanimous agreement to Dr Peter Wood.

A move to include Birkdale in the new borough was not successful, but Southport continued to expand northwards and in 1875 Hesketh and Scarisbrick Wards were created when the boundary was extended to include Churchtown, Crossens and High Park.

The inhabitants of the older parts of North Meols parish could hardly be expected to welcome this takeover by a town which had not even existed within the living memory of the older inhabitants. Conversely, some residents of the new town were ignorant of the agricultural pursuits and ancient rural traditions of North Meols parish, and a clash between the

Early Victorian Lord Street

Southport expanded eastwards from the cluster of buildings around the Duke's Folly, into a natural valley between the sandhills. Houses were built well back from the chain of 'slacks' or pools which flooded the valley after heavy rain. It was the accident of these pools which determined the great width of Lord Street, but the lords of the manor accepted that a natural building line had been created. By the 1820s the street was well formulated and by 1830, at about the time Lord Street first acquired its name, a ditch was excavated to drain the slacks. All the houses on the south side were given long gardens which were fenced around with wooden palings, access to each house being over a little wooden bridge with brick supports. The ditch was later culverted and the little bridges disappeared, but the long gardens can be seen illustrated in the engravings here.

Left - *A splendid early engraving which captures the atmosphere of early Victorian Lord Street.* (Botanic Gardens Museum)
Below - *Lord Street in 1849. This view shows local names Blundell, Hodge, Robinson and Whitehead established in business as some of Southport's early tradesmen. The site is very central on Eastbank Street Square. The Scarisbrick Arms was formerly called the Hesketh Arms and was built by Thomas Mawdesley in 1821. The shops were demolished when the entrance to Scarisbrick Avenue was created later in the 19th century.* (E.W. Collection)

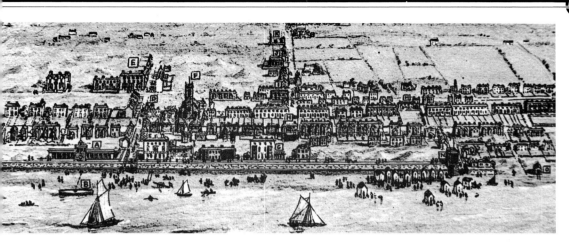

Top - Almost every Southport home is on Lord Street in 1849, as this splendid illustration shows. Fine terraces with long gardens, Christ Church and the Victoria Market can all be seen.
(Southport Library)

Right - Donkey carriages were popular with the early visitors to Southport. This picture, dated 1858, shows the Russell Hotel (behind the driver) and Boothroyds store to the right.
(Photo, Botanic Gardens Museum)

Centre right - A top-hatted gent hires a donkey carriage outside the Town Hall in 1858.
(Photo, Botanic Gardens Museum)

Above - The Scarisbrick Arms Hotel sports a tall flagpole; top hats and crinolenes are the fashion and Christ Church can be seen in the distance.
(E.W. Collection)

Right - The Victoria Market carries the date 1848, and the picture is dated 1850. This was the first covered market in Southport; it remained until 1857 when a larger covered market was opened in Chapel Street. The site is the corner of London Street and Lord Street, now occupied by Lloyds Bank.
(E.W. Collection)

Edwardian Lord Street

or much of the 19th century, Southport was the most popular seaside resort in the north of England, and it is therefore of great importance in the history of seaside development. But Southport continues to confuse the seaside historian; it is the country's most blatant exception to the rule that the more select resorts are further from the centres of population. Unlike the majority of resorts, it did not grow from the seafront but from Lord Street, which is more a feature of the inland spa towns, from which the early seaside resorts developed. The segregation of Lord Street, an all-year-round feature, from the seasonal holiday trade was very evident by Edwardian times when the boulevard was fully matured and the souvenir shops and other seaside paraphernalia had been relegated to the side streets.

Below - London Square and an evocative Edwardian scene. The Monument was not built until 1923 but Parrs Bank and the Post Office can be seen. Horse-drawn carriages and bath chairs are available for hire.
(E.W. Collection)

Above - Two general views of Lord Street in the early part of this century.
(E.W. Collection)

Above - *This view of Lord Street evokes the atmosphere of the shopping area better than any form of words. The trees are not yet fully mature but they provide shade and are a very attractive complement to the street scene.*
(E.W. Collection)
Right - *The Cambridge Hall.*
(Valentine Collection, St. Andrews University Library)
Below - *Another view showing the whole range of municipal buildings on the east side of Lord Street.*
(Photo, Southport Library)

differing interests of old and new was inevitable. In the nineteenth century much of England was still so rural that a village like Churchtown was not seen as picturesque or in any way worthy of note; a contemporary account described it as one long serpentine street, lined by old-fashioned thatched low mud cottages, with here and there a more respectable house, and the usual ramifications of the irregularly built hamlets.

The annual Churchtown Fair, described as a cattle and pig fair, was viewed by some people with disfavour. 'The occasion being taken advantage of for a drunken bout', wrote the *Southport News Guide,* 'when a Mayor is chosen with great pomp by the ale-tasters, whose term of office commences and terminates with the fair'. The Rev Charles Hesketh Knowlys supported the views of the newspaper and asked that the fair be suppressed on the grounds that it was too conducive to immorality. After witnessing a few more performances of the Churchtown Fair the majority of the Town Council were in agreement with the charges of drunkenness and immorality and in 1884 they decided that it was time the fair was banned.

Placards and press notices appeared announcing the Council decision, but the instigators soon found that they had misjudged local opinion. Other notices soon appeared pasted over the placards and printed beneath the press announcements:

> 'CHURCHTOWN FAIR. The fair having been held for centuries before the Southport Corporation existed, WILL TAKE PLACE as usual on MONDAY NEXT, THE 18TH AUGUST.

Edward Fleetwood Hesketh, the lord of the manor, announced that the decision to ban the fair was quite illegal and declared that it showed a total lack of concern for the needs of those employed in agriculture. Councillor James Linaker claimed that there was just as much drunkenness in the fashionable parts of Southport as in Churchtown. Support for the fair came from all quarters, and it was held in defiance of the council decision and continued to be held, unmolested, for many more years.

On the wider political front Southport was formerly part of the extensive constituency of South Lancashire, which was represented by Gladstone for several years in the 1860s during which time he delivered several election speeches in the town. There is a story, probably true but exaggerated, that as a boy William Gladstone nearly ended his young life in Southport. He and a schoolfriend dug out such a deep excavation in the sand that it collapsed on the future prime minister and practically buried him alive.

Southport was created a separate constituency in 1885 and was generally reckoned to be a safe Conservative stronghold. The first elected Member of Parliament, however, was Dr George Pilkington, a Liberal, who was elected with a narrow majority of 160. At the general election in 1886 it was apparent that the Conservatives had an excellent chance of gaining the seat, and the ambitious young Lord Curzon put himself forward as a prospective candidate. The local Conservative Association suggested that he pay the full election costs which amounted to about one thousand pounds, plus an annual contribution of £200. Lord Curzon protested, with some degree of truth, that he could not afford to pay for the election and, after some wrangling, the local association suggested a sum of £600 towards the election costs and to settle for a contribution of £50 per annum towards their funds. Lord Curzon won the seat with a majority of 461 over George Pilkington.

> The Rads were positively astounded at our victory, as they counted on winning by eighty. Their agent showed me his figures during the counting. I believe against any other candidate but Pilkington, whose local popularity is prodigious, I should have won by twice as many[1].

The Southport Conservatives were so pleased with the success that they agreed to pay the whole of the election costs — a welcome move to the new MP who had temporary financial problems at the time.

George Nathaniel Curzon won the Southport seat for the Conservatives by 461 votes in 1886 and retained it, not without some difficulty, until 1898 when he was appointed Viceroy of India. His superior attitude did not endear him to his political opponents, but he always took a deep interest in his constituency and came back to speak in Southport after his return from India.

(Photo, Botanic Gardens Museum)

George Nathaniel Curzon represented Southport for twelve years; according to his biographer neither Southport nor its MP ever regretted their compact[2]. Lord Curzon had a brilliant political mind, but he was a very controversial and ambitious man known to everybody as a most superior person and described by his political enemies as the most pompous and supercilious man in England. The local liberal press gave him a hard time, especially during the election years, but this did not rattle his confidence.

'I think my seat at Southport is fairly safe', he wrote to his future wife before the 1892 election. 'I judge so from the extravagant denunciation of the radical paper, whose last number accuses me of brag, bluster, blatancy, bombast, buffoonery, foppishness, malignity, and other political virtues' – his judgement proved sound and his majority increased to 604. The 1895 election was again bitterly fought, George Curzon had recently married and his beautiful and sensitive young wife, a desperately homesick American straight from her honeymoon, was thrown straight into the brutal realities of British politics. The Conservative candidate's political enemies claimed that his wife's beauty gave him an unfair advantage over his opponent – but the electors expected Mary Curzon to support her new husband. She dutifully smiled her way through a rough and hardfought election campaign, but she privately hated every minute of it. George Curzon's majority increased to 764. In 1898 Lord Curzon was appointed Viceroy of India. He was the youngest person ever to be offered the post, but the cynics said it was offered to get him out of the way. His superior attitude had created so many enemies even within his own party that he had thwarted his chances of achieving his great ambition to become prime minister. It is hard to believe that the proud George Nathaniel Curzon touted from door to door in Banks asking the people to give him their vote, and it is not surprising to find that they did not extend to him the warm welcome which they gave to the homely Rev William Bulpit. Lord Curzon summed up his constituency in a letter to his successor, Edward M Hall, who fought for the seat in 1900.

> Except in times of imperial crisis it unquestionably inclines to the Radical side. Therefore you cannot take too much trouble about it . . . Banks is quite hopeless. For twelve years I laboured at that place. I visited every house in it over and over again. I tramped along those muddy flats all to no purpose. I got fewer votes there in my last election than in my first. I should not waste much time there . . . The place in which to strike out and build up your future majority is in the radical suburbs of Southport. Get the women and the young men on your side, and you can afford to disregard the soured radicals of middle life . . . The constituency is exacting in petty demands, and placed a great strain upon my correspondence. In larger matters it was singularly lenient. It never cost me more than £250 a year during the twelve years I represented it, except in election years.[3]

Lord Curzon obviously saw the advantages of getting the women on his side, but when he was a member of parliament women did not have a vote. Women's suffrage became a great issue a few years later when Winston Churchill came to speak in Southport. Churchill himself was not opposed to giving women the vote, but in 1909 he felt there were more urgent matters to attend to and he became one of the targets for the suffragettes. When he began to address the meeting at Southport some observant members of the audience noticed his wife Clementine waving cheerfully from the platform to somebody high above. As Winston started to speak a high pitched voice from somewhere in the rafters shouted loudly 'VOTES FOR WOMEN' and continued to heckle his speech from a godlike position, out of reach of the stewards, up on high.

The incident did not dismay Winston Churchill, but the stewards were infuriated because disturbances by the suffragettes had been anticipated and two hundred and fifty pounds had been spent on precautions to try and prevent them from disturbing the meeting. What the organisers did not realise was that Dora Marsden and her colleagues had hidden in the

Mary Leiter was the daughter of a wealthy industrialist. She married George Curzon in 1895. She privately hated British politics and her appearances in Southport were only out of duty. This picture, taken towards the end of the nineteenth century, shows her as Vicerine of India - in a sense it was the highest position ever achieved by an American in the British Empire.
(Author's collection)

roof of the building for twenty four hours so as to be able to make their point. 'Enraged Liberal stewards sent them rolling down the steep roof', wrote Sylvia Pankhurst, 'and two of them were saved only through colliding with a cistern'. Dora Marsden very nearly became a martyr to the cause, a policeman seized her by the foot and prevented her from falling to what would have been certain death. 'If I had not caught you, you would have gone to glory', he said. The women were arrested and taken to court, but the magistrate had no wish to press the charges and the case was dismissed.[4] Churchill was back in Southport for the general election in the following year. One morning he decided to go for a walk on the beach with his wife, and he made the mistake of wearing a tiny felt hat which looked quite ridiculous perched on the expansive Churchillian features – this was long before the cigar had become his hallmark for the cartoonists. Churchill described the incident in some detail:

> One of the most necessary features of a public man's equipment is some distinctive mark which everyone learns to look for and recognise. Disraeli's forelock, Mr Gladstone's collars, Lord Randolf Churchill's moustache, Mr Chamberlain's eyeglass, Mr Baldwin's pipe – the properties' have the greatest value. I have never indulged in any of them, so to fill the need the cartoonists have invented the legend of my hats . . . A very tiny felt hat – I do not know where it came from – had been packed with my luggage. It lay on the hall table, and without thinking I put it on. As we came back from our walk, there was the photographer, and he took a picture. Ever since, the cartoonists and paragraphists have dwelt on my hats; how many they are, how strange and queer; and how I am always changing them, and what importance I attach to them, and so on. It is all rubbish, and it is founded on a single photograph.[5]

The Southport seat oscillated from Liberal to Conservative many more times than Winston Churchill; between 1898 and 1924 it changed hands no less than six times.

The 1910 general election was one of the earliest memories of the prominent historian Alan John Percival Taylor; he remembered shaking hands with Baron de Forest, the Liberal candidate for Southport, who was attired in an Austrian greatcoat right down to his ankles. Percy Lees Taylor, father of AJP, was a dedicated Liberal worker, and in his autobiography Alan Taylor described his father's attitude to the suffragette movement and provides an interesting sidelight to the Churchill incident:

> Women's suffrage, or rather the sufragettes, provided greater excitement. Many of the big meetings my parents attended were wrecked by suffragettes. My father was entirely on their side. Women, he thought, were entitled to the vote, and it was for them to judge what was the best way of getting it – an attitude he took later towards the working-class demand for Socialism. My mother was less approving, perhaps to cover a twinge of conscience that she ought to be demonstrating. Such twinges were to carry her far later. In her immediate reactions she was highly respectable – moralistic, teetotal, censorious of others. Inside there was a Madame Bovary struggling to get out.[6]

The Taylors frequently provided functions to raise money for the Liberals at their home in Crosby Road, Birkdale. The historian's brief description of one such gathering shows that women's suffrage was not the only disturbance which the Liberal gatherings had to tolerate:

> On one occasion my mother gave a garden party on the front lawn for the Liberal Women of Southport. I had just acquired a Red Indian suit. My cousin Margery and I painted our faces and burst on the Liberal Women through the conservatory, shrieking war cries. We were not well received. At a big dinner party, I was told, my father, an expert carver, announced that he had learnt his skill from an uncle who was a butcher. My mother was much offended by this revelation of 'low' relations. I expect most Birkdale families had similar skeletons in their cupboards.

The proposal to include Birkdale as part of Southport re-appeared every few years and became a reality in 1912. 'For some obscure reason, connected with the sewage', wrote Alan Taylor. The merger was a radical

Opposite

Top left - This picture of Station Road in Ainsdale shows just how much the popular and fashionable Lord Street was emulated locally. The iron canopies and tree-lined boulevard are very reminiscent of those which are so evocative of Southport's famous shopping mall.
(E.W. Collection)

Top right - A splendid view of Thom's tea rooms at 291 Lord Street. It was here that the young AJP Taylor spent many boring hours on his best behaviour in his mother's company. Thom had several other tea rooms, including one outside the Town Hall and one at the end of the pier.
(E.W. Collection)

Bottom left - Southport pier saw many eccentrics performing strange acts. Here a cyclist, perhaps the infamous Professor Powsey, waits to launch off the specially-constructed ramp.
(E.W. Collection)

Bottom right - And a high diver performs much the same feat without the aid of a bicycle.
(E.W. Collection)

cause, and my father's campaigning for it is one of my earliest political recollections. To the outsider nothing could be more obvious or beneficial to both places than the merger of Southport and Birkdale, but to many who lived in the latter town the issue was seen as a takeover to be resisted at all costs. Francis Bailey describes some of the moves in the very deliberate game of chess between Southport Corporation and Birkdale Council, showing that it was indeed the problem of sewage disposal which eventually gave Southport a checkmate. Birkdale's objections were very naturally founded on a sense of local pride allied to the fear of a loss of identity — there existed a subtle difference between the two towns in that Southport originated as a place of resort where Birkdale's origins were entirely residential. Ainsdale and even Formby had, at different times, formulated ideas for attracting visitors to their shores, but Birkdale alone always existed for residents and had never seriously entertained any thoughts in the other direction. In the long term Birkdale's attitude proved to be very fortunate for the area, and must be seen as one of the greatest single factors which ensured the preservation of the sandhills and the natural coastline.

In his mother's company young Alan Taylor was expected to be well-dressed and to behave himself, she took him to Thom's Japanese Tea Rooms in the Lord Street arcade where he, and sometimes his father as well, were expected to make polite and empty conversation. Saturday expeditions with his father, however, were of a rather different nature:

> Thanks to me he could escape from Thom's Japanese Tea Rooms. We had two regular treats. One was Funland, a miniature railway in a dark tunnel, where we saw such delights as dwarves working a corn mill and devils roasting sinners in Hell. The other was Professor Powsey, a deep sea diver — the first Professor in my acquaintance. For this we took a train along the pier until we reached the remote sea.

Thoms' Lounge, 291, Lord St., Southport.

Pier Head, Southport

Attractions

rom donkey riding, seaside bathing and strolling along the Promenade on a lovely summer's afternoon, to the antics of the 'mad Professors' at the end of the Pier, Southport has always been synonymous with entertainment and holidaymaking. Visitors would make the canal, railway and later the road journey to the town from far and wide and Southport was not slow in catering for the wide-ranging whims of its patrons. However, Southport has never become over-commercialised and much of the town centre retained a graciousness and elegance which are still admired by visitors to the town today and which still generates the love and affection of those who live here.

Right - The Lakeside Miniature Railway was opened in 1911 and ran from Pleasureland to the pier. It was always very popular with children and adults too because the locomotives were genuine miniature steam engines. (E.W. Collection)

Below left - A pier diver, no doubt one of the Professors, about to launch into the Irish Sea from atop Thom's Tearooms.

Below right - The redoubtable Professor Powsey with his Bamber bicycle at the very moment of departure 52 feet above the water. Both stunts look a pretty bad insurance risk. (Both pictures, E.W. Collection)

A view of the north end of the Marine Lake between the wars, the site of the Floral Hall. Note the bandstand near the tall flagpole.
(Valentine Collection, St. Andrews University Library)

Left - *A very serious-looking donkey handler together with her charges makes a very typical seaside scene.*
(E.W. Collection)

Centre left - *H. Wallis's motor switchback, Ainsdale.*
(E.W. Collection)

Centre right - *The New Promenade, seen here soon after the King's Gardens were opened by George V and Queen Mary. The landscaping is beautifully done, with flower beds, Italian-style summer houses, stone balustrades and curved flights of steps.*
(St. Andrews University Library)

Bottom - *Southport's big attractions included the water shute which deposited holidaymakers into the Marine Lake at high speed and the Maxim flying machine which whirled them around until they were dizzy.*
(St. Andrews University Library)

In the summer months all the resorts on the Irish Sea were connected by a regular service of paddle steamers, and the pier head was the place where day trippers from other resorts disembarked for Southport. The arrival of the paddle steamer *Belle* was a fine sight; she was accompanied by clouds of black smoke from her twin funnels, mixed with plumes of white steam hissing from her escape valves and siren. She manoeuvered into position by reversing one of her paddles and churning the water into an angry white froth beneath it. As she edged nearer to the berth the deck hands stooped in readiness to throw the hawsers over the pier bollards. Agile sailors lept across the gap and criss-crossed the ropes skilfully around the bollards; there was an ominous and strange creaking as the taught hemp took up the inertia of the steamer, the pier thrilled through its iron legs as it took up the strain, the gangplank was thrown across for the holidaymakers to disembark and there was a sudden relative silence as the *Belle* stopped churning her paddles.

Passengers arriving from the steamers, and those like Alan Taylor who were prepared to make the long journey to the end of the pier, could be entertained by the redoubtable Professor Powsey who held a chair of his own making in bicycle diving. The Professor was attired in a very modern bathing suit, like a pair of longjohns with a fashionable hooped design. He made a few formal poses before the spectators, then mounted his velocipede at the top of a curved ramp. There followed a flurry of pedalling as potential and muscular energy was converted into kinetic, the Professor launched himself off the pier and into the firmament, performing gyrations which demonstrated Euler's Dynamical Equations for Rotating Bodies, and ended up a sorry mess in the Irish Sea. When Professor Powsey's wet head resurfaced, however, it was to claps and cheers from the onlookers craning over the edge of the pier to see him.

The holiday trade saw some extravagant additions to Southport. An example was the Winter Gardens, a building complex next to the Cheshire Lines Railway Station on the north side of Lord Street and dating from the 1870s. The Winter Gardens complex was built to rival the Crystal Palace at Sydenham. At one end was a Conservatory 180 feet long with a roof eighty feet high. It housed tropical trees, hot house plants and exotic flowers. From one side of the Conservatory ran a long hall called the Promenade, built with colonnades supporting galleries beneath a hammer beam ceiling; it led to another great hall called the Pavilion which architecturally balanced the Conservatory. The Pavilion was an auditorium built to seat 2,500 people where visitors could sit and listen to a thirty piece orchestra which gave two performances a day.

Palladium, Southport

Even Churchtown was affected by the holiday trade and the Strawberry Gardens near the bridge over the Old Pool were re-landscaped and became known by the impressive title of the Botanical Gardens. These gardens were on land donated by the Rev Charles Hesketh who served the community as both squire and rector. The gardens sprouted rockeries, fountains and grottos, the Old Pool was widened to form a boating lake, and the Botanic Gardens eventually acquired a fernery, a magnificent conservatory, and a refreshment room which served breakfast, dinner, and afternoon teas. The first visitors to the Botanic Gardens arrived from Southport by horse drawn tram, and Paul Lloyd described the trams as he remembered them in the winter months passing through the village on their grooved rails.

> Tramcars were pulled by a pair of general purpose horses hitched to a single-tree on a double-tree which was attached to the tram by a draw bolt at either end of the vehicle. The tramcars were double deckers with a stairway at each end. The driver sat on a three-legged stool and in winter he was wrapped in blankets. He always had a red face. In very cold weather straw was thickly laid on the floor of the lower deck which was closed, the upper deck was open to the weather.*

The first of the electric trams ran in July 1900 and by 1902 the whole of the tramway system had been converted to electric traction. The railways, too, were quick to adopt electrification and the line to Liverpool was electrified in 1903. The Lancashire and Yorkshire Railway Company wanted it to become the first electrified line in the country but narrowly failed to achieve this ambition.

The first electricity generating station opened in 1894, and the trees and

---

The Albany Buildings.
(Engraving, Botanic Gardens Museum)

*Paul Lloyd's first job was on the tramways, which explains his attention to the details of the tractive mechanism.

gardens in front of the Town Hall were illuminated by incandescent electric lamps in the same year. In 1902, at the coronation festivities for Edward VII, coloured lamps were introduced in the trees, and these proved to be so popular and attractive that the corporation decided to keep them as a permanent summer feature.

It was Lord Street which was the main attraction of Southport, and as the Edwardian age gained momentum Lord Street gained a little more in stature every year. Visitors arriving at the east end of Lord Street were greeted by the perspective of a long tree-lined avenue stretching into the distance over a mile away. Here was a panorama to equal any in England.

The boulevard was ninety yards wide from frontage to frontage. On the north side were the fashionable shops selling wares of every kind and built in a grand Victorian medley of architectural styles. Mock Tudor stood alongside Gothic, Jacobean, and Classical buildings, with an assortment of Flemish, Greek, Italian and even Muslim styles. Ornate cast iron canopies lined the frontages along practically the whole length of the boulevard, hanging baskets with colourful floral displays hung from the canopies every few yards, a broad pavement ran down to the road and kept the traffic at a respectable distance. On the south side were houses with long gardens running down to another tree-lined pavement; they shared the frontage with churches, civic buildings and public gardens.

In London Square a policeman in a blue uniform with a handlebar moustache stood in a box and directed the traffic with the motions of his white-gloved hands. His polished buttons and the brasses on his helmet gleamed in the sunshine. Down the centre of the street ran the electric trams. They were small vehicles with helical staircases and platforms at each end and they had open toast rack seats on the top. Their sides were covered with notices and advertisements which made the destination signs seem insignificant. The trams competed with horse drawn traffic, but the

The six pictures on these pages give some idea of the enormous range of styles which stand side by side on Lord Street. Thankfully, much of the best architecture of the late Victorian and Edwardian periods remains and still constitutes one of the main assets of the town.

Transport

he nineteenth century saw the development of the railway as the main mode of transport to the seaside, but the twentieth century brought with it many other revolutions in transport. By 1900 the electric trams were running in Southport. These, fondly remembered by many people, were a familiar feature of many an early photograph. Two years later the Vulcan car was coming off the production lines in the town and within a few years motor vehicles had arrived in great numbers to pose new difficulties for the town centre. And even before the decade was out, primitive heavier-than-air-flying machines made their debut on Southport sands, using the flat expanses towards Freshfield as a basic runway.

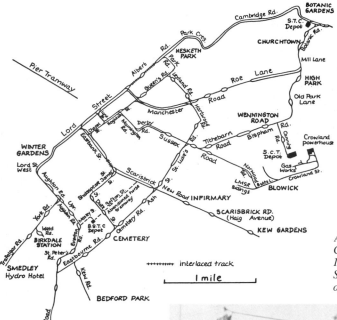

Above - *Number 6 tram, photographed outside the Cambridge Hall some time between 1900 and 1904, in the dark green and white livery of the Southport Tramways Company which had a fleet of twenty trams and a depot at Churchtown.*

Above - *A sketch plan of the tramway system of Southport based on the work of C. Greenwood. The lines were an amalgamation of two main tramway companies and the various depots can be identified. The last tram ran on December 31st, 1934.*

Right - *A familiar sight earlier this century.*
(E.W. Collection)

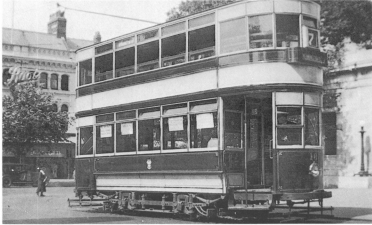

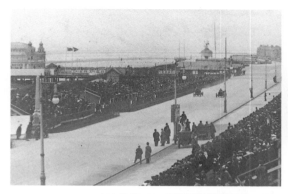

Above left - *The beach was used for motor racing. In this picture the course is along the Promenade and continued to Rotten Row. The slope at Weld Road was used to help the vehicles stop. In 1926 Major Henry Segrave created a new land speed record of 160 mph on the beach at Birkdale.*
(E.W. Collection)

Above right - *The beach was also ideal as a runway. The Farman biplane went into production in 1909 and the Bristol Boxkite (1910) was an unashamed reproduction of Farman's machine. Mr King's plane shown here is the original article.*
(E. W. Collection)

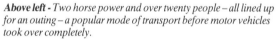

Above left - *Two horse power and over twenty people – all lined up for an outing – a popular mode of transport before motor vehicles took over completely.*
(E.W. Collection)

Above right - *A pre-war bus waits for passengers at the Shore Road Terminus in Ainsdale. The popular scarlet and cream livery of the Southport Corporation continued until the early seventies when the buses were repainted in the rather insipid green livery of the new County of Merseyside.*
(E.W. Collection)

Right - *A fine selection of veteran cars line up for a meet in Edwardian Southport. Many of the cars are of 1890s' vintage, of dog-cart construction with tiller steering. The Vulcan foundry at Crossens was one of the first British motor car factories; Vulcan cars were manufactured from 1902 to 1929.*
(Photo, Botanic Gardens Museum)

Above left - _This picture shows the unveiling ceremony of Frampton's statue of Queen Victoria by the Mayor of Southport, Councillor Brown, on 5th July, 1904. In the background is the Atkinson Library and Art Gallery._
(E.W. Collection)

Above right - _The statue stood in the Municipal Gardens for over 8 years but was moved to the Promenade in December, 1912, in which position we see it in this picture._
(E.W. Collection)

Right - _In Edwardian times the Southport Town Band in their smart uniforms and headgear was nearly forty strong and sported two double basses as well as a fine selection of wind instruments. This photograph, taken around 1905, appears to be from the bandstand outside the Cambridge Hall. William Rimmer is seated in the centre in different attire._
(Photo, Botanic Gardens Museum)

occasional horseless carriage had made its appearance — brightly painted vehicles with open chasses and spoked wheels, and with an assortment of polished brass horns and brake levers outside the driver's seat. The driver himself was an enthusiast in a heavy coat, driving gloves and goggles, striving to keep his underpowered vibrating vehicle out of the way of the horses and the tramlines.

Centrally situated on Lord Street was the classical Town Hall, the Atkinson Library, and the typically Victorian Cambridge Hall with its steep tower housing a four-faced public clock. In front of these buildings were gardens with trees and terra cotta fountains, presided over by a solid statue of her late majesty standing on a high pedestal. In the gardens stood a bandstand; people sat or strolled as they listened to the music of a splendidly attired military band with a repertoire of patriotic marching tunes. The soldiers and bandsmen wore red uniforms and sported military sidewhiskers, they were the guardians of that world-wide empire on which the sun never set . . .

A man in a tweed suit and matching deerstalker hat strode purposefully across the road to do business in the bank. A tattle of elderly ladies made towards one of the teashops, gossiping so fast that nobody could get a word in edgeways. A nursemaid in a white starched uniform pushed a perambulator with a small charge inside it — the charge was a baby boy in his frilly petticoats. A crocodile of schoolgirls wearing white dresses and straw hats with long ribbons was chaperoned by daunting spinsters severely attired in black. The girls put their noses in the air and tried to ignore the grins and grimaces of a clutch of peak-capped schoolboys. An open horse-drawn carriage came by with an Edwardian family, father and

The remarkable thing about this early photograph of Lord Street is that it is instantly recognisable today by the Midland Bank frontage and the entrance to the Wayfarers Arcade. There appear to be tramlines but no overhead cables; this would date it close to the turn of the century, before the electrification in 1900.
(E.W. Collection)

mother, two small boys in sailor suits and a teenage sister waving happily to a friend on the pavement, grandfather beamed ruddily through his whiskers as a tiny granddaughter, totally engrossed by the scene, sat on his knee.

To be seen promenading on Lord Street it was considered necessary to be attired in the best possible display of finery. Men wore bowler hats with fancy waistcoats of bright colours, and some had striped blazers and straw boaters. The older men favoured top hats with darker suits and tails, and carried walking sticks with silver handles. But it was the ladies who excelled in this Edwardian fashion parade. Some were attired in smart, closely tailored suits with shaped ankle length skirts, others favoured white blouses with lace frills at the neck and at the wrists of their wide sleeves. Slender silken gloves were the fashion with matching silk parasoles, and with carefully chosen bracelets, necklaces and ear rings. The ladies were crowned with elaborate hairstyles and large fanciful hats trimmed with lace and fine feathers. Their male escorts were mere appendages to these doyens of fashion who promenaded along the wide pavement of the boulevard.

At the south end of the street was a stone tablet set into a wall. It had an inscription consisting of one long rambling sentence which related to a house which no longer existed:

IN THE YEAR OF OUR LORD
1792
THIS HOUSE WAS BUILT
IN MEMORY of D. W. SUTTON
of North Meols who was the first Founder Executor of
South-Port which was call'd his
Folly for many Years and it proves
that his foresight was his wisdom
which should be remembered with
Gratitude by the LORDS of this
Manor and by the Inhabitants of this
PLACE ALSO

Even though it only came into existence at the beginning of the nineteenth century, A J P Taylor wrote flippantly on the first page of his autobiography. 'The origins of Southport are as legendary as those of Troy'.

Above - *Chapel Street, 1840. Christ Church, on the right of the picture, is the only building in this scene which now survives. On the left can be seen the Congregational Chapel, built in 1823, which gave Chapel Street its name.*
(E.W. Collection)

Right - *The Congregational Chapel, seen here in an early photograph. Here the Rev Greatbatch preached to his loyal flock. The chapel was a great improvement on the wooden structure where the Congregationalists previously met – and when umbrellas were sometimes needed during the service!*
(E.W. Collection)

Bottom - *A lively winter scene of hectic activity is captured by W.G. Herdman at Peter's Slack. This area was badly drained and liable to flooding. It provided an excellent skating rink in times of hard frost. The site is where the Fire Station now stands in Manchester Road.*
(Botanic Gardens Museum)

Above and centre - *Two views of Nevill Street. Both pictures show a vast amount of detail; tradesmen and shops of all descriptions will be remembered by many a Sandgrounder. Note the splendid lack of vehicular traffic in both these views, a peace which would be shattered only a few years later.*
(E.W. Collection)

Bottom - *The Market Hall and Eastbank Street. The Market Hall was built in 1881 and stood at the junction of Chapel Street and Eastbank Street. Other entrances were in King Street and Market Street. The dome was a familiar sight for about 30 years but the building was destroyed by fire in 1913.*
(E.W. Collection)

Top - *Looking down Chapel Street the facade of Broadbents can be seen on the left, and the canopy of the station is visible just behind tram number 12. Chapel Street apparently never had more than a single tram line in spite of the volume of traffic.*
(E.W. Collection)

1

2

3

4

5

6

This page

Top - *An Infirmary and Local Dispensary was built in Virginia Street in 1870 and served until 1895 when the new Infirmary was opened with great ceremony in Scarisbrick New Road.*

Centre - *The Promenade Hospital, one of the most distinctive buildings on the Promenade. The older parts of the hospital date from 1853 but the grand frontage was built between 1880 and 1883 and partly financed by the surplus from the Lancashire Cotton Relief Fund.*

Bottom - *The Cemetery was opened in December, 1865, at a site on Snuttering Lane, and the latter henceforth became known as Cemetery Road. The gatehouses and chapel are virtually unchanged.*

(All photos, E.W. Collection)

Opposite

1 – A view of Turner's yard in Hawesside Street between the wars.

2 - Harry Ellans, of 5 Gordon Street; a second-hand shop hidden in the back streets, a common sight between the wars.

3 – A London Street coal merchant does his rounds between the wars.

4 – A splendid early photograph of a shopping scene on Lord Street with the familiar facade of Wayfarers Arcade standing proudly on the right.

5 – Two patient housewives wait for the proprietor to pose for the photographer, outside Robinson's shop.

6 – London Street. The mock-Tudor building on the left still exists, now Goffey & Co., solicitors.

(All photos, E.W. Collection)

This page

Top - *Early in the 20th century, Southport had four large hydropathic establishments. They offered Russian and Turkish baths, oscillatory and vibratory massage, Galvanism and radiant heat treatments. The largest was the Smedley, built in extensive grounds in Birkdale. This picture shows the Kenworthy's, which still exists as private residences in Bath Street; the frontage is virtually unchanged.*

Centre - *A group of war wounded line up in the grounds of Grange Hospital in 1915.*

Bottom - *A World War One tank provides a platform for wartime speakers. The Lusitania was torpedoed and sunk in 1915, which dates this picture in May 1918. (All photos, E.W. Collection)*

Opposite

1 – The Municipal Gardens were again redesigned in 1911. The distinctive circular bandstand was built in 1913 and is remembered with great affection. The circular bandstand was demolished in 1969 and Lord Street continued without a bandstand until 1984 when a new one was built to Martin Perry's design on the opposite side of Eastbank Street Square.

2 – The interior of the Southport Palais de Danse on Lord Street in the 1920s, showing the Chinese decor, the lanterns and the balconies around the huge dance floor.

3 – The Alexandra Hotel on Scarisbrick New Road dates from about 1860 and became the nucleus of Alexandra Gardens. This engraving is from the 1870s, when the hotel sported a dance floor; it was renamed the Richmond in 1884.

4 – An engraving of the Prince of Wales Hotel in the 1870s.

5 – A very early photograph of the Promenade.

(Botanic Gardens Museum)

6 – A view of the Promenade at the turn of the century, showing the Victoria Hotel and Victoria Baths.

(Valentine Collection, St Andrews University Library)

(All photos, except 5 and 6, E.W. Collection)

UNDED PATIENTS AT THE GRANGE HOSPITAL, AUG 4TH 1915

Left - *The Municipal Gardens were redesigned in 1877; the terra cotta fountains were a popular feature of the gardens. The octagonal bandstand can be seen in many early views and first appears in Edwardian times. Note the bathchair in front of the fountain.*
(E.W. Collection)

Right - *A fine panoramic view of Lord Street taken from the Town Hall. The statue of Queen Victoria dates this scene between 1904 and 1912.*
(Valentine Collection, St Andrews University Library)

Below left - *The Monument; an early view showing the striking white Portland stone with which it was built.   (E.W. Collection)*

Below right - *The water shute, Maxim flying machine and the Aerial Flight with crowds of holidaymakers on the sands.*
(E.W. Collection)

Right - *An evocative scene at the turn of the century of promenading along the pier. The pier railway can be seen over the barrier on the right.*

Bottom left - *Rotten Row, which was previously described as 'a very indifferent thoroughfare', was in line with Southport Promenade and became a fashionable parade for Birkdale.*

Bottom right - *Shore Road, Ainsdale, in the 1920s.*
(All photos, E.W. Collection)

Chapter Sixteen

The Twentieth Century

N the twentieth century Southport was claimed to be the only place in England where the number of churches and chapels exceeded the number of licensed houses. Whether this was due to sobriety or to an excessive zeal for religion is a point which has yet to be determined, but all the major denominations were well represented and the residents certainly found plenty of competition for the care of their souls. The new rector of North Meols, Canon James Denton Thompson, decided that it was time to close down and demolish the old parish church. The new and beautiful church of Emmanuel was one of the finest and most modern in the country, and as he considered St Cuthbert's to be a place quite unsuitable for public worship, he recommended that Emmanuel be made the new parish church of North Meols.

To outsiders Canon Thompson was not a new rector at all. He had served for over a decade at his post but, considering that he was only the fifth rector since the death of Edward Shakespeare in 1748, he still had over twenty years to serve before he could achieve even the average length of incumbency expected of him. When, in 1906 he was offered the post of Rector of Birmingham, many people in his parish were delighted that he accepted his new appointment.

The Reverend Robert Bibby Blakeney was appointed as successor, and remained for a respectable 42 years as rector. It was generally agreed that Canon Thompson had made a point about the parish church: the over-enthusiastic reconstructions of the nineteenth century had left St Cuthbert's as a clumsy place of worship. Robert Blakeney immediately applied himself to the task of rebuilding the church and on 8th February 1909 Frank Cheetham came to look at the reconstruction which was then in progress. 'With Mr Bulpit this morning at St Cuthbert's Churchtown', he wrote. 'To have a look at the new chancel now building, and the alterations in progress. The roof is being put on the chancel, and the whole body of the church is practically gutted. Just four walls and a roof. There is nothing to regret, the new work seems in character. Mr Bulpit was anxious for me to see some fragments of the older building found in the walls, but these do not appear to be more than bits of sixteenth century mullioned windows with moulded heads.'[1]

It is surprising that Cheetham, who was the finest and most professional of local historians, was not more excited by these finds - virtually nothing is known of the church fabric in the sixteenth century and from this evidence an expert may have been able to give at least an opinion on the construction of the windows. Cheetham and Bulpit were probably

Above - *The Rev Mr Hall was an Independent clergyman whose Calvanistic doctrines were not acceptable to the Rev George Greatbatch. But Pastor Hall found a wealthy sponsor in a Liverpool builder called Bartin Haid, and was able to set up his own 'Independent Mission'. This site is now Hall Street. The railway was a temporary line laid to service the limekilns alongside from the main line of the Lancashire and Yorkshire Railway.*
(E.W. Collection)

Right - *A late photograph of the chapel with the windows sadly bricked up and the thatch in disrepair.*
(Photo, Botanic Gardens Museum)

motivated to search for more clues about the older church, but nothing more came to light.

At this time the rectory in Roe Lane was still the residence of the Hesketh family, and when the First World War broke out Meols Hall was used as a military hospital. In 1919, when the war had ended, the Heskeths moved from the Rookery to take up residence in Meols Hall and the old manorial hall regained its status after a gap of 186 years. It was also after the Great War that the town took the opportunity to raise a memorial to 1,133 local people who died in the service of their country, and in 1923 The Monument became the centre piece of Lord Street. Built from white Portland stone, it consists of a simple obelisk rising to 67 feet, flanked by twin colonnades each supported by Doric columns. The colonnades have coffered ceilings and sanctums at each end where the names of the dead are inscribed on marble tablets.

The decade after the Great War saw many new attractions in Southport. The opening of Pleasureland brought the rides and fairbooths which clustered around the Marine Lake into a self contained, purpose built site. In 1928 the new Sea Bathing Lake replaced an earlier, less impressive, bathing pool. In the 1930s Ainsdale Bathing Centre was opened and

The Monument. Built of white Portland Stone in 1923 to the designs of Hastewell and A.L. McMillan. The names of 1133 dead are inscribed in the sanctums.

The limitations of Southport as a place for sea bathing were very obvious. The first alternative to sea bathing was a pool built on the north side of the Marine Drive in 1914. It was very popular but was unsheltered and had a poor water purification system. When the new Sea Bathing Lake was opened in 1928 no expense was spared to rectify the earlier deficiencies and the pool was probably the finest in the country. It proved to be a very worthwhile investment and a big attraction for the town.
(E.W. Collection)

provided an alternative to Southport for bathing. The twenties also saw two very sad events which were the end of an era for the town. One was the departure of the last steamer from the end of Southport Pier in 1923 and the other was the closing of the lifeboat station in 1926. The last North Meols Court Leet and Court Baron was held in July 1926 and marked the end of a much older era.

In 1927 Southport played host to a gathering of the world's astronomers who assembled to observe a total eclipse of the sun. The town happened to lie right on the path of totality. Measurememts of the bending of light by the sun's gravitational field, to vindicate Einstein's General Theory of Relativity, had been made by Eddington from the eclipse of 1919 which was observed in Brazil. The 1927 eclipse was the first occasion on which the measurements could be taken in this country. The Round House at Hillside, built by Luke Highton in 1924/5, was the highest point in the town and became a popular observation point. Another conglomeration of telescopes and cameras appeared at the recently built King George V School on Scarisbrick New Road.

It was in 1926 that the boys' secondary school moved from its site at the Woodlands to a new building opened by the Earl of Derby, and became

Above left - *The round house at Hillside has always attracted interest. It was built in 1924-25 by Luke Highton (1850-1931). The round dome on the top has now been replaced. It is a good observation point and is the highest in Southport. The Solar Eclipse of 1927 was observed from here.*

(E.W. Collection)

Above right - *Mount Street gaily decorated for the Coronation of 1937.*

(Photo, Botanic Gardens Museum)

known as King George V School. The new building happened to be in the road where the school had begun life in temporary accommodation two years before moving to the Woodlands in 1920. The new building was a fine classical design of the decade. It was built in a large rectangle with classrooms on two levels, and with a central assembly hall creating two quadrangles. Exceptions to the two level design were the single storey science laboratories situated at the rear of the school and the music and art rooms, the only second floor classrooms, situated centrally above the school library.. Two wings were added to the main building, one containing the gymnasium and a wood and metal working block, and balanced on the other side by a wing housing the school kitchens and dining room.

King George V School chose the red rose of Lancashire for its emblem. The building was designed to float on a reinforced concrete raft on land which had bordered the mere many centuries earlier – but even twentieth century technology was unable to subdue Martin Mere and after sixty years the school had suffered so badly from subsidence that it had to be demolished. It became a grammar school after the 1944 Education Act and it is of interest that Kenneth Baker, the Conservative Minister of Education, was a pupil for a short time after the war – most of his primary education was at Trinity School in Southport.

The Girls' High School was founded in 1907 and was therefore an older foundation than the boys' school. It, too, occupied premises in Scarisbrick New Road for many years and did not move to purpose built accommodation at Greenbank in Hillside until the 1950s. The Southport Technical College was opened in 1935, and a School of Arts and Crafts was added in 1938.

The growth of the town still continued between the wars, but less rapidly than in the previous generation. Fields and sandhills still existed between Southport and Churchtown in the 1920s, but in 1927 a portion of the Hesketh estate was sold for private development and houses were built in the area bounded by Roe Lane, Bibby Road and the railway to Preston. The new housing development meant that one of the few surviving portions of the Churchgate footpath would be lost, and the *Southport Visiter* described the changeover from footpath to road.

> The portion of this old footpath between Roe-Lane and Bibby-Road was officially closed, or stopped, about a year ago. That meant that building could proceed on the land occupied by the footpath, but until recently the path has been interfered with only near the Roe-lane end, the rest of it being frequently used by pedestrians and cyclists. Last week, however, the boundary walls of the back garden of a house in the new Churchgate, the name of the new road parallel with the old footpath, were begun, cutting across the path at about mid-length, and enclosing a part of it in the garden.[2]

Transport developed rapidly in the years between the wars and Southport was served by a very comprehensive network of tramlines and railways. The last electric tram ran on New Year's Eve 1934, and was replaced by a motor bus in the new year. Air transport too was commonplace in the thirties and the firm sands of the beach made an ideal natural runway. In 1937 the first pictures of George VI's Coronation were rushed from London to Southport where they were put aboard Merrill and Lambie's aircraft. The plane took off from the beach for a transatlantic flight to America and the pictures appeared in the *New York Times* the following morning.

During the Second World War air raid warnings were very frequent when the Luftwaffe followed the coast to bomb the docks at Liverpool, but the town suffered very few bombs. The main contribution to the war effort was the use of the larger hotels for government departments evacuated from Westminster, the use of other hotels for military purposes and the large number of refugees who were accommodated by the people of the town.

One wartime story worth repeating concerns a busload of refugees from Liverpool which was approaching the top of Meols Cop Bridge during the blackout. The conductor was counting up his money and had a satchel loaded with coppers and silver, a whole day's takings. The bus hit a ramp where the road was under repair and the jolt caused the strap of the conductor's satchel to break. The satchel fell to the platform and bounced onto the road; money and tickets were scattered all over the bridge in the darkness. All the passengers dismounted and for half an hour everybody searched in the blackout for coins and tickets. The conductor had to find all the missing money from his own pocket, and the next day he was out at dawn to search in the daylight. When he eventually sat down to work out his losses he found that every one of the refugees possessed the wartime spirit of honesty - his money was short by about three pence.

The fifties and the sixties were prosperous decades and 1955 saw the publication of Francis Bailey's *History of Southport*. This was not the first definitive history of the town but it was by far the most professional. Bailey made full use of the material accumulated by Frank Cheetham, and produced a highly valued masterpiece which combined historical accuracy with readability in a way which is seldom equalled. Francis Arthur Bailey was born at Lutterworth in 1904, he came to Lancashire in 1926 as a teacher of history at Prescot Grammar School and many of his publications are on the history of Prescot. F T Wainwright, one of his few close friends, tells us something of his character:

> . . . he had a dry sense of humour which made even his enthusiasms curiously restful and which, in a lighter convivial vein, made him an ideal companion. There was a solid permanent quality about his friendship. With him one could pick up the threads of a conversation dropped a year before, without retracing steps or re-stating the bases of the argument − all that could be taken for granted on the assumption that time alone had not changed fundamental principles and attitudes. He remained himself against changing backgrounds − in his study with his hundreds of carefully written notebooks, at a meeting summoned to launch some new project, on the wrong bus in a wartime black-out, at a hilarious party in Aberdeen, climbing to see a hill-fort in Cheshire, or balancing precariously on a windswept cliff overlooking Moray Firth . . .[3]

It was a tragedy that Frank Bailey did not live long enough to enjoy the respect which he earned through his finest work, for he died just as his history was going to press.

The inevitable decline of traditional industries was very evident in the fifties. The last fishing boats had disappeared, but the shrimping industry just managed to survive and a few shankers were still earning a diminishing living by putting for shrimps. The last of the horse drawn shrimping carts disappeared in the 1960s but the industry soldiered on using mechanised vehicles.

The North Meols dialect was still commonly spoken by the older

Parks and Gardens

outhport has spawned a gardener to rival Lady Chatterley's', wrote the film critics when the film *Mr Love* was released. Postcards from the early part of this century often featured the various gardens, depicting them from all aspects and at different times of the year. The town owes much to its municipal gardens and it has always taken immense pride in its parks, gardens and floral displays. The Southport Flower Show was inaugurated in 1924 and within a few years became established as second only to Chelsea in terms of scope and appeal. Ornamental gardens were built in Victoria Park every year in August as part of the show and the herbacious borders of Rotten Row became a permanent feature. When a conference centre opened on the Promenade in 1930, it was given the name of the Floral Hall.

Right - *A fine engraving of Hesketh Park showing the weather observatory and the lake. The trees are still very small and do not obscure the houses on the skyline, but they are well established.*
(Botanic Gardens Museum)

Left - *Hesketh Park was opened by the mayor, Dr Peter Wood, on May 1, 1868. Here the flags fly near the entrance lodge (which still survives). Many people doubted that the sandhills of the park would ever be able to grow trees and flowers.*
(Photo, Botanic Gardens Museum)

Top left - *This absorbing little group with their beautiful hats captures the spirit of a walk in the park better than any form of words.*
(E.W. Collection)

Top right - *The site of this magnificent conservatory is now a display of spring bedding flowers, but the fernery which stood behind it still exists.*
(E.W. Collection)

Centre - *A delightful picture of boating in the Botanic Gardens.*
(E.W. Collection)

Right - *The Floral Hall, built in 1930 with the object of providing a better conference facility for Southport.*
(E.W. Collection)

generation in the decades after the war, and it lingered on far longer in a large number of families. In 1982, long after everybody thought the dialect was dead, Richard Sutton recorded it in a booklet about Marshside. He attempted to identify pronunciations and figures of speech which were peculiar to the area and produced a dictionary of about 1500 dialect words. With the help of his older brother, William Sutton, he produced a table of about 200 nicknames listed against proper names. It was very heartening to find that his book became an immediate sellout in Southport.

The preservation of Churchtown has been treated with consideration and affection, and it still retains much of the character which it had as the main village of North Meols — much of the credit for this must go to the late Roger Hesketh, a very considerate and responsible lord of the manor. The same cannot be said for the newer Churchtown shopping centre where the closing of the railway to Preston gave modern planners an opportunity for small scale redevelopment. It would be difficult to find a better example with which to illustrate the 'twentieth- century decline in standards' than this development - there does not even seem to be a building line. The only consolation is that given sufficient time planning errors of this kind can be corrected, unlike the inexplicable decision to demolish Birkdale Town Hall with its accompanying library and law courts — a blunder which can never be corrected. It was unfortunate that Cedric Greenwood's book *Thatch, Towers and Colonnades,* which did more than any previous publication to make the public aware of the architecture of Southport, appeared just after Birkdale Town Hall had been demolished.

To these post-war woes must be added the loss of a football league club which, with very limited financial resources, did much for the town, put the name of Southport in the football results every Saturday and even on the league's honours list. To win a fourth division championship was a fine achievement for a team with the slender resources of Southport Football Club, but the demise of Southport FC is a good example of a self made problem. The players, the directors and all the staff gave their everything to keep league football in Southport, as did a few thousand very loyal supporters. But the town simply did not give the club the support it deserved. At Wigan the people did support their club and few could honestly argue that Wigan did not merit their place in the Football League more than did Southport. Here the influence of the times is very evident and the loss of league football must be seen in the perspective of the region as a whole. It is a minor consolation to find that there are places where the loss of first division football is a greater blow than the loss of fourth division football is to Southport. Will we ever again have the pleasure of seeing a town with the population of Burnley boasting the finest football team in the country?

When the controversial decision was taken to desert Lancashire and become part of the new metropolitan county of Merseyside the reasons given were weak and unconvincing. The population around Southport was for some reason considered insufficient to form a metropolitan borough on its own, and the area became part of the borough of Sefton with its clumsy bimodal distribution of population. The decision to become part of Merseyside was by no means an easy one. Liverpool has always thought highly of Southport and under different circumstances the decision might have had much happier consequences, but it transpired that Southport was left without its own local government and with greatly reduced control over local affairs. Liverpool's social and unemployment problems unfortunately proved to be so severe that any suggestion to the effect that Southport suffered a loss of identity cut no ice at all.

Southport has a very definite identity, and this sense of identity is one of the many theories which have been put forward to explain the success of Ronnie Fearn for the Liberals in the 1987 general election. The result was a great personal success for the new member of parliament, but it was also a vote by a town wanting to be represented by a man with a real interest in his native constituency. The vote was against the national swing because much of it was not for a political party; in many ways it was similar to the vote which gave Roger Hesketh such large majorities in the 1950s. It came as no surprise to find that in the first months of 1988 a strong campaign was launched for the improvement of the local government situation with a proposal to create a new borough council based on Southport and Formby.

Some of the other problems facing Southport in the twentieth century are the greatly exaggerated traditional problems. One of these problems is the loss of the sea − a retreat which is real enough but which has generated bad jokes for much too long. Thomas Glazebrook in 1809 wrote that the sea was distant two miles at low tide, Gimcrack's holidaymakers had to take the waters before breakfast, and throughout the nineteenth century the sea was only suitable for bathing at high tide. It is wrong to assume that the retreating coastline is a recent problem; visitors know exactly what to expect and have always been prepared to make the most out of it and to treat high tide at Southport as an event to be savoured and enjoyed.

The time has come for somebody to point out the advantages of a retreating sea. The Marine Lake, the Promenade Gardens, Princes Park, Pleasureland, the Sea Bathing Lake, Happiland, the Municipal Golf Links − these are all built on land which the sea has released, and there is more land available. Southport would never have been able to build such an impressive pier if the beach had not been so shallow. Whether the tide is in or out, the Marine Lake provides water sports facilities which the sea cannot provide, without the problems of sea pollution, and provides them in full view of the Promenade. The retreat of the sea creates exciting planning opportunities near the town centre which would be the envy of many seaside resorts. Land can be developed to create more sporting and leisure facilities which, as free time becomes more common, will become an asset to the town. To the north, at Crossens and Marshside, reclaimed land has been used for housing developments and has thereby released some of the pressure on the conservation areas to the south.

It is often said that the large number of retired people in the town creates a problem and a strain on resources. Like many coastal resorts, Southport has always been a popular place for retirement; it has an active elderly population and there is some evidence to support the traditional claims of longevity. Southport is fortunate, however, in that it is also able to attract younger people who are prepared to travel daily to Liverpool or Manchester for their work. The percentage of retired people is thus lower than in the South Coast resorts and in some of the resorts on the Fylde. Concern for the elderly is a national problem. It is good to see this concern in Southport. People generally are enjoying better medical care and nutrition and are living longer, but it is misleading to suggest that the problem of the elderly is more acute in Southport than in other seaside places.

It is important to ensure that the town is still able to attract young people and the new blood which makes a welcome contribution to the social life. To attract couples with children is essential, and schooling and other educational aspects are of great importance. The introduction of comprehensive education proved to be difficult and painful in Southport where a very successful grammar and secondary modern school system was in operation until 1978. Many people feel that Southport must do more to meet the difficult and exacting requirements of a good secondary education − another point in favour of strong local government.

The loss of league football has not affected the enthusiasm for actually playing the game, and the traditional English games of both football and cricket have always been well represented by flourishing local leagues. The Southport and Birkdale Cricket Club was founded in 1859, and soon after celebrating its centenary it was able to stage an annual game of first-class cricket with Lancashire as the host side. Tennis, too, has always been well represented at high levels, and Red Rum has assured Birkdale of a place in the history of the Grand National. If preference is to be given to any one sport, however, then it must go to the one which found the sandhills ideal for its requirements. The Hesketh Golf Club, founded in 1885, predates Birkdale by four years, Southport Old Links has its origins around the turn of the century, the Southport and Ainsdale Club dates from 1907, Hillside from 1912 and the Municipal Golf Links from 1913. Thus, from before the First World War up to the present time the town has boasted no fewer than six full scale golf courses within its boundaries. The Southport and Ainsdale Golf Course has been the scene of many great golfing moments. One of the most exciting matches to be played there must be the Ryder Cup of 1937 between Britain and the United States. The outcome hung in the balance until the last putt, Easterbrook playing for Britain:

> Easterbrook putted first and lay dead; Shute gave the hole a chance, ran four feet past it, and missed the return putt. Easterbrook holed his short putt, and players, green, and all were engulfed in people. Britain had pulled through after all.

The Royal Birkdale is an even better known course, but did not reach its prime as a championship course until after the war. Peter Dobereiner describes the course as seen by the modern golfer:

> The links of Royal Birkdale divide the world of golf. Those who adhere to the Pilgrim's Progress school of architecture, insisting that a round of golf should test a man's character as he battles against hidden perils, hold Birkdale in low esteem. It is unfaithful to the links' tradition and not fit to be mentioned in the same breath as, say, Old Prestwick. The opposing view of modernists, much influenced by professional golf, claims that golf should be primarily a test of skill, and a fair test at that. For them Birkdale is the greatest of the English championship links. The argument can be encapsulated in the simple incident of a drive directed truly down the middle of a fairway and then being deflected by a hump into the rough. Is that golf? Yes, say the traditionalists in unison, for the player must now summon up those worthy qualities of stoicism, patience and fortitude and shrug off his misfortune with no more than a wry smile. No, say the modernists. If a player has the skill to hit a straight drive he is morally entitled to his due reward of finding the ball on the fairway. It is specially irksome to traditionalists that Birkdale has the natural endowments of towering dunes to create a course which would try the patience of a saint. But Birkdale is uncompromisingly modern, with fairways level enough to eliminate rub of the green bounces. Similarly, the greens are not perched on top of dunes, which is where the masochists would have them, but for the most part nestle in the hospitable cleavage between the dunes. Above all, you can see what you are at when you play Birkdale. The challenge is squarely presented before you and in all conscience it is challenging enough without the lottery of blind shots . . .

J. H. Taylor and Fred Hawtree redesigned the original course in the early thirties but as a championship course Birkdale really came into its own after the Second World War. It enjoys to a degree higher than any other of the major championship courses the incidental amenities necessary for a major sporting occasion, such as space for parking and tented villages, easy road access and local hotel facilities. Birkdale has therefore attracted more than its share of great events; the Amateur Championship, English Amateur Championship, Walker and Ryder Cup matches and regular Open Championships. The history which accrues from these events adds noticeably to the enjoyment of playing Royal Birkdale. Who could suppress a feeling of awe at seeing a plaque in the rough celebrating a titanic recovery shot by Arnold Palmer in the 1961 Open, or fail to be moved by Jack Nicklaus's sporting gesture in conceding to Tony Jacklin a short but eminently missable putt on the last green to tie the result of the 1969 Ryder Cup match? Then there is the indelible memory of Lee Trevino failing to thread his drive through the dunes at the 17th and nearly dishing his chances in the 1971 Open, with

SP1.222F.   Royal Birkdale Golf Club. Southport.

(E.W. Collection)

the grinning, hat-doffing Lu Liang Huan almost sneaking home on the
post. It was here also that the teenaged Severiano Ballesteros of Spain
first gave notice of his coming greatness when he disputed the climax of
the 1976 Open shot for thrilling shot with Johnny Miller. The quality and
stature of Royal Birkdale will undoubtedly be disputed for years to come
but by one test of a golf course, the capacity to inspire exciting and
dramatic golf, it has certainly earned its reputation for greatness.[4]

Thus, in the age of golf, the Meols came into their own. Strictly from
a conservation point of view, the use of the sandhills for golf courses does
not guarantee the preservation of the natural environment — but from
a practical viewpoint the golf courses make Southport into a golfing mecca
and a glance at the map is sufficient to show that it is the golf courses
which have saved the area between Birkdale and Ainsdale from becoming
a continuous housing development.

One of the most fortunate accidents of the last century was that Formby,
with one of the best beaches in the county and one of the nearest for much
of the population, remained residential and never developed into a holiday
resort. Formby Promenade, built late in the 1870s, is today well buried
under the sandhills. If such had not been the case then it is very doubtful
that the golf courses and the nature reserve would have been sufficient
to hold back the spread of housing and recreational development along
the coast. The Meols have survived, but more by accident than by design.

There is a great future in the leisure industry, and Southport has all
the requirements needed to develop as a modern holiday centre with leisure
and sporting facilities for all age groups. Southport has matured into a
reserved and dignified town, still claiming a place among the leading seaside
resorts of Great Britain, still striving to meet the needs of holidaymakers
as well as the residents, but with concern and reservations about the
problems of preservation and the environment. In the town centre the
question of preservation is more important than any other issue because
it is Lord Street which raises Southport above the level of the ordinary
seaside resort.

With few notable exceptions, much of the best of the past still remains
today. The pride and care of previous generations has left us with a town
which is now of great historical importance, the more so because it is
situated in a part of England with a strong industrial heritage and which
still bears the scars of the Industrial Revolution. In Southport there is a
Civic Society and an active Family History Society. Birkdale has an
Historical Research Society which includes Ainsdale and whose publication

Old Birkdale and Ainsdale has done much towards filling in the history of these two places. The Birkdale Civic Society is another body which helps to promote local interest, as anybody who has joined a walkabout and listened to the unfailing enthusiasm of Geoffrey Barnes will know. Pictures of Southport hang in houses all over the world; it is a place which generates great loyalty and nostalgia. An American doctor with North Meols ancestry photo-copied the whole of Bailey's *History* because he was unable to purchase a copy of his own — there are many who understand his problem and suffer from the same disease.

The Edwardian and Victorian atmosphere remains intact in the arcades and canopies of Lord Street. Portland Hall, where William Gladstone delivered his election speech on the Abyssinian War and election reform, remains more as less as he found it. Birkdale Lodge still stands as a symbol of Birkdale Park from the mid-nineteenth century. The Town Hall survives from the same decade, as do some of the buildings on the Promenade. The pier has lost its magnificent oriental pavilion, but much of the original iron fabric of the first of the seaside pleasure piers can still be seen. The lifeboat memorials on the Promenade have their own stories to tell.

The Cottage, 74 Liverpool Road, Birkdale, with the late James Rimmer, who was born in this cottage, as was his father. He owned and operated horsedrawn and motor hackney carriages. He was photographed here at the age of 77 in 1971.
(Photo, C. Greenwood)

The bathing village atmosphere disappeared long ago, but a little of it survives in the Regency terrace of Wellington Parade which looks out on where the village green used to be, and at the end of the long drive of The Willows in Lord Street West can be seen one of the original and most beautiful of the marine villas of early Southport. Both these buildings are close to the place where Southport was born, and memorial tablets to William Sutton are set into the wall near the junction of Lord Street and Duke Street — it used to be said that one of these was cut by the Old Duke himself, but it seems more likely that his son, John Sutton, cut

it as a memorial to his father. Many personal reminders of early Southport can be found at Churchtown where memorials to the lords of the manor abound, and a careful search will reveal gems like the burial place of two infant children of George Greatbatch — a discovery which thrills and saddens at the same time. The churchyard contains a wealth of memories from the eighteenth century — the gravestone of John Grayson, captain of the slaving vessel; Thomas Rimmer the Barbary captive; Robert and Esther Shorlicar; the village stocks by John Linaker; and an abundance of memorials belonging to local families. Those prepared to travel further afield will find the grave of Doctor Miles Barton of Nile Cottage, with three generations of his family, in the churchyard at Hoole.

At Churchtown buildings from the eighteenth and seventeenth centuries help to keep the village atmosphere alive. Other pockets of North Meols can be found in unexpected places like the group of cottages in Roe Lane; the cottages with their backs to the sea hiding snugly in the hollows at Marshside; and the oldest of all the cottages, the Birkdale Cottage with its Tudor fabric and with its cruck construction visible on the inside.

Meols Hall retains its seventeenth-century gable and also retains some Tudor fabric in its interior, the dovecote in the grounds may well date back to Elizabethan times. For those who seek relics of the Middle Ages there is very little left to see, but the single remaining medieval buttress of St Cuthbert's might well have been familiar to Katherine de Coudray and Millicent Comyn. Inside the church can be found the names of the rectors throughout the ages, men like James Starkie, Matthew French, Lawrence Waterward, John de Lyverpool, back to Adam the Clerk of Meols. The medieval family names of North Meols have become thinner on the ground, but they still survive and promise to do so for many more generations. Older still are the place names - some of these are pre-Conquest and go back to the time before the written record of North Meols began. For those prepared to search for it, there are times when the aboriginal Meols can still be found, much as it was a thousand years before the keel of the first Viking longboat scraped on the sands of the beach.

In the early spring when the beach is empty and deserted, a white line of distant breakers lies on the horizon and a brisk sou-westerly blows the salt-scented air from off the Irish Sea. Wisps of fine sand blow in eddies along the shore and a few grains lodge at the base of the dunes to add to the accumulated masses of the ages. The wind lightly bends the blades of the marram grass and whispers through the willow scrub. The harsh call of the seabirds sounds over the remote rumbling of the sea. 'Ye guize of those chaffe sands which doe in mountains rize on shore' is pleasure to behold. The brackish water fills the slacks in the sheltered valleys and the dunes are the province of the native flora and fauna. The sand lizard bathes his grey-green scales in the rays of the morning sun and the first delicate wild flowers of the spring bravely show their faces to the skies. Something of the primeval state of the Meols returns, land and sea belong once more to nature and the world is young again.

References

Many sources have been consulted during the research for this book. Many original documents, some of them published, some at the Lancashire Record Office and elsewhere, are available for the earlier period. For the history of Southport itself, the pioneering work of several prominent local historians, like Bailey and Bland, is invaluable. The various historical societies have published many of the main original sources; in some cases, like the seventeenth-century court leet and court baron records, the originals can no longer be traced. Unfortunately, some of the earlier writers, like Bland and Bulpit, do not give the sources of their information so that some of it becomes difficult to confirm. This information has been treated with care. In the case of Farrer, however, the converse is the case, and the full texts of many early documents have been published. For the later chapters data has been taken from newspaper accounts. The main source for the family tree information is the parish registers, supplemented by census returns for the nineteenth century and family records.

Main Reference Works

F.A. Bailey	A History of Southport (1955).
E. Bland	Annals of Southport (1st edn 1887, 2nd edn 1903).
H. Brierley	The Parish Registers of North Meols (1594-1731). Lancs Parish Register Society (vol 66).
W. Farrer	A History of the Parish of North Meols (1903).
T.K. Glazebrook	A Guide to South-Port, North Meoles, in the County of Lancaster (1st edn 1809, 2nd edn 1826).
A. Sparke	The Parish Registers of North Meols (1731-1812). Lancs Parish Register Society (vol 72).

Other Reference Works

N. Blundell	The Great Diurnal of Nicholas Blundell (ed Frank Tyrer, RS vol 110, 112 and 114).
J.H.L. Booth	A History of the Southport Lifeboats (1949).
W.T. Bulpit	Notes on Southport and District (1908).
C. Greenwood	Thatch, Towers and Colonnades (1971).
S. Harrop	Old Birkdale and Ainsdale (published 1985).
N. Hawthorne	English Notebooks (ed Randall Stewart, 1941).
P. Lloyd	Paul Lloyd's Memoirs (unpublished, Atkinson Library).
F. Robinson	A Descriptive History of Southport (1848).
R. Sutton	Marshside and its Dialect (1981).
Miss E. Weeton	The Journal of a Governess (ed Edward Hall, 1936).
P. Whittle	Marina, an Historical and Descriptive Account of Southport, Lytham and Blackpool (1831).

References to Historical Societies, Periodicals, Records Offices etc.

CS   Chetham Society
LFH   Liverpool Family Historian
LRO   Lancashire Record Office, Preston
PRO   Public Records Office
RS   Record Society of Lancashire and Cheshire
SV   Southport Visiter
THSL&C Transactions of the Historic Society of Lancashire and Cheshire
VCH   Victoria County History of Lancashire

Chapter One

1 J.J. Bagley, The Story of Merseyside (1968).
2 Farrer, p5
3 Farrer, p6
4 Farrer, p8
5 Close Rolls 4 Henry III
6 Bailey, p28

Chapter Two

1 Farrer, p11
2 PRO, Tithe Map (1939) North Meols, w/e 549; Tithe Apportionment, IR 30/18/218
3 RS, vol 41
4 Farrer, p15
5 VCH, vol III; RS, vol 39
6 Farrer, p16
7 VCH, Warwickshire; Dugdale, "Antiquities of Warwickshire"
8 PRO, Map no 3234 (Eliz I) PL 31/24
9 Farrer, p19
10 Lawrence Hill, Gentlemen of Courage - Forward (1987)
11 Exchequer Lay Subsidies PRO, ref 179/130/24 CP/744
12 Pal. of Lancs. Plea Roll no 1

Chapter Three

1 Bland and Bulpit
2 A.R. Rimmer, The Rimmers (Botanic Gardens Museum)
3 F.H. Cheetham, THSL&C, vol 75
4 Farrer, p21
5 R.C. Clare, A Short History of North Meols (1952)
6 Palat. of Lancs. Plea Roll no 28 (1465)
7 Farrer, p23
8 Ibid
9 LRO, DDSc 56/9

Chapter Four

1 C. Haigh, Reformation and Resistance in Tudor Lancashire (1975)
2 State Papers of Henry VIII, vol XI, no 1251
3 State Papers of Henry VIII, vol XI, no 786
4 Farrer, p30

5 Ibid
6 Bland
7 Bland and Farrer give excellent complementary accounts of the Baldemeryhokes affair
8 LRO, Will of Barnaby Kitchen, 1603
9 VCH, vol III
10 J.J. Bagley, A History of Lancashire (6th edn 1976).
11 Bland
12 Ibid
13 F.H. Cheetham, THSL&C, vol 65
14 Farrer has published a full transcript, pp31-34
15 Farrer, p29
16 LRO, DDIn 45/6
17 LRO, Will of Alexander Houghton, 1578

Chapter Five

1 VCH, vol III
2 LRO, Wills and Inventories, Mathew French, 1615
3 Farrer, p78
4 LRO, QSB 1/99/68
5 F.H. Cheetham, THSL&C, vol 84
6 CS VII, Iter Lancastrense, also published in Bland (1903)
7 RS, vol 110 appendix H
8 A.B. Whatton, Memoir of the Rev Jeremiah Horrox (1850) (Very few accounts add anything original to Whatton, amongst the few are: THSL&C, vol 106; British Astronomical Association, vol 47 (1937) and vol 64 (1954))

Chapter Six

1 LRO, Moore MSS
2 F.H. Cheetham, SV (May 1933)
3 CS LXII, A Discourse of the Warr in Lancashire
4 Farrer, p50
5 Harrop
6 VCH, vol III
7 Farrer, p80
8 LRO, QSP 48/10
9 LRO, QSP 416/22
10 North Meols Grammar School, SV, Aug 28 1981
11 Aughton of North Meols - A

Family History (Botanic Gardens Museum, unpublished).

12 CS XXI, Notatia Cestriensis
13 The Journeys of Celia Fiennes
14 Farrer, p85
15 LRO, QSP 766/15

Chapter Seven

1 LRO, QSP 653/45
2 The Great Diurnal of Nicholas Blundell, RS 110, 112, 114
3 LRO, Cross MSS
4 Bailey
5 LRO, QSP 223/3
6 LRO, QSP 1171/9
7 LRO, QSP 1183/6
8 J. Beck, Inundation of the Lancashire Coast (1720); THSL&C, vol 105
9 Bulpit
10 Farrer, p83
11 F.H. Cheetham, North Meols Church Lancashire; THSL&C, vol 83

Chapter Eight

1 SV, May 13 1848
2 Bland
3 Glazebrook
4 LFH, The King of the Cocklers, vol 7 no 2
5 Glazebrook
6 Quoted by Bland
7 Letters in SV, 1857
8 F.H. Cheetham, North Meols Church, Lancashire; THSL&C, vol 83
9 Bland

Chapter Nine

1 Bailey
2 Glazebrook
3 Ellen Weeton
4 Richard Holden, A Northern Tour in 1808 (published in the 'Manchester Guardian', Sept 1953)
5 R. Ayton, A Voyage round Great Britain, vol 2, 1815
6 Bland
7 Whittle

Chapter Ten

1 Liverpool Mercury, Dec 8 1820
2 Ellen Weeton
3 Sir George Head, A Tour through the Manufacturing Districts of England in the Summer of 1835
4 Whittle

Chapter Eleven

1 Robinson's Guide, 1848
2 SV, May 4 1844
3 Robinson

4 Bland
5 Harrop
6 Greenwood
7 SV, Feb 1854

Chapter Twelve

1 Hawthorne
2 SV, Feb 1857
3 LFH, Nathaniel Hawthorne's Housemaid, vol 5 no 4
4 S.H. Adamson, Seaside Piers (1977)
5 SV, March 1857
6 Mannex Directory of Mid-Lancashire, 1866 (Figures quoted by the resorts themselves are notoriously unreliable)
7 Turner and Palmer, The Blackpool Story (1976)

Chapter Thirteen

1 B. and R. Yorke, Britain's First Lifeboat Station (1982)
2 Bailey
3 Mrs C. Winter, Journal of an Invalid (1871)
4 J.H.L. Booth, A History of the Southport Lifeboats (corrected by Atkinson Library, Southport)
5 The Times, Dec 1886
6 Punch, Dec 25 1886

Chapter Fourteen

1 Paul Lloyd's Memoirs, Atkinson Library, Southport
2 Sutton
3 For a list of local nicknames see Sutton
4 Sutton
5 Bulpit

Chapter Fifteen

1 Letter, G.N. Curzon to John Broderick (1886)
2 Kenneth Rose, Superior Person (1969)
3 Ibid
4 Sylvia Pankhurst, The Suffragette Movement
5 W.S. Churchill, Cartoon and Cartoonists (essay 1932)
6 A.J.P. Taylor, A Personal History (1983)

Chapter Sixteen

1 Papers of F.H. Cheetham
2 SV, Jul 30 1929
3 Obituary, THSL&C, 1955
4 P. Dobereiner, Down the Nineteenth Fairway (1982

Appendices

Appendix 1
The Hearth Tax Returns
(Ladyday 1664)

These lists, preserved in the Public Record Office (PRO E179/250/11), are invaluable in showing who was resident in each parish in the middle of the 17th century and in giving at least some indication of their relative prosperity.

Church Towne

Thomas Selby Esq	6
Tho Owen Esq	4
James Starkie, rector	3
Adam Bannester	1
John Jumpe	1
Robt Breckell	1
Peter Wright	1
Hugh Hesketh	1
Tho Aughton	1
Hugh Haworth	1
Richard Wright	1
Hugh Hodges	1
Wm Johnson	1
John Mathew	1
Wm Rimmer	1

Bankes

Robert Rymer	1
Tho Ball	1
Jo Ball	1
Jo Rymer	1
Law Abram	1
Ric Abram	1
Wm Bond	1

Crossens

Edmund Wright	1
John Copeland	1
Tho Thomasson	1
James Blevin	1
Ric Breckell	1
John Rymer	1
Ric Sutch	1
Jo Blundell	1
Ric Blevin	1

Widdowe Mosse	1
John Haworth	1
Robert Rymer	1
Peter Wright	1
Robt Wright	1
Widdow Boond	1
Hugh Wignall	1
Thomas Wright	1
Henry Linnaker	1

Rowe

Thomas Hodges	1
John Haworth	1
Tho Ball	1
John Ball	1
Jo Rymmer	1
Edw Wright	1
James Rymmer	1
John Ball	1
John Richardson	1
Widd Wright	1
John Boond	1

Hawes

Thomas Rymer	1
Ric Buckley	1
Jo Aughton	1
Ric Rymer	1
Tho Ayndoe	1
John Wright	1

Blowicke

John Ball	1
John Gilbertson	1
Ric Ball	1
Wm Wilkinson	1
John Rymmer	1
Willm Lunt	1
Widdow Ball	1
Mary Ball	1
Robert Wright	1
Richard Ball	1

Birkdale

Jo Rymmer & Ellis	1

Wm Rymmer Jun	1
John Rymmer Jun	1
Hugh Mathew	1
Dorothy Rymer vid	1
Edmund Jumpe	1
James Wilkinson	1
James Birch	1
Wm Ball	1
Robert Jumpe	1
Wm Blashawe	1
Nich Rymer	1
James Rimmer	1
Gilbert Rymmer	1
Hugh Johnson	1
Richard Rimmer	1
John Richardson	1
James Blashaw	1
Wm Johnson	1
Tho Rymmer Sen	1

Not Chargeable

John Aspinwall	1
Richard Wright	1
Edward Rymmer	1
Hugh Rymmer	1
Widd Johnson	1
Widd Bamford	1
Tho Rymmer	1
Henry Sutch	1
Richard Ball	1

[Ainsdale]

John Rimmer	1
Wm Sutton	1
Peter Jumpe	1
James Balshall	1
Rich Norris	1
Wm Jumpe	1
Ellizab Harrison	1
Peter Jumpe Sen	1
Izabell Aindoe	1
Cicely Aindoe	1
Tho Warton	1
Elizab Rimmer	1
John Eadee	1
Tho Norris	1
Nick Reynold	1
Gilbert Rimmer	1

Appendix 2
Placenames of
North Meols and Southport

The study of placenames and their derivation is one of the main techniques of research open to the local historian. Places get their names in many different ways and the list which follows gives some examples from the North Meols and Southport area.

The lords of the manor are commemorated by a number of Southport street names: for example, Blundell Avenue, Crescent and Drive; Bibby Road; Bold Street; Coudray Road; Fleetwood Road; Hesketh Drive and Road; Hoghton Street and Scarisbrick Avenue.

Many street names come from the names of families who lived in them at one time. Examples are: Baker's Lane; Ball's Place; Blundell's Lane; Brade Street; Bradshaw's Lane; Carr Lane; Hargreaves Street; Hodge Street; Hodges Brow; Hodson Street; Hulme Street; Hunt's Cottages; Johnson Street; Peet's Lane; Rimmer's Avenue; Segar's Lane; Shaw's Avenue and Road; Simpson's Place, Threlfall's Lane; Watkinson's Lane (now Larkfield Lane); Wright Street and Terrace.

Some places are named after individuals, often by nicknames, and the individuals can only rarely be identified. They are often of great antiquity and some pre-date Southport by more than a century. Some examples are: Clenger's Brow; Boss's Brow; Cockle Dick's Lane; Cotty's Brow; Croston's Brow; Fine Jane's Brook and Way; Hosker's Brow; Knob Hall Lane; Manx Jane's Lane; Mat's Brow; Nabb's Cop; Ralph's Wife's Lane; Sally's Lane and Slackey's Lane.

There are also many obsolete names, of which only a few are mentioned here. The early Ordnance Survey maps are a very good source of information for their whereabouts. Most of the following are mentioned in the text and are of historical interest.

Ainsdale:
'Einulvesdael' is mentioned in the Domesday Survey of 1086. It was a detached part of the parish of Walton on the Hill. The name itself may well come from the Old English personal name Aegenwulf and 'dael', meaning Aegenwulf's valley.

Anderson's Square:
Situated at the Lord Street end of Scarisbrick Avenue, it seems to have been completely overwhelmed by sand in the 1830s. Several South Hawes cottages stood in the square and were buried up to the ridge tiles in drifting sand. A party of practical jokers dropped the carcass of a black greyhound into 'Long Nan's chimney', which was the only part of her cottage showing above the sand - when the teeth and eyes of the greyhound appeared in the fireplace poor Nan thought the devil himself had come for her at last.

Argarmeols Close:
Argarmeols was the lost township inundated by the sea in about 1400. It was on the seaward side of Birkdale, not where the close is today. The name is derived from the Old Norse personal name 'Erengr' and 'meols', giving a meaning of 'Erengr's sand hill'.

Aughton Road:
This was named after John Aughton (1814 - ?), who built the first houses in Birkdale Park at the north end of the road.

Baker's Lane:
On Bankes' survey of 1736, Hugh Baker is shown as farming a field at one end of the lane, but it is referred to as 'Nelly Baker's Lane' in the 1871 census.

Bankfield Lane:
This lane has a strong claim to be the oldest lane in the parish, though Churchgate could be older still. Bankfield Lane, as its name implies, follows the line of the sea embankment built by the monks of Sawley in about 1210.

Belmont Street and Castle Walk:
Near the site of Belmont Cottage which was originally occupied by Mary Leigh in 1801. Belmont Castle, built by Robert Holt in 1820, was also in this neighbourhood.

Birkdale:
This Old Norse name, meaning 'birch dale', is not mentioned in the Domesday Book but was in use by the 13th century. Birkdale is essentially the surviving portion of Argarmeols, which was lost to the sea around 1400. Its name was still undergoing development until quite late and the spelling was not finally fixed in its present form until the 18th century. Dialect speakers continued to call it 'Birtle' well into the present century.

Blowick:
'Bla-vik, 'the dark bay' of the mere. Prior to 1500 it was usually referred to simply as 'The Wyke'.

Brade Street:
This is the suggested site of a skirmish between villagers and some Cavaliers in 1644. 'Bradelond' is mentioned in a deed of around 1180. There was also a Brade family in North Meols.

Butts Lane:
'Butt' can often mean the end of a field, the turning area for the plough. We cannot rule out the possibility, however, that the parish archery butts were here it the Middle Ages.

Churchgate:
A bridlepath and footpath of very great antiquity running originally from Sefton church to St Cuthbert's in Churchtown and serving all the places in between. The path is still shown clearly on 19th-century maps but only a very short stretch in Churchtown retains some of its original character.

Coronation Walk:
Named when the bathing village celebrated the Coronation of George IV in July 1821.

Crossens:
This name is derived from the Old Norse which means 'headland on which a cross or crosses stand'.

Duke Street:
Named after the 'Old Duke', William Sutton (1752-1840). The Duke's Folly stood at the junction of Duke Street and Lord Street.

Eastbank Street:
Formerly East Bank Lane. This is actually a very ancient placename, for 'Le Estbankfield' is mentioned in 1550.

Fine Jane's Brook:
Whoever she really was, 'Fine Jane' has generated much folklore. She must have been quite a lady. In 1721 the bridge spanning the Otter Pool in Churchtown was referred to as 'Fine Jane's Bridge' and the 'Church Bridge' is mentioned in the Court Baron records of 1640. It is possible that she was the daughter of Matthew Travers, who married John Bold in 1582.

Foul Lane:
Known locally as 'Red Lane', it is difficult to believe that this was the original access road to South Port which was used by visitors alighting from the canal at Scarisbrick. The route then followed Wennington Road, Roe Lane, Manchester Road and Lord Street.

Hall Street:
After Hall's Chapel. The Rev Hall was an independent clergyman whose doctrines were not acceptable to the Rev George Greatbatch, he set up his own independent chapel at Hawes Side sponsored by Bartin Haigh, a Liverpool builder.

Hawesside Street:
Formerly Hawes Side Lane, with only 'Hawes', or sandhills, to seaward.

Hoghton Street:
Dorothea Bold married Sir Henry Bold-Hoghton in around 1820 and the Hoghtons became part owners of the Bold half of the manor. Around 1840 forty cartloads of stone setts had been laid from the London Street end as far as the foot of a sandhill, where they were left lying about in confusion. From this point to the old Trinity church (built in 1837) was a group of huge sandhills, one of which was so large that the whole roof of the church could be seen from the top. Mary Bold, sister of Dorothea and another part owner of the Bold moiety, married Prince Eustace Sapieha of Dereczyn in the Duchy of Lithuania; it is surprising that this obscure but fascinating royal connection is not commemorated by a street name.

Kew:
In the 1880s, horse trams took visitors to Kew Gardens. Named after the Botanical Gardens in Surrey, these gardens covered 12 acres and attractions included the lake with gondoliers, a pavilion to cater for 1000 diners, a zoo and the Alexandra Hotel. The latter was renamed the Richmond in 1884 and is the only surviving memento of the gardens.

King Street:
Whitehead recollected that Upper King Street was 'the Mecca of the bona-fide Sandgrounders'. It was peopled by many native families, including several branches of the Balls, who were formerly occupants of South Hawes. It was probably the last outpost of thatch in the town centre.

Little London:
A fascinating placename. Although not mentioned in the parish registers until the early 18th century, 'Londehay' appears as early as 1489. The most likely derivation is that it was here that the London merchants, or their representatives, came to collect the fleeces of wool from North Meols, indicating what was once an important component of the local economy.

London Street
Formerly London Lane. It did not lead to the capital, but to the humbler settlement of Little London (qv). Before 1850 it was residential on the north side as far out as Wright Street. On the south side was a gently sloping bank formed by trimming up the sandhills and planted with shrubs and wallflowers.

Lord Street:
Named 'Lords Street' after the lords of the manor. On Bankes' survey of 1736 the site was a marsh; indeed, a chain of shallow pools which lingered until 1842 dictated the great width of Lord Street. On Leigh's plan of 1824 it is still unnamed and the earliest written reference is in the rate assessment book of 1831.

Mill Lane:
This is derived from the site of the Churchtown windmill since the 16th century. The medieval water mill which it replaced was situated on the Old Pool which ran past the opposite side of Meols Hall.

Mill Road (Ainsdale):
Similarly, this represents the site of the Ainsdale windmill, which is shown on Yates' map of 1786 near White Otter Pool, but probably far older than

this date.

Nevill Street:
Named after James Nevill, one of the earliest residents of Southport. He was a Wigan man, thought to have built Nile Bank Cottage in 1803. He was a member of the Marine Fund of 1817 and was a leading light in the Society of Friends.

Nile Square:
This is now Lord Street West and recalls the diminutive River Nile.

Pilkington Road:
Dr (later Sir) George Pilkington (Liberal) was the first MP for the Southport constituency. He lost his seat to Lord Curzon in 1886 by 3,723 votes to 3,262. He regained the seat against Mr C.B. Balfour in 1899 by 5,635 to 5,052 but lost it again the following year. On 9th December 1886, as local secretary to the RNLI, he rushed from a ball in the town hall to try and join the crew of the Eliza Fernley, but he arrived too late to go to the assistance of the Mexico.

Pinfold Lane:
The pinfold was an enclosure where stray cattle were impounded by the pinder (or pounder) and returned to the owner after the payment of a fine.

Ralph's Wife's Lane:
The traditional story (as told by Bulpit) is that Ralph was a smuggler and the lane was where his wife perished from exposure when waiting for him to return from one of his expeditions. The story might be true but Ralph was long before Bulpit's time, for the lane is shown as 'Ralph Lane' by Bankes in 1736.

Roe Lane:
New Row appears in about 1605; it was a row of cottages and tenements south of Churchtown. By 1700 it had become known simply as 'Row' or 'Roe'. It is interesting that the mis-spelling is the one which has survived.

Shellfield Road:
This was formerly Danglus Lane. Shells could be found only a little way under the soil. The land was beneath the high water mark in the 17th century.

Tithebarn Road:
Formerly Tithe Barn Lane. North Meols had several tithe barns, the earliest of which would have been nearer Churchtown but there is some evidence that there was one here in the Middle Ages.

Vulcan Street:
It was here that the Vulcan Cars rolled off the production line in 1902.

Winter Gardens Terrace:
The Southport Winter Gardens covered eight acres between Lord Street Station (the Ribble Bus Terminal) and Coronation Walk. Demolished in 1933 when Kingsway was built through the middle of the site.

Yellow House Lane:
The correct name for the Yellow House was East Bank House, shown on Walker's plan of 1834. It was lime-washed in yellow instead of the usual white-wash. Superstitious locals would not pass by the Yellow House after dark - they believed it to be haunted by a 'boggart'.

Appendix 3
Selected family trees

Abram

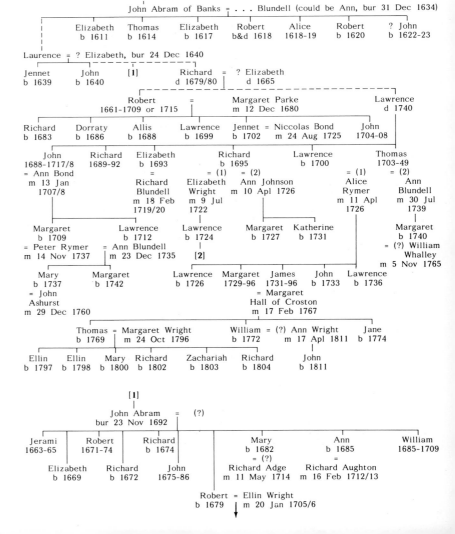

Richard Abram of Crossens bur 18 Apl 1635

John Abram of Banks = . . . Blundell (could be Ann, bur 31 Dec 1634)

Elizabeth	Thomas	Elizabeth	Robert	Alice	Robert	? John
b 1611	b 1614	b 1617	b&d 1618	1618-19	b 1620	b 1622-23

Laurence = ? Elizabeth, bur 24 Dec 1640

Jennet	John	[1]	Richard = ? Elizabeth
b 1639	b 1640		d 1679/80 d 1665

Robert	=	Margaret Parke	Lawrence
1661-1709 or 1715		m 12 Dec 1680	d 1740

Richard	Dorraty	Allis	Lawrence	Jennet = Niccolas Bond	John
b 1683	b 1686	b 1688	b 1699	b 1702 m 24 Aug 1725	1704-08

John	Richard	Elizabeth	Richard	Lawrence	Thomas
1688-1717/8	1689-92	b 1693	b 1695	b 1700	1703-49
= Ann Bond		=	= (1) = (2)	= (1)	= (2)
m 13 Jan		Richard	Elizabeth Ann Johnson	Alice	Ann
1707/8		Blundell	Wright m 10 Apl 1726	Rymer	Blundell
		m 18 Feb	m 9 Jul	m 11 Apl	m 30 Jul
		1719/20	1722	1726	1739

Margaret	Lawrence	Lawrence	Margaret	Katherine	Margaret
b 1709	b 1712	b 1724	b 1727	b 1731	b 1740
= Peter Rymer	= Ann Blundell				= (?) William
m 14 Nov 1737	m 23 Dec 1735	[2]			Whalley
					m 5 Nov 1765

Mary	Margaret	Lawrence	Margaret	James	John	Lawrence
b 1737	b 1742	b 1726	1729-96	1731-96	b 1733	b 1736
= John				= Margaret		
Ashurst				Hall of Croston		
m 29 Dec 1760				m 17 Feb 1767		

Thomas = Margaret Wright	William = (?) Ann Wright	Jane
b 1769 m 24 Oct 1796	b 1772 m 17 Apl 1811	b 1774

Ellin	Ellin	Mary	Richard	Zachariah	Richard	John
b 1797	b 1798	b 1800	b 1802	b 1803	b 1804	b 1811

[1]

John Abram	=	(?)
bur 23 Nov 1692		

Jerami	Robert	Richard	Mary	Ann	William
1663-65	1671-74	b 1674	b 1682	b 1685	1685-1709
			= (?)	=	

Elizabeth	Richard	John	Richard Adge	Richard Aughton
b 1669	b 1672	1675-86	m 11 May 1714	m 16 Feb 1712/13

Robert = Ellin Wright
b 1679   m 20 Jan 1705/6

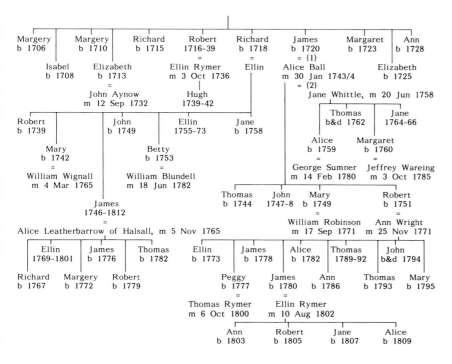

| Margery b 1706 | Margery b 1710 | Richard b 1715 | Robert 1716-39 | Richard b 1718 | James b 1720 | Margaret b 1723 | Ann b 1728 |

Isabel b 1708
Elizabeth b 1713 = John Aynow m 12 Sep 1732
Ellin Rymer m 3 Oct 1736
Ellin
Alice Ball m 30 Jan 1743/4 = (1)
Elizabeth b 1725

= (2) Jane Whittle, m 20 Jun 1758

Hugh 1739-42

Robert b 1739
John b 1749
Ellin 1755-73
Jane b 1758

Thomas b&d 1762 | Jane 1764-66

Mary b 1742
Betty b 1753
Alice b 1759
Margaret b 1760

William Wignall m 4 Mar 1765
William Blundell m 18 Jun 1782
George Sumner m 14 Feb 1780
Jeffrey Wareing m 3 Oct 1785

James 1746-1812 = Alice Leatherbarrow of Halsall, m 5 Nov 1765

| Thomas b 1744 | John 1747-8 | Mary b 1749 | Robert b 1751 |

William Robinson m 17 Sep 1771 | Ann Wright m 25 Nov 1771

| Ellin 1769-1801 | James b 1776 | Thomas b 1782 | Ellin b 1773 | James b 1778 | Alice b 1782 | Thomas 1789-92 | John b&d 1794 |

| Richard b 1767 | Margery b 1772 | Robert b 1779 | Peggy b 1777 | James b 1780 | Ann b 1786 | Thomas b 1793 | Mary b 1795 |

Thomas Rymer m 6 Oct 1800 | Ellin Rymer m 10 Aug 1802

| Ann b 1803 | Robert b 1805 | Jane b 1807 | Alice b 1809 |

[2]

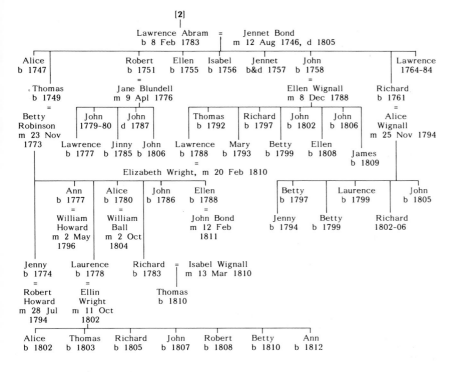

Lawrence Abram b 8 Feb 1783 = Jennet Bond m 12 Aug 1746, d 1805

| Alice b 1747 | Robert b 1751 | Ellen b 1755 | Isabel b 1756 | Jennet b&d 1757 | John b 1758 | Lawrence 1764-84 |

Thomas b 1749
Jane Blundell m 9 Apl 1776
Ellen Wignall m 8 Dec 1788
Richard b 1761

Betty Robinson m 23 Nov 1773
John 1779-80 | John d 1787
Thomas b 1792 | Richard b 1797 | John b 1802 | John b 1806
Alice Wignall m 25 Nov 1794

| Lawrence b 1777 | Jinny b 1785 | John b 1806 | Lawrence b 1788 | Mary b 1793 | Betty b 1799 | Ellen b 1808 | James b 1809 |

Elizabeth Wright, m 20 Feb 1810

| Ann b 1777 | Alice b 1780 | John b 1786 | Ellen b 1788 | Betty b 1797 | Laurence b 1799 | John b 1805 |

William Howard m 2 May 1796
William Ball m 2 Oct 1804
John Bond m 12 Feb 1811
Jenny b 1794 | Betty b 1799
Richard 1802-06

| Jenny b 1774 | Laurence b 1778 | Richard b 1783 | = Isabel Wignall m 13 Mar 1810 |

Robert Howard m 28 Jul 1794
Ellin Wright m 11 Oct 1802
Thomas b 1810

| Alice b 1802 | Thomas b 1803 | Richard b 1805 | John b 1807 | Robert b 1808 | Betty b 1810 | Ann b 1812 |

Aughton

Aughton of Meols
Sable, three garbs or
The Aughtons were lords of the
manor of North Meols for two
hundred years. In the 1380s
William de Aughton married
Millicent Comyn and adopted the
arms of his wife's family. The
Comyns claimed descent from
King Duncan 1 of Scotland.

At the time of the Domesday Survey (1087) Aughton, with Skelmersdale, Uplitherland, and many other places in the area, was held by a Saxon thane called Uctred. The name Richard son of Uctred appears in about 1190; the father is possibly a descendant of the earlier Uctred.

Baines states that Madoc de Hacton (Aughton) was an elder brother of William de Coudray, and that they were sons of William Fitzwilliam. He traces the descent of William Fitzwilliam from Richard son of Uctred.

Farrer, in the Victoria County History (1908), takes the male line of the Aughtons back to Rhuddlan in Wales. A study of the Welsh names in the early manorial family of Aughton shows that Farrer is almost certainly correct, but the people identified by Baines may well be ancestors through one of the female lines.

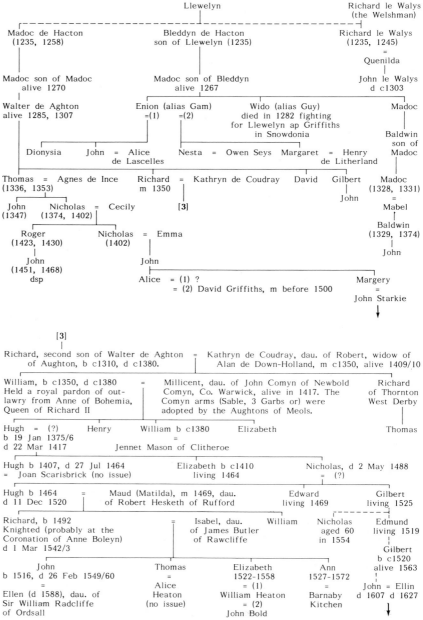

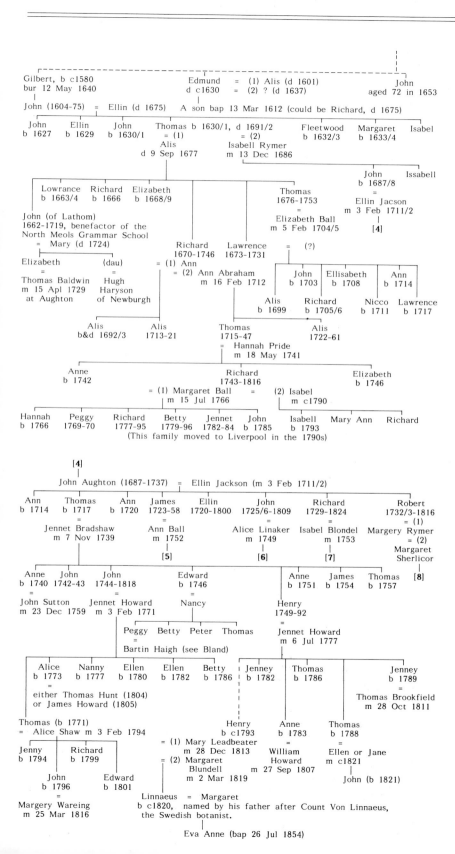

Gilbert, b c1580
bur 12 May 1640

Edmund = (1) Alis (d 1601)
d c1630 = (2) ? (d 1637)

John
aged 72 in 1653

John (1604-75) = Ellin (d 1675)   A son bap 13 Mar 1612 (could be Richard, d 1675)

John b 1627   Ellin b 1629   John b 1630/1   Thomas b 1630/1, d 1691/2   Fleetwood b 1632/3   Margaret b 1633/4   Isabel

Thomas = (1) Alis d 9 Sep 1677 = (2) Isabell Rymer m 13 Dec 1686

John b 1687/8   Issabell
= Ellin Jacson m 3 Feb 1711/2
[4]

Lowrance b 1663/4   Richard b 1666   Elizabeth b 1668/9

Thomas 1676-1753 = Elizabeth Ball m 5 Feb 1704/5

John (of Lathom) 1662-1719, benefactor of the North Meols Grammar School = Mary (d 1724)

Richard 1670-1746 = (1) Ann = (2) Ann Abraham m 16 Feb 1712

Lawrence 1673-1731 = (?)

John b 1703   Ellisabeth b 1708   Ann b 1714
Alis b 1699   Richard b 1705/6   Nicco b 1711   Lawrence b 1717

Elizabeth = Thomas Baldwin m 15 Apl 1729 at Aughton
(dau) = Hugh Haryson of Newburgh

Alis b&d 1692/3   Alis 1713-21   Thomas 1715-47 = Hannah Pride m 18 May 1741   Alis 1722-61

Anne b 1742   Richard 1743-1816 = (1) Margaret Ball m 15 Jul 1766   (2) Isabel m c1790   Elizabeth b 1746

Hannah b 1766   Peggy 1769-70   Richard 1777-95   Betty 1779-96   Jennet 1782-84   John b 1785   Isabell b 1793   Mary   Ann   Richard
(This family moved to Liverpool in the 1790s)

[4]
John Aughton (1687-1737) = Ellin Jackson (m 3 Feb 1711/2)

Ann b 1714   Thomas b 1717   Ann b 1720   James 1723-58   Ellin 1720-1800   John 1725/6-1809   Richard 1729-1824   Robert 1732/3-1816

Jennet Bradshaw m 7 Nov 1739   Ann Ball m 1752 [5]   Alice Linaker m 1749 [6]   Isabel Blondel m 1753 [7]   = (1) Margery Rymer = (2) Margaret Sherlicor [8]

Anne b 1740   John 1742-43   John 1744-1818   Edward b 1746   Anne b 1751   James b 1754   Thomas b 1757   [8]

John Sutton m 23 Dec 1759   Jennet Howard m 3 Feb 1771   Nancy   Henry 1749-92

Peggy   Betty   Peter   Thomas   = Bartin Haigh (see Bland)

Henry 1749-92 = Jennet Howard m 6 Jul 1777

Alice b 1773   Nanny b 1777   Ellen b 1780   Ellen b 1782   Betty b 1786   Jenney b 1782   Thomas b 1786   Jenney b 1789
= either Thomas Hunt (1804) or James Howard (1805)
Thomas Brookfield m 28 Oct 1811

Thomas (b 1771) = Alice Shaw m 3 Feb 1794

Henry b c1793   Anne b 1783   Thomas b 1788

Jenny b 1794   Richard b 1799

John b 1796   Edward b 1801

Margery Wareing m 25 Mar 1816

Henry b c1793 = (1) Mary Leadbeater m 28 Dec 1813 = (2) Margaret Blundell m 2 Mar 1819
Anne b 1783   William Howard m 27 Sep 1807
Thomas b 1788   Ellen or Jane m c1821   John (b 1821)

Linnaeus = Margaret
b c1820, named by his father after Count Von Linnaeus, the Swedish botanist.

Eva Anne (bap 26 Jul 1854)

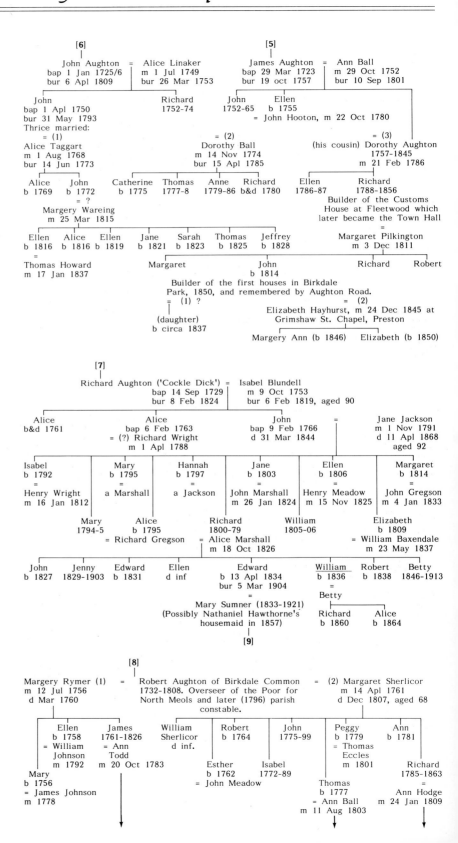

[6]
|
John Aughton = Alice Linaker
bap 1 Jan 1725/6 | m 1 Jul 1749
bur 6 Apl 1809 | bur 26 Mar 1753

[5]
|
James Aughton = Ann Ball
bap 29 Mar 1723 | m 29 Oct 1752
bur 19 oct 1757 | bur 10 Sep 1801

John
bap 1 Apl 1750
bur 31 May 1793
Thrice married:
= (1)
Alice Taggart
m 1 Aug 1768
bur 14 Jun 1773

Richard
1752-74

John
1752-65

Ellen
b 1755
= John Hooton, m 22 Oct 1780

= (2)
Dorothy Ball
m 14 Nov 1774
bur 15 Apl 1785

= (3)
(his cousin) Dorothy Aughton
1757-1845
m 21 Feb 1786

Alice   John
b 1769   b 1772
= ?
Margery Wareing
m 25 Mar 1815

Catherine   Thomas   Anne   Richard
b 1775   1777-8   1779-86   b&d 1780

Ellen   Richard
1786-87   1788-1856
Builder of the Customs
House at Fleetwood which
later became the Town Hall
=
Margaret Pilkington
m 3 Dec 1811

Ellen   Alice   Ellen   Jane   Sarah   Thomas   Jeffrey
b 1816   b 1816   b 1819   b 1821   b 1823   b 1825   b 1828
=
Thomas Howard
m 17 Jan 1837

Margaret

John
b 1814
Builder of the first houses in Birkdale
Park, 1850, and remembered by Aughton Road.
= (1) ?   = (2)
| Elizabeth Hayhurst, m 24 Dec 1845 at
(daughter)   Grimshaw St. Chapel, Preston
b circa 1837

Richard   Robert

Margery Ann (b 1846)   Elizabeth (b 1850)

[7]
|
Richard Aughton ('Cockle Dick') = Isabel Blundell
bap 14 Sep 1729 | m 9 Oct 1753
bur 8 Feb 1824 | bur 6 Feb 1819, aged 90

Alice
b&d 1761

Alice
bap 6 Feb 1763
= (?) Richard Wright
m 1 Apl 1788

John
bap 9 Feb 1766
d 31 Mar 1844

=

Jane Jackson
m 1 Nov 1791
d 11 Apl 1868
aged 92

Isabel
b 1792
=
Henry Wright
m 16 Jan 1812

Mary
b 1795
=
a Marshall

Hannah
b 1797
=
a Jackson

Jane
b 1803
=
John Marshall
m 26 Jan 1824

Ellen
b 1806
=
Henry Meadow
m 15 Nov 1825

Margaret
b 1814
=
John Gregson
m 4 Jan 1833

Mary   Alice
1794-5   b 1795
= Richard Gregson

Richard
1800-79
= Alice Marshall
m 18 Oct 1826

William
1805-06

Elizabeth
b 1809
= William Baxendale
m 23 May 1837

John   Jenny   Edward   Ellen
b 1827   1829-1903   b 1831   d inf

Edward
b 13 Apl 1834
bur 5 Mar 1904
=
Mary Sumner (1833-1921)
(Possibly Nathaniel Hawthorne's
housemaid in 1857)
|
[9]

William   Robert   Betty
b 1836   b 1838   1846-1913
=
Betty

Richard   Alice
b 1860   b 1864

[8]
|
Margery Rymer (1) = Robert Aughton of Birkdale Common = (2) Margaret Sherlicor
m 12 Jul 1756 | 1732-1808. Overseer of the Poor for | m 14 Apl 1761
d Mar 1760 | North Meols and later (1796) parish | d Dec 1807, aged 68
                 constable.

Ellen
b 1758
= William
Johnson
m 1792

James
1761-1826
= Ann
Todd
m 20 Oct 1783

William
Sherlicor
d inf.

Robert
b 1764

John
1775-99

Peggy
b 1779
= Thomas
Eccles
m 1801

Ann
b 1781

Mary
b 1756
= James Johnson
m 1778

Esther   Isabel
b 1762   1772-89
= John Meadow

Thomas
b 1777
= Ann Ball
m 11 Aug 1803

Richard
1785-1863
=
Ann Hodge
m 24 Jan 1809

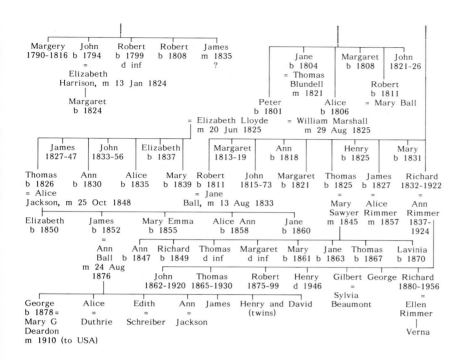

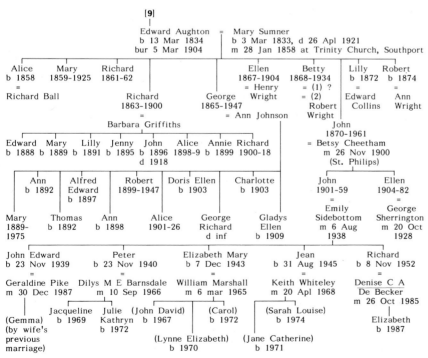

Barton

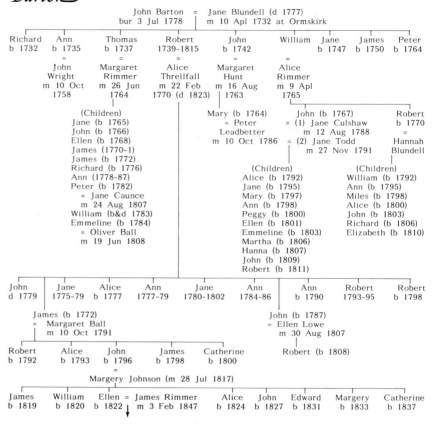

```
                    John Barton  =  Jane Blundell (d 1777)
                    bur 3 Jul 1778  |  m 10 Apl 1732 at Ormskirk

Richard   Ann      Thomas    Robert     John      William  Jane    James    Peter
b 1732    b 1735   b 1737    1739-1815  b 1742    b 1747   b 1750  b 1764
          =        =         =          =         =
          John     Margaret  Alice      Margaret  Alice
          Wright   Rimmer    Threlfall  Hunt      Rimmer
          m 10 Oct m 26 Jun  m 22 Feb   m 16 Aug  m 9 Apl
          1758     1764      1770 (d 1823) 1763    1765
                   |                      |
                   (Children)          Mary (b 1764)   John (b 1767)        Robert
                   Jane (b 1765)       = Peter         = (1) Jane Culshaw   b 1770
                   John (b 1766)       Leadbetter        m 12 Aug 1788      =
                   Ellen (b 1768)      m 10 Oct 1786   = (2) Jane Todd      Hannah
                   James (1770-1)                        m 27 Nov 1791      Blundell
                   James (b 1772)                                          |
                   Richard (b 1776)    (Children)        (Children)
                   Ann (1778-87)       Alice (b 1792)    William (b 1792)
                   Peter (b 1782)      Jane (b 1795)     Ann (b 1795)
                   = Jane Caunce       Mary (b 1797)     Miles (b 1798)
                   m 24 Aug 1807       Ann (b 1798)      Alice (b 1800)
                   William (b&d 1783)  Peggy (b 1800)    John (b 1803)
                   Emmeline (b 1784)   Ellen (b 1801)    Richard (b 1806)
                   = Oliver Ball       Emmeline (b 1803) Elizabeth (b 1810)
                   m 19 Jun 1808       Martha (b 1806)
                                       Hanna (b 1807)
                                       John (b 1809)
                                       Robert (b 1811)

John   Jane     Alice   Ann      Jane      Ann      Ann      Robert   Robert
d 1779 1775-79  b 1777  1777-79  1780-1802 1784-86  b 1790   1793-95  b 1798

     James (b 1772)                              John (b 1787)
     = Margaret Ball                             = Ellen Lowe
     m 10 Oct 1791                               m 30 Aug 1807

Robert    Alice   John    James   Catherine      Robert (b 1808)
b 1792    b 1793  b 1796  b 1798  b 1800
                   =
            Margery Johnson (m 28 Jul 1817)

James    William  Ellen  = James Rimmer   Alice   John    Edward   Margery   Catherine
b 1819   b 1820   b 1822 | m 3 Feb 1847    b 1824  b 1827  b 1831   b 1833    b 1837
```

Blundell

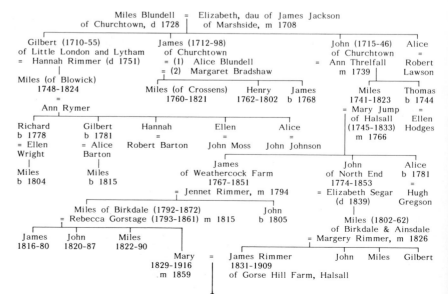

```
                    Miles Blundell  =  Elizabeth, dau of James Jackson
                    of Churchtown, d 1728 |  of Marshside, m 1708

Gilbert (1710-55)              James (1712-98)              John (1715-46)    Alice
of Little London and Lytham    of Churchtown                of Churchtown     =
= Hannah Rimmer (d 1751)       = (1) Alice Blundell         = Ann Threlfall   Robert
|                              = (2) Margaret Bradshaw        m 1739          Lawson
Miles (of Blowick)                                          |
1748-1824          Miles (of Crossens)  Henry    James     Miles     Thomas
=                  1760-1821            1762-1802 b 1768    1741-1823  b 1744
Ann Rymer                                                   = Mary Jump
                                                              of Halsall    Ellen
Richard    Gilbert   Hannah     Ellen       Alice           (1745-1833)    Hodges
b 1778     b 1781    =          =           =               m 1766
= Ellen    = Alice   Robert Barton  John Moss  John Johnson
Wright     Barton
|          |              James                    John              Alice
Miles      Miles         of Weathercock Farm       of North End      b 1781
b 1804     b 1815        1767-1851                  1774-1853         =
                        = Jennet Rimmer, m 1794   = Elizabeth Segar   Hugh
                                                    (d 1839)          Gregson
            Miles of Birkdale (1792-1872)    John               |
            = Rebecca Gorstage (1793-1861) m 1815  b 1805       Miles (1802-62)
                                                                of Birkdale & Ainsdale
                                                                = Margery Rimmer, m 1826

James    John     Miles                                    
1816-80  1820-87  1822-90          Mary    =  James Rimmer        John   Miles   Gilbert
                                   1829-1916   1831-1909
                                   m 1859      of Gorse Hill Farm, Halsall
```

```
                                    |
        ┌───────────────────────────┴───────────────────────────┐
Miles Rimmer of Scarisbrick Hall Farm       James Gilbert of Warren Farm, Ainsdale
   1870-1933  =  Jane Marshall (d 1956)        1873-1930  =  Kathleen Cardwell, d 1973
        │                                              │
   Miles James                                   James  =  Alice Taylor
   b 1911, dsp 1970                             b 1922  │  b 1922, m 1950
                                                        │
                                              John  =  Christine Lowry
                                             b 1952 │  b 1951, m 1977
                                                    │
                                           Miles John, b 1982
```

Bond

```
                        William Bond of Rowe  =  Alice Ball
                           bur 9 Sep 1697        m 12 Jan 1663/4
   ┌──────┬──────┬──────┬──────────┴──────────┐
  Ann   Margery  Cicely  Margaret      John (1675-1735)
 b 1664 b 1666  b 1668  b 1674    =  (1)            =  (2)
                              Ann Stevenson       Ann Johnson
                            m 15 May 1698, d 1699  m 23 Oct 1705
                                  │                    │
                            William      Ann    Gilbert   Gilbert   John    James
                            b 1699      b 1705  1709-10   1711-67   b 1712  b 1714
                                                               =
                                              Ann Moss, m 6 May 1740
   ┌─────────────────────────┬─────────────────────────────────────┐
  John = Catherine Fazakerly      Ann  = Gilbert Rimmer      Ellen = Martin Rimmer
 1740-93  m 5 Jul 1762          1744-74  m 1 Feb 1768        1747-91  m 1 Feb 1768
Gilbert  Gilbert   James   John   Ann      Thomas      Ellen    Jenney
b&d 1765 1766-1813 b 1768 b 1771 b ?     1774-1858     b 1777  1780-1806
              =                               =
   Mary Golbourne of Altcar          Margery Wright
        m 30 Jan 1792                m 28 May 1805
 ┌─────┬──────────┬─────┬─────┬────────┬─────────┐
John  Betty  Catherine  Ann  Alice  Thomas   (a son)
b 1792 b 1794 b 1796  b 1798 b 1801 b 1803    b 1807
Jenny  John  Catherine  Margery      Thomas          Gilbert      James
b 1807 b 1808 b 1813?   b 1815       b 1818          b 1821       b 1824,
        =              =                               =                dsp
      Alice      William Marshall      Jane    Ann Todd   Sarah Can
                 m 7 Dec 1848       Marshall  m 9 Apl 1849  m 24 Jun 1856
 ┌─────┬───────┬───────┬──────┬──────┬──────┐                    │
Alice James  Margery  Mary  John  Peter                      Margery
b 1832 b 1834 b 1836 b 1838 b 1846 b 1849                      Ann
                                                              b 1857
Thomas
b 1830                         Emma   Thomas  Margery       Elizabeth
  =  ?                        b 1849  b 1850  b 1852         1862-1936
 ┌────┬──────┬──────┐     ┌──────┬──────┬──────────┬──────┬──────┐        =
Mary Alice  John  Roger  Margery Thomas Elizabeth Margaret Ann    James
b 1857 b 1859 b 1862 b 1864 b 1845 b 1846 b 1849  b 1851  b 1853  Rimmer
                                                            m 13 Jun 1885
```

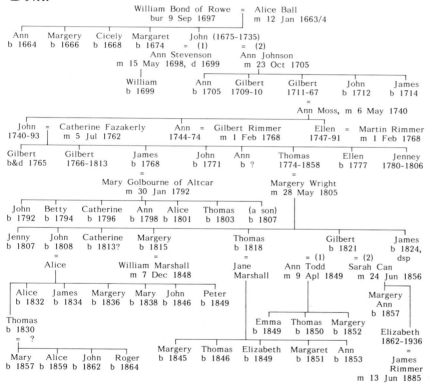

Breakill

```
                   Richard Breakill  =  Ann (d 1634)
                       d 1621           m circa 1580
  ┌──────────┬──────────────┬──────────────┬──────────────┬──────────┐
Thomas      Alis          Jane          William         Ann
= (1)      = (2) ?          =            d 1608            =
Ann         John Moss   William Watkinson                John Ball
          m 28 Jan 1604/5 m 17 Jan 1613/4   =         m 18 Jul 1616
(Children)                              Margery
John (b 1616)  Richard  John   Hugh   Thomas   Rymer
(illeg.)       b 1627  b 1630 1635-94 b 1636  m 16 Jan 1602/3
Ann (b 1619)     = ?    = ?                        │
Ellen (b 1621)                                William = ?
Richard (b 1623)  Elizabeth Richard William Jennet  b 1606
John (b 1623)     b 1672   b 1675 1678-1718 b 1680
 (twins)                     =                        William
                    Alice Smalley, m 11 Jul 1706
```

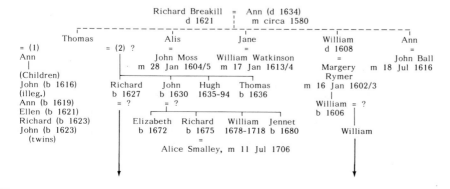

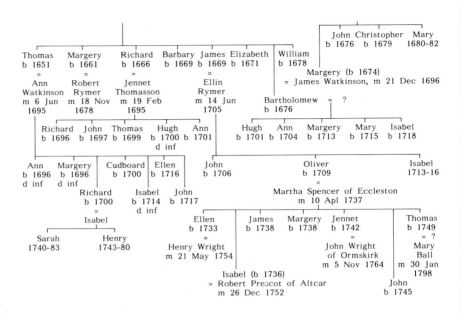

Brookfield

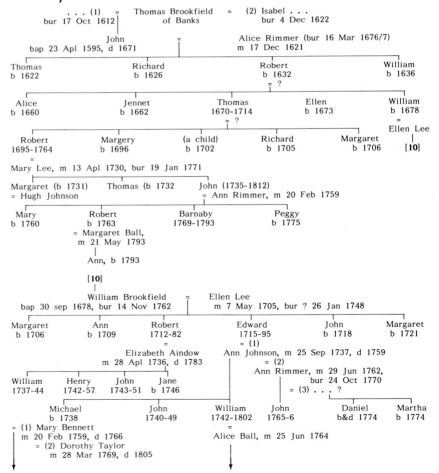

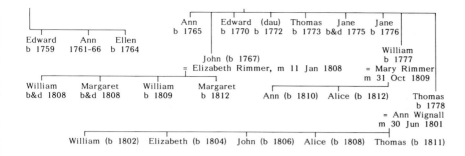

```
                              Ann      Edward  (dau)  Thomas   Jane    Jane
                              b 1765   b 1770  b 1772 b 1773  b&d 1775 b 1776
Edward    Ann      Ellen                                              William
b 1759  1761-66   b 1764              John (b 1767)                   b 1777
                                  = Elizabeth Rimmer, m 11 Jan 1808   = Mary Rimmer
                                                                      m 31 Oct 1809
William   Margaret  William  Margaret
b&d 1808  b&d 1808  b 1809   b 1812    Ann (b 1810)  Alice (b 1812)   Thomas
                                                                      b 1778
                                                                      = Ann Wignall
                                                                      m 30 Jun 1801

       William (b 1802)  Elizabeth (b 1804)  John (b 1806)  Alice (b 1808)  Thomas (b 1811)
```

Coudray/Meols of Meols

```
                  Coudray of Meols              Meols of Meols
(Sable, ten billets, 4, 3, 2 and 1 argent)   (Argent, 3 torteux in fesse within a bordure gules)

Jordan, chamberlain of Coudray     =    ?        Alan de Meols     =    ?
who gave the church of Coudray                   alive in 1220 when he held a fourth part of
to Lesnes Abbey, Kent                            the manor of Meols

Robert de Coudray  = ?   (a sister to Robert)    Robert    =  ?   Gilbert, dsp before 1276
Praepositus of Domfront,  = William (?) Russel   d c1240
Normandy c1170, d c1220   d c1220
                                                      William   =   ?
William Russel          =   Amabel Blundel           (1242, 1270)
alias William de Coudray    of Ince
(1224, 1246)                            Robert (1298)     John de Farrington
                                        d before 1311     = Avice, dau of Robert Bussel
Robert (1278)          William, rector       |                    |
= Anota de Wittingham  of Halsall        Alan de Meols          Thomas
of Thistleton,                           (1311, 1346)             |
Amounderness                               = ?                  William
                                             |                    |
William de Coudray (1311, 1338)  =   Joan de Meols              Adam

Robert      John        Lawrence     Thomas        Richard      William
d c1350    dsp 1350     dsp          alive 1354                  |
= Eleanor                                                      Katherine
                                                               = Otes of
William   Eleanor     Katherine  =  (1) Alan de Downholland    Halsall
dsp       d c1350     de Coudray      m c1341, d c1345
          = Henry      alive 1410  =  (2) Richard de Aghton
          de Scarisbrick               m c1350, d c1380, Second son of Walter de Aghton
          alive 1388
             |                        [see Aughton]
          (Isabel)
```

Meols of Meols
Argent, 3 torteaux within a bordure gules
Little is known about the Meols or Meales family, but they certainly existed early in the thirteenth century and their arms appear in the pedigrees of their descendants. The arms are sometimes described as 'Argent, 3 torteaux in fesse'.

Gregson

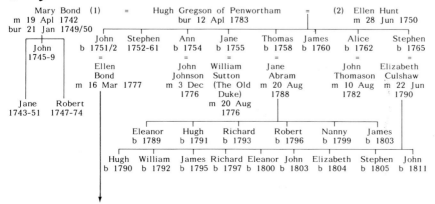

```
     Mary Bond (1)     =    Hugh Gregson of Penwortham    =    (2) Ellen Hunt
m 19 Apl 1742                    bur 12 Apl 1783                m 28 Jun 1750
bur 21 Jan 1749/50

         John    Stephen   Ann     Jane    Thomas  James   Alice    Stephen
 John   b 1751/2 1752-61  b 1754  b 1755  b 1758  b 1760  b 1762   b 1765
 1745-9
         Ellen            John    William  Jane            John    Elizabeth
         Bond             Johnson Sutton   Abram           Thomason Culshaw
         m 16 Mar 1777    m 3 Dec (The Old m 20 Aug        m 10 Aug m 22 Jun
Jane   Robert            1776    Duke)    1788            1782     1790
1743-51 1747-74                  m 20 Aug
                                 1776
                 Eleanor  Hugh   Richard  Robert  Nanny   James
                 b 1789   b 1791 b 1793   b 1796  b 1799  b 1803

    Hugh   William  James  Richard Eleanor John  Elizabeth Stephen  John
   b 1790  b 1792  b 1795 b 1797  b 1800 b 1803 b 1804    b 1805   b 1811
```

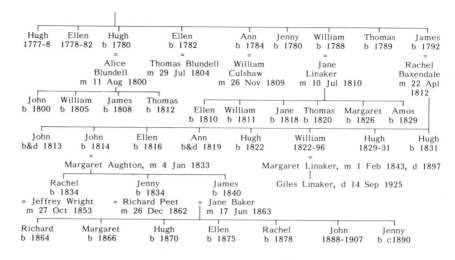

| Hugh 1777-8 | Ellen 1778-82 | Hugh b 1780 | Ellen b 1782 | Ann b 1784 | Jenny b 1780 | William b 1788 | Thomas b 1789 | James b 1792 |

= Alice Blundell m 11 Aug 1800   = Thomas Blundell m 29 Jul 1804   = William Culshaw m 26 Nov 1809   = Jane Linaker m 10 Jul 1810   = Rachel Baxendale m 22 Apl 1812

| John b 1800 | William b 1805 | James b 1808 | Thomas b 1812 | Ellen b 1810 | William b 1811 | Jane b 1818 | Thomas b 1820 | Margaret b 1826 | Amos b 1829 |

| John b&d 1813 | John b 1814 | Ellen b 1816 | Ann b&d 1819 | Hugh b 1822 | William 1822-96 | Hugh 1829-31 | Hugh b 1831 |

= Margaret Aughton, m 4 Jan 1833   = Margaret Linaker, m 1 Feb 1843, d 1897

| Rachel b 1834 | Jenny b 1834 | James b 1840 | Giles Linaker, d 14 Sep 1925 |

= Jeffrey Wright m 27 Oct 1853   = Richard Peet m 26 Dec 1862   = Jane Baker m 17 Jun 1863

| Richard b 1864 | Margaret b 1866 | Hugh b 1870 | Ellen b 1875 | Rachel b 1878 | John 1888-1907 | Jenny b c1890 |

Hesketh

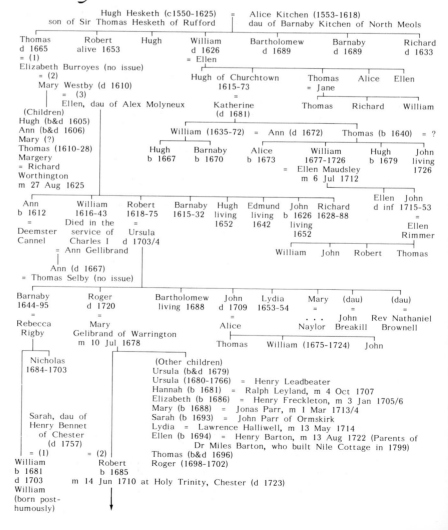

Hugh Hesketh (c1550-1625)   =   Alice Kitchen (1553-1618)
son of Sir Thomas Hesketh of Rufford   dau of Barnaby Kitchen of North Meols

| Thomas d 1665 | Robert alive 1653 | Hugh | William d 1626 | Bartholomew d 1689 | Barnaby d 1689 | Richard d 1633 |

Thomas d 1665
= (1) Elizabeth Burroyes (no issue)
= (2) Mary Westby (d 1610)
= (3) Ellen, dau of Alex Molyneux

(Children)
Hugh (b&d 1605)
Ann (b&d 1606)
Mary (?)
Thomas (1610-28)
Margery = Richard Worthington m 27 Aug 1625

William d 1626 = Ellen

Hugh of Churchtown 1615-73 = Katherine (d 1681)

Thomas = Jane → Thomas, Richard, William

Alice, Ellen

William (1635-72) = Ann (d 1672)   Thomas (b 1640) = ?

| Hugh b 1667 | Barnaby b 1670 | Alice b 1673 | William 1677-1726 = Ellen Maudsley m 6 Jul 1712 | Hugh b 1679 | John living 1726 |

Ellen, John d inf 1715-53

| Ann b 1612 = Deemster Cannel | William 1616-43 Died in the service of Charles I | Robert 1618-75 = Ursula d 1703/4 | Barnaby 1615-32 | Hugh living 1652 | Edmund living 1642 | John b 1626 living 1652 | Richard 1628-88 |

John = Ellen Rimmer → William, John, Robert, Thomas

Robert 1618-75
= Ann Gellibrand
|
Ann (d 1667)
= Thomas Selby (no issue)

| Barnaby 1644-95 = Rebecca Rigby | Roger d 1720 = Mary Gelibrand of Warrington m 10 Jul 1678 | Bartholomew living 1688 | John d 1709 = Alice | Lydia 1653-54 | Mary = ... John Naylor | (dau) = John Breakill | (dau) = Rev Nathaniel Brownell |

Thomas   William (1675-1724)   John

Nicholas 1684-1703

Sarah, dau of Henry Bennet of Chester (d 1757)
= (1) William b 1681 d 1703 William (born posthumously)
= (2) Robert b 1685 m 14 Jun 1710 at Holy Trinity, Chester (d 1723)

(Other children)
Ursula (b&d 1679)
Ursula (1680-1766) = Henry Leadbeater
Hannah (b 1681) = Ralph Leyland, m 4 Oct 1707
Elizabeth (b 1686) = Henry Freckleton, m 3 Jan 1705/6
Mary (b 1688) = Jonas Parr, m 1 Mar 1713/4
Sarah (b 1693) = John Parr of Ormskirk
Lydia = Lawrence Halliwell, m 13 May 1714
Ellen (b 1694) = Henry Barton, m 13 Aug 1722 (Parents of Dr Miles Barton, who built Nile Cottage in 1799)
Thomas (b&d 1696)
Roger (1698-1702)

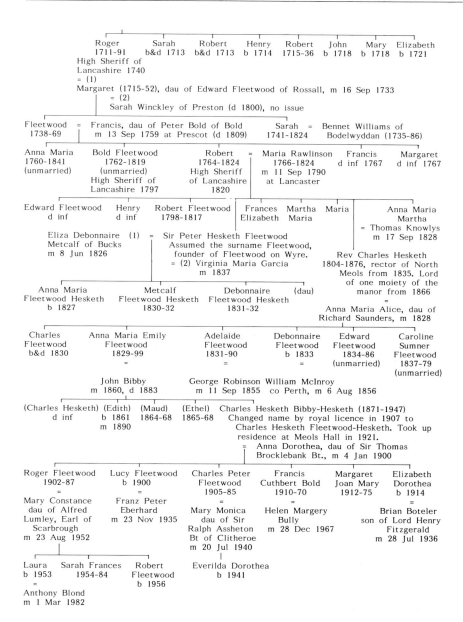

Roger 1711-91 | Sarah b&d 1713 | Robert b&d 1713 | Henry b 1714 | Robert 1715-36 | John b 1718 | Mary b 1718 | Elizabeth b 1721

Roger 1711-91
High Sheriff of
Lancashire 1740
= (1)
Margaret (1715-52), dau of Edward Fleetwood of Rossall, m 16 Sep 1733
= (2)
Sarah Winckley of Preston (d 1800), no issue

Fleetwood 1738-69 = Francis, dau of Peter Bold of Bold m 13 Sep 1759 at Prescot (d 1809) | Sarah 1741-1824 = Bennet Williams of Bodelwyddan (1735-86)

Anna Maria 1760-1841 (unmarried)

Bold Fleetwood 1762-1819 (unmarried) High Sheriff of Lancashire 1797

Robert 1764-1824 High Sheriff of Lancashire 1820 = Maria Rawlinson 1766-1824 m 11 Sep 1790 at Lancaster

Francis d inf 1767

Margaret d inf 1767

Edward Fleetwood d inf | Henry d inf | Robert Fleetwood 1798-1817 | Frances Elizabeth | Martha Maria | Maria | Anna Maria Martha = Thomas Knowlys m 17 Sep 1828

Eliza Debonnaire (1) Metcalf of Bucks m 8 Jun 1826 = Sir Peter Hesketh Fleetwood Assumed the surname Fleetwood, founder of Fleetwood on Wyre. = (2) Virginia Maria Garcia m 1837

Rev Charles Hesketh 1804-1876, rector of North Meols from 1835. Lord of one moiety of the manor from 1866 = Anna Maria Alice, dau of Richard Saunders, m 1828

Anna Maria Fleetwood Hesketh b 1827 | Metcalf Fleetwood Hesketh 1830-32 | Debonnaire Fleetwood Hesketh 1831-32 | (dau)

Charles Fleetwood b&d 1830 | Anna Maria Emily Fleetwood 1829-99 = | Adelaide Fleetwood 1831-90 = | Debonnaire Fleetwood b 1833 = | Edward Fleetwood 1834-86 (unmarried) | Caroline Sumner Fleetwood 1837-79 (unmarried)

John Bibby m 1860, d 1883 | George Robinson m 11 Sep 1855 | William McInroy co Perth, m 6 Aug 1856

(Charles Hesketh) d inf | (Edith) b 1861 m 1890 | (Maud) 1864-68 | (Ethel) 1865-68 | Charles Hesketh Bibby-Hesketh (1871-1947) Changed name by royal licence in 1907 to Charles Hesketh Fleetwood-Hesketh. Took up residence at Meols Hall in 1921. = Anna Dorothea, dau of Sir Thomas Brocklebank Bt., m 4 Jan 1900

Roger Fleetwood 1902-87 = Mary Constance dau of Alfred Lumley, Earl of Scarbrough m 23 Aug 1952

Lucy Fleetwood b 1900 = Franz Peter Eberhard m 23 Nov 1935

Charles Peter Fleetwood 1905-85 = Mary Monica dau of Sir Ralph Assheton Bt of Clitheroe m 20 Jul 1940

Francis Cuthbert Bold 1910-70 = Helen Margery Bully m 28 Dec 1967

Margaret Joan Mary 1912-75 =

Elizabeth Dorothea b 1914 = Brian Boteler son of Lord Henry Fitzgerald m 28 Jul 1936

Laura b 1953 = Anthony Blond m 1 Mar 1982 | Sarah Frances 1954-84 | Robert Fleetwood b 1956

Everilda Dorothea b 1941

Hooton

William Hooton = (?) Elizabeth

Margaret b Jul 1695 | John b Mar 1702/3 = (?) = John Ottley, m 15 Jun 1731 | Elizabeth | Isabell b Jan 1707/8

Thomas (a weaver of Marshside) 1728-1793 = Jane Rymer (1733-1804) m 21 Jan 1753/4

Jennet = Richard Wignall m 21 Feb 1754

Elizabeth (b Nov 1736) = John Sutch, m 10 May 1752

Margery 1755-73 | John 1758-1836 Credited with the introduction of handloom weaving into North Meols during the 1790s = Ellen Aughton m 22 Oct 1780 | Frances b Sep 1760 = Richard Rowbottom of Hoole m 14 May 1781 | Thomas b 1763 = Martha Ball m 27 Apl 1789 | James b Jan 1769 = Jenny Sutton m 30 Apl 1805 | Jane b Oct 1772 = Nicholas Wright m 2 Nov 1795

Ellen	Thomas	Margery = James Blundell	John	William	Ann	Jane
d May 1781	b 1784	b Jan 1787 m 30 Oct 1805	b Jun 1789	b Aug 1792	b 1795	b 1798

Hunt

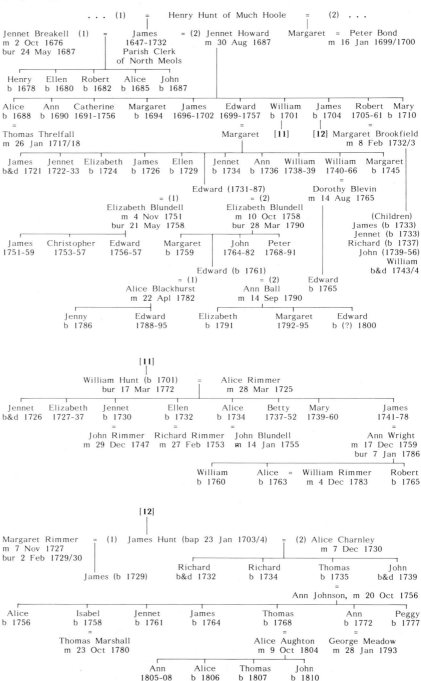

. . . (1)   =   Henry Hunt of Much Hoole   =   (2) . . .

Jennet Breakell (1) =   James   = (2) Jennet Howard   Margaret = Peter Bond
m 2 Oct 1676   1647–1732   m 30 Aug 1687   m 16 Jan 1699/1700
bur 24 May 1687   Parish Clerk
           of North Meols

Henry   Ellen   Robert   Alice   John
b 1678   b 1680   b 1682   b 1685   b 1687

Alice	Ann	Catherine	Margaret	James	Edward	William	James	Robert	Mary
b 1688	b 1690	1691–1756	b 1694	1696–1702	1699–1757	b 1701	b 1704	1705–61	b 1710
=									
Thomas Threlfall					Margaret	[11]		[12]	Margaret Brookfield
m 26 Jan 1717/18									m 8 Feb 1732/3

James	Jennet	Elizabeth	James	Ellen	Jennet	Ann	William	William	Margaret
b&d 1721	1722–33	b 1724	b 1726	b 1729	b 1734	b 1736	1738–39	1740–66	b 1745

Edward (1731–87)   Dorothy Blevin
                         =
= (1)   = (2)   m 14 Aug 1765
Elizabeth Blundell   Elizabeth Blundell
m 4 Nov 1751   m 10 Oct 1758
bur 21 May 1758   bur 28 Mar 1790   (Children)
                                    James (b 1733)
                                   Jennet (b 1733)

James   Christopher   Edward   Margaret   John   Peter   Richard (b 1737)
1751–59   1753–57   1756–57   b 1759   1764–82   1768–91   John (1739–56)
                                            William
                                            b&d 1743/4

Edward (b 1761)
= (1)   = (2)   Edward
Alice Blackhurst   Ann Ball   b 1765
m 22 Apl 1782   m 14 Sep 1790

Jenny	Edward	Elizabeth	Margaret	Edward
b 1786	1788–95	b 1791	1792–95	b (?) 1800

[11]

William Hunt (b 1701)   =   Alice Rimmer
bur 17 Mar 1772   m 28 Mar 1725

Jennet	Elizabeth	Jennet	Ellen	Alice	Betty	Mary	James
b&d 1726	1727–37	b 1730	b 1732	b 1734	1737–52	1739–60	1741–78
		=	=	=			=
		John Rimmer	Richard Rimmer	John Blundell			Ann Wright
		m 29 Dec 1747	m 27 Feb 1753	m 14 Jan 1755			m 17 Dec 1759
							bur 7 Jan 1786

William	Alice	=	William Rimmer	Robert
b 1760	b 1763		m 4 Dec 1783	b 1765

[12]

Margaret Rimmer = (1)   James Hunt (bap 23 Jan 1703/4)   = (2)   Alice Charnley
m 7 Nov 1727   m 7 Dec 1730
bur 2 Feb 1729/30

	Richard	Richard	Thomas	John
James (b 1729)	b&d 1732	b 1734	b 1735	b&d 1739

                                      =
                               Ann Johnson, m 20 Oct 1756

Alice	Isabel	Jennet	James	Thomas	Ann	Peggy
b 1756	b 1758	b 1761	b 1764	b 1768	b 1772	b 1777
	=			=	=	
	Thomas Marshall			Alice Aughton	George Meadow	
	m 23 Oct 1780			m 9 Oct 1804	m 28 Jan 1793	

Ann	Alice	Thomas	John
1805–08	b 1806	b 1807	b 1810

Johnson

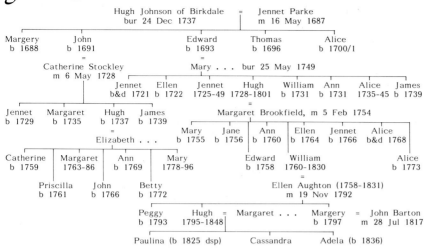

Hugh Johnson of Birkdale = Jennet Parke
bur 24 Dec 1737 / m 16 May 1687

Margery b 1688 — John b 1691 = Catherine Stockley m 6 May 1728 — Edward b 1693 — Thomas b 1696 = Mary . . . bur 25 May 1749 — Alice b 1700/1

Jennet b&d 1721 — Ellen b 1722 — Jennet 1725-49 — Hugh 1728-1801 = Margaret Brookfield, m 5 Feb 1754 — William b 1731 — Ann b 1731 — Alice 1735-45 — James b 1739

Jennet b 1729 — Margaret b 1735 — Hugh b 1737 = Elizabeth . . . — James b 1739 — Mary b 1755 — Jane b 1756 — Ann b 1760 — Ellen b 1764 — Jennet b 1766 — Alice b&d 1768

Catherine b 1759 — Margaret 1763-86 — Ann b 1769 — Mary 1778-96 — Edward b 1758 = Ellen Aughton (1758-1831) m 19 Nov 1792 — William 1760-1830 — Alice b 1773

Priscilla b 1761 — John b 1766 — Betty b 1772

Peggy b 1793 — Hugh 1795-1848 = Margaret . . . — Margery b 1797 = John Barton m 28 Jul 1817

Paulina (b 1825 dsp) — Cassandra — Adela (b 1836)

Leadbetter

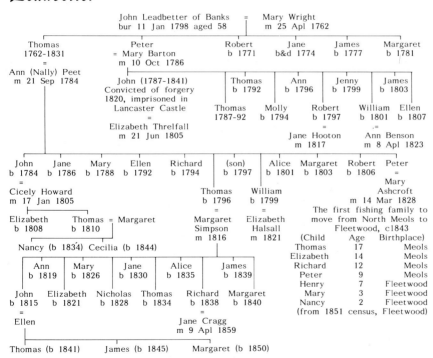

John Leadbetter of Banks = Mary Wright
bur 11 Jan 1798 aged 58 / m 25 Apl 1762

Thomas 1762-1831 = Ann (Nally) Peet m 21 Sep 1784 — Peter = Mary Barton m 10 Oct 1786 — Robert b 1771 — Jane b&d 1774 — James b 1777 — Margaret b 1781

John (1787-1841) Convicted of forgery 1820, imprisoned in Lancaster Castle = Elizabeth Threlfall m 21 Jun 1805 — Thomas b 1792 — Ann b 1796 — Jenny b 1799 — James b 1803

Thomas 1787-92 — Molly b 1794 — Robert b 1797 = Jane Hooton m 1817 — William b 1801 = Ann Benson m 8 Apl 1823 — Ellen b 1807

John b 1784 = Cicely Howard m 17 Jan 1805 — Jane b 1786 — Mary b 1788 — Ellen b 1792 — Richard b 1794 — (son) b 1797 — Alice b 1801 — Margaret b 1803 — Robert b 1806 — Peter = Mary Ashcroft m 14 Mar 1828

Thomas b 1796 = Margaret Simpson m 1816 — William b 1799 = Elizabeth Halsall m 1821

The first fishing family to move from North Meols to Fleetwood, c1843

Elizabeth b 1808 — Thomas b 1810 = Margaret

Nancy (b 1834) Cecilia (b 1844)

Margaret Simpson m 1816 — Elizabeth Halsall m 1821

Ann b 1819 — Mary b 1826 — Jane b 1830 — Alice b 1835 — James b 1839

John b 1815 = Ellen — Elizabeth b 1821 — Nicholas b 1828 — Thomas b 1834 — Richard b 1838 — Margaret b 1840 = Jane Cragg m 9 Apl 1859

Thomas (b 1841)   James (b 1845)   Margaret (b 1850)

(Child	Age	Birthplace)
Thomas	17	Meols
Elizabeth	14	Meols
Richard	12	Meols
Peter	9	Meols
Henry	7	Fleetwood
Mary	3	Fleetwood
Nancy	2	Fleetwood
(from 1851 census, Fleetwood)		

Peter Leadbetter (1736-1797)
He is possibly the brother of John Leadbetter at the beginning of this tree.
The Leadbetters probably came from Tarleton where Peter and Jane Leadbetter
married on the 15th of June 1736 and subsequently moved to North Meols.
=
Margaret Blundell (1738-1822)
married 1760

Alice (b 1762)   Hannah (b 1764)   Peter (b 1768) = Betty Watkinson m 6 Nov 1804   Jane b 1770   Betty b 1780

Peter b 1805 — Richard 1805-31 — James b&d 1807 — Christopher b 1810 = Margaret . . .

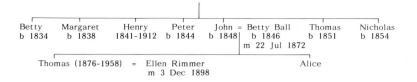

| Betty b 1834 | Margaret b 1838 | Henry 1841-1912 | Peter b 1844 | John = Betty Ball b 1848 \| b 1846 m 22 Jul 1872 | Thomas b 1851 | Nicholas b 1854 |

Thomas (1876-1958) = Ellen Rimmer m 3 Dec 1898
Alice

Linaker

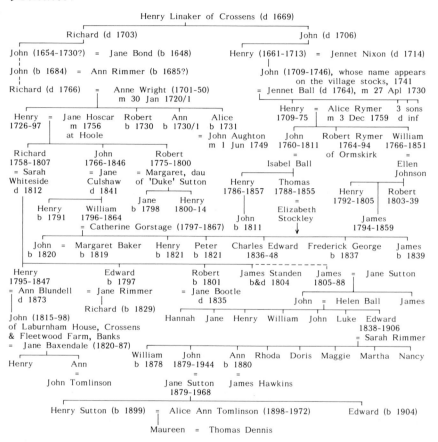

Henry Linaker of Crossens (d 1669)

Richard (d 1703) — John (d 1706)

John (1654-1730?) = Jane Bond (b 1648) Henry (1661-1713) = Jennet Nixon (d 1714)

John (b 1684) = Ann Rimmer (b 1685?) John (1709-1746), whose name appears on the village stocks, 1741 = Jennet Ball (d 1764), m 27 Apl 1730

Richard (d 1766) = Anne Wright (1701-50) m 30 Jan 1720/1

Henry = Jane Hoscar Robert Ann Alice Henry = Alice Rymer 3 sons
1726-97 \| m 1756 b 1730 b 1730/1 b 1731 1709-75 \| m 3 Dec 1759 d inf
at Hoole = John Aughton m 1 Jun 1749

Richard John Robert John Robert Rymer William
1758-1807 1766-1846 1775-1800 1760-1811 1764-94 1766-1851
= Sarah = Jane = Margaret, dau = of Ormskirk =
Whiteside Culshaw of 'Duke' Sutton Isabel Ball Ellen
d 1812 d 1841 Johnson

Henry William Jane Henry Henry Thomas Henry Robert
b 1791 1796-1864 b 1798 1800-14 1786-1857 1788-1855 1792-1805 1803-39
= Catherine Gorstage (1797-1867) = Elizabeth Stockley James
John b 1811 1794-1859

John = Margaret Baker Henry Peter Charles Edward Frederick George James
b 1820 b 1819 b 1821 b 1821 1836-48 b 1837 b 1839

Henry Edward Robert James Standen James = Jane Sutton
1795-1847 b 1797 b 1801 b&d 1804 1805-88
= Ann Blundell = Jane Rimmer = Jane Bootle John = Helen Ball James
d 1873 Richard (b 1829) d 1835
John (1815-98) Hannah Jane Henry William John Luke Edward
of Laburnham House, Crossens 1838-1906
& Fleetwood Farm, Banks = Sarah Rimmer
= Jane Baxendale (1820-87)

Henry Ann William John Ann Rhoda Doris Maggie Martha Nancy
= b 1878 1879-1944 b 1880
John Tomlinson = =
Jane Sutton James Hawkins
1879-1968

Henry Sutton (b 1899) = Alice Ann Tomlinson (1898-1972) Edward (b 1904)

Maureen = Thomas Dennis

Lloyd

Peter Lloyd = Mary Charnley, m 5 Feb 1734

John Richard Richard Richard George
1739-1824 b 1742, d inf b 1743 1744-1811 1747-1819
= d inf no issue Wrongfully convicted of arson in
Elizabeth Johnson in 1776 (see Bland)
m 19 Sep 1763 =
Sussannah Rainford of Halsall

Richard Peter John Thomas Richard Robert Mary Robert James
1764-70 b 1766 b 1768 1770-1808 b 1772 b&d 1775 b 1776 1775-1786 1779-1841

Alice Jackson
1779-1832
↓

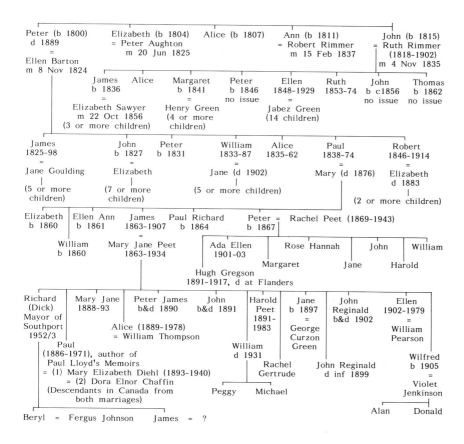

Peter (b 1800)   Elizabeth (b 1804)   Alice (b 1807)   Ann (b 1811)   John (b 1815)
d 1889   = Peter Aughton   = Robert Rimmer   = Ruth Rimmer
=   m 20 Jun 1825   m 15 Feb 1837   (1818-1902)
Ellen Barton   m 4 Nov 1835
m 8 Nov 1824

James Alice   Margaret   Peter   Ellen   Ruth   John   Thomas
b 1836   b 1841   b 1846   1848-1929 1853-74 b c1856 b 1862
=   =   no issue   =   no issue no issue
Elizabeth Sawyer Henry Green   Jabez Green
m 22 Oct 1856   (4 or more   (14 children)
(3 or more children)   children)

James   John   Peter   William   Alice   Paul   Robert
1825-98   b 1827   b 1831   1833-87   1835-62   1838-74   1846-1914
=   =   =   =
Jane Goulding Elizabeth   Jane (d 1902)   Mary (d 1876) Elizabeth
| | d 1883
(5 or more   (7 or more   (5 or more children) |
children)   children)   (2 or more children)

Elizabeth Ellen Ann James Paul Richard   Peter = Rachel Peet (1869-1943)
b 1860   b 1861   1863-1907 b 1864   b 1867
            =
William   Mary Jane Peet   Ada Ellen   Rose Hannah   John   William
b 1860   1863-1934   1901-03
                             Margaret   Jane   Harold
                    Hugh Gregson
            1891-1917, d at Flanders

Richard   Mary Jane Peter James John   Harold Jane   John   Ellen
(Dick)   1888-93   b&d 1890   b&d 1891 Peet b 1897 Reginald 1902-1979
Mayor of   1891- =   b&d 1902 =
Southport   Alice (1889-1978)   1983 George   William
1952/3   = William Thompson   Curzon   Pearson
Paul   William Green
(1886-1971), author of   d 1931   Wilfred
Paul Lloyd's Memoirs   Rachel   John Reginald b 1905
= (1) Mary Elizabeth Diehl (1893-1940)   Gertrude d inf 1899   =
= (2) Dora Elnor Chaffin   Violet
(Descendants in Canada from Peggy Michael   Jenkinson
both marriages)   Alan   Donald

Beryl = Fergus Johnson   James = ?

Sutton

Robert Sutton
Parish constable of North Meols and tenant of the water mill in 1594
|
(two generations)

Robert Sutton (1640-1720) = Alis Williamson, m 14 Jan 1666, d 1679

William (b 1668)   Robert (b 1672)   John (b 1674)   = Ann Jumpe, m 1706   Ellin (b 1677)

Thomas (1709-60) John   Ellin   William   William (b 1712) Matthew Jane
= (1) Ellin Dobson b 1709 b 1709 b 1709   =   b 1715 b 1727
of Croston   d inf   d inf   Elizabeth Blundell
m 1732, d 1640   m 1734
= (2) Mary . . .

                             John   Robert John   William (1752-1840)
Isabel   Jennet   John   Mary   d inf   b 1738 b 1741 'The Old Duke'
b 1743 b 1745 1747-1818 b 1754   =   Known as the
=   =   =   Ann   founder of
Robert John   Elizabeth Watkinson   Aughton Southport
Capwell Howard 1747-89, m 25 Feb 1771   m 23 Dec 1759 =
m Jul   m 9 Apl   Jane Gregson
1764   1767   m 20 Aug 1776

        Peggy (b 1777) John (b 1781) Ellen (b 1783) Hugh   Jane
        = Robert Linaker = Ann Peet = William Gass b 1786 b 1790
        m 1798   m 1810   m 1804

Mary (b 1771) Betty (b 1774) Anne (b 1776) Alice (b 1779) Thomas (1782-1833) Richard
                                                 b 1786
=   =   =   =   =
William Wright James Waring Henry Blundell Robert Cropper Betty Baker
m 15 Feb 1796 m 25 Jan 1795 m 8 Sep 1798 m 2 Aug 1803 1784-1877
                                     m 12 May 1807
                                     ↓

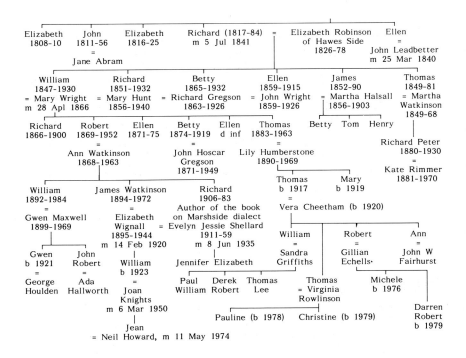

Elizabeth 1808-10   John 1811-56   Elizabeth 1816-25   Richard (1817-84) m 5 Jul 1841 = Elizabeth Robinson of Hawes Side 1826-78   Ellen = John Leadbetter m 25 Mar 1840

=
Jane Abram

William 1847-1930 = Mary Wright m 28 Apl 1866   Richard 1851-1932 = Mary Hunt 1856-1940   Betty 1865-1932 = Richard Gregson 1863-1926   Ellen 1859-1915 = John Wright 1859-1926   James 1852-90 = Martha Halsall 1856-1903   Thomas 1849-81 = Martha Watkinson 1849-68

Richard 1866-1900   Robert 1869-1952 = Ann Watkinson 1868-1963   Ellen 1871-75   Betty 1874-1919 = John Hoscar Gregson 1871-1949   Ellen d inf   Thomas 1883-1963 = Lily Humberstone 1890-1969

Betty   Tom   Henry

Richard Peter 1880-1930 = Kate Rimmer 1881-1970

William 1892-1984 = Gwen Maxwell 1899-1969   James Watkinson 1894-1972 = Elizabeth Wignall 1895-1944 m 14 Feb 1920   Richard 1906-83 Author of the book on Marshside dialect = Evelyn Jessie Shellard 1911-59 m 8 Jun 1935

Thomas b 1917   Mary b 1919

Vera Cheetham (b 1920)

Gwen b 1921 = George Houlden   John Robert = Ada Hallworth   William b 1923 = Joan Knights m 6 Mar 1950   Jennifer Elizabeth

William = Sandra Griffiths   Robert = Gillian Echells·   Ann = John W Fairhurst

Paul William   Derek Robert   Thomas Lee   Thomas = Virginia Rowlinson   Michele b 1976

Jean
= Neil Howard, m 11 May 1974

Pauline (b 1978)   Christine (b 1979)   Darren Robert b 1979

Thomasson

Thomas Thomason of Crossens, bur 11 Mary 1699

Richard (d Feb 1698) = Lydia Ball (subsequently married to James Rimmer)   Thomas (1661-94) = Jennet   John (b 1662) living 1698   Nicholas (b 1665) living 1698

Ellen (d 1702)

Thomas (1684-1746), of Roe Lane = Elizabeth (d 1729)   John (1696-1729) = Elizabeth Wright, m 1724

Richard 1724-51 = Mary Ball m 1750   Richard (of Banks), 1725-62 = Anne Rymer, m 1749, d 1766

Thomas (b 1748)   John (1755-97) = Alice Gregson, m 1784   Thomas (b 1760) = Margaret Culshaw m 1782

Richard (b 1787) = Isabel Baker, m 1812

James (b 1815) = Alice Ball, m 1837

John (1842-1901) = Alice Gorstage Linaker (1846-1912)

Harry Henshaw

Todd

John Todd = Jane Halsall, m 31 Mar 1725
bur 14 Jan 1754   bur 3 Sep 1751

John = Margery Rimmer
bap 10 Aug 1726, bur 18 Sep 1808   m 19 Jan 1752, bur 12 Sep 1775

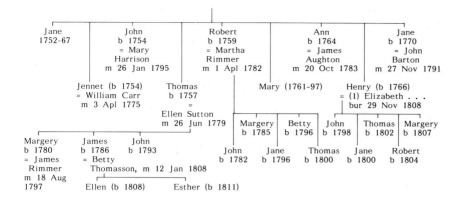

Watkinson

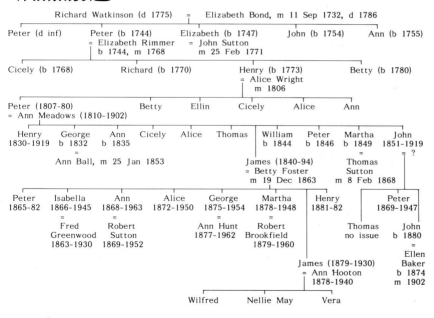

Subject Index

Numbers in bold type refer to illustrations or their accompanying captions.
An asterisk (*) denotes two or more references on the same page.

Name Index

Numbers in bold type refer to illustrations or their accompanying captions.
An asterisk (*) denotes two or more references on the same page.